IRAQ
Policy and Percepti

The Institute for the Study of Diplomacy (ISD), founded in 1978, is part of Georgetown University's Edmund A. Walsh School of Foreign Service and is the School's primary window on the world of the foreign affairs practitioner.

ISD studies the practitioner's craft : how diplomats and other foreign affairs professionals succeed and the lessons to be learned from their successes and failures. Institute programs focus on the foreign policy process: how decisions are made and implemented.

ISD conducts its programs through a small staff and resident and nonresident "associates." Associates, primarily U.S. and foreign government officials, are detailed to or affiliated with the Institute for a year or more. The Institute seeks to build academic-practitioner collaborations around issues using associates and Georgetown faculty. ISD staff and associates teach courses, organize lectures and discussions, mentor students, and participate on university committees.

In addition, ISD's Pew Case Studies in International Affairs are used in over 1,000 courses across the country and around the world.

IRAQ
Policy and Perceptions

RICHARD J. SCHMIERER

Institute for the Study of Diplomacy
Edmund A. Walsh School of Foreign Service
GEORGETOWN UNIVERSITY

DISCLAIMER: The author is a Foreign Service Officer of the Department of State, currently assigned by the department as a senior advisor at the Institute for the Study of Diplomacy of the Edmund A. Walsh School of Foreign Service at Georgetown University. Any views expressed herein are solely those of the author, and not necessarily those of the U.S. government, the Department of State, or the Institute for the Study of Diplomacy.

Cover photograph credit: Residents of Baghdad Go to the Polls BAGHDAD, IRAQ–JANUARY 30: An Iraqi woman shows that her finger has been marked after voting at a polling station in the Sadr City neighborhood of Baghdad on January 30, 2005 in Iraq. Iraq's first multiparty elections in half a century began at 7:00 am on Sunday. (Photo by Majid Saeedi/Getty Images). Copyright: 2005 Getty Images.

Institute for the Study of Diplomacy
Edmund A. Walsh School of Foreign Service
Georgetown University, Washington, D.C. 20057–1025
© 2007 by the Institute for the Study of Diplomacy.

All rights reserved by the publisher. No part of this Monograph may be reproduced, stored in a retrieval system, or transmitted in any form or by any means—electronic, electrostatic, magnetic tape, mechanical, photocopying, recording, or otherwise—without permission in writing from the Institute for the Study of Diplomacy. Material contained in this Monograph may be quoted with appropriate citation.

ISBN 0-934742-99-5
Printed in the United States of America

Contents

Dedication   ix

Foreword   xii

Introduction   1

1
Iraq and 9/11   9
The Paradigm Shift   12
The Westphalian World   13
The (New) U.S. National Security Strategy   14
The Geneva Conventions in the Post-Westphalian World   15
Urgent U.S. Post-9/11 Policy Goals   16
Weapons of Mass Destruction   17
Alternate Scenarios?   20
The Post-Westphalian Challenge   25

2
The End of the Cold War and the Emergence of a Unipolar World   26
The Unipolar World   31
The Realism versus Idealism Debate   33

3
The Arab World and the Information Revolution   37
Asymmetric Propaganda   40
The Blogosphere   44
Proving Motives   47

4
Democracy and its Discontents   55

Democratic Gridlock   55
A Mushroom Cloud as "Smoking Gun"   58
Hard Power and Soft Power   59
Democratic Debate   61
Politics as Policy   63
Staying Power   64
Governance and Politics   65
The Bureaucracy: Even Paranoids Have Enemies   71
Institutional Dysfunction   76
Government by Accountability Review Board   76
The Case of Tariq Ramadan   82
Partisanship and the Water's Edge   85
Elections   88
The Iraq Study Group   90

5
Iraq and the U.S. Military   93

Attitudes toward the United States   94
The Roles in Iraq   96
Preemptive Capitulation and Insurgency   98
Insufficient Troops   101
The Impact of Foreign Jihadists and Escaped Baathists   105
The Absence of a Northern Front   106
The U.S. Military through Others' Eyes   106
Who Is Fighting This War?   108
Sacrifice, Heroism, and "Baghdad ER"   110
Savagery and Absolute Savagery   113

6
The Coalition of the Unwilling   115

A Bitter Media Environment   119
Capital Punishment   129
Hostage Policy   131
The Absence of International Institutions   132

7
Violence in Iraq:
The Insurgency/Sectarian Conflict   134
The Nature of the Insurgency in Iraq   134
The Iraqi "Fence Sitters"   135
Economically Driven "Insurgency"   136
An Eye for an Eye   137
Criminality   138
Ruthlessness and Religiously Inspired Fanaticism   139
Sectarian Conflict   142

8
Iraq and the Media   145
Covering Iraq   151
The Post-Al-Jazeera Era   154
Media Evolution within Iraq   156
The Iraqi Media Network and the
    Ministry of Information Mentality   157
Censorship   159

9
Inside Iraq   161
The Kurdish Community   162
Kirkuk   163
Iraqi Kurdistan   164
The Sunni Community   165
The Shi'a Community   167
The Iraq War: Phase IV   169
Internal Dynamics inside Iraq   176
Reconciliation among Iraq's Communities   176
Economic Reform   179
Corruption   182
Dismembering Iraq   185
Iraq as Switzerland   188

10
Iraq's Neighborhood   192
Fear, or Loathing?   192
Regional Democratic Reform   197
Iran   200
Turkey   202

11
American Competence and Commitment   204
Competence   204
The Army You've Got   206
Transformational Diplomacy   209
In Iraq, the Enlightenment Meets Rambo   211
(Dis-)Connection   212
Commitment   216
Yet another Perfect Storm   217
The Approaching End Game   219

Summary and Conclusions   221

Notes   225

Acknowledgements   236

Dedication

In a more than quarter-century diplomatic career I have had many memorable encounters and experiences. I have had the opportunity to meet presidents, kings, and movie stars. I have worked with hundreds of well-known journalists—from Christiane Amanpour to Fareed Zakaria—who represent the media stars of my generation. My foreign service experiences have included being on hand in Germany in 1981when the freed U.S. hostages from Iran touched down on the tarmac at Rhein-Main Air Base, to experiencing the jolt of an arrested landing on an aircraft carrier in the Arabian Sea, to walking the ruins of ancient Babylon in Iraq.

In all of these years, and through all of these experiences, I have never in my diplomatic career been more exhilarated than I was in being present in the Convention Center in Baghdad's International Zone on January 30, 2005, witnessing Iraqis—officials, politicians, journalists, and members of my own embassy staff—all proudly thrusting their purple-stained index fingers in the air after voting in the first free Iraqi elections in their lifetimes. Having participated in this scene in person, and having repeatedly been inspired during my year in Iraq by the courage, resilience, and determination of the hundreds of Iraqis I encountered, I remain optimistic on the future of Iraq, and I am pleased to dedicate this work to the heroic people of that country.

Source: Central Intelligence Agency, file: iraq_pol_2004.jpg.
Accessed http://www.lib.utexas.edu/maps/iraq.html, February 2007.

Foreword

Through the tumultuous period from the "end of combat operations" in Iraq on May 1, 2003, to the "surge" to secure Baghdad announced by President Bush in January 2007, America's efforts in that long-suffering country have come to define the challenge of the current decade, and perhaps generation.

Since August 2005, the Institute for the Study of Diplomacy (ISD) has been fortunate to have Dr. Richard J. Schmierer, a Foreign Service Officer with more than a quarter century of diplomatic experience, in residence to teach, speak, research, and write. Dr. Schmierer joined ISD following a one-year tour, from June 2004 through June 2005, as the minister-counselor for public affairs at the U.S. embassy in Baghdad. He was on hand as the U.S. embassy was reopened, as sovereignty was restored to the Iraqi government, and as Iraqis voted in their first free elections in decades. As head of the embassy's public affairs operation, Dr. Schmierer played a key role in the U.S. government's "hearts and minds" efforts in Iraq during what was then still the early stage of the Iraqi insurgency.

In conjunction with his teaching and research here at Georgetown University, Dr. Schmierer has written an insightful and eye-opening personal account of the Iraq issue and all of the complexity in which it has revealed itself since the U.S.-led coalition ousted Saddam Hussein from power in 2003. He explores the fundamentals that underlie U.S. policies and perceptions vis-à-vis Iraq, examining the motives, interests, and circumstances in the world that affect and define the U.S. approach to Iraq. In exploring everything from post-Cold War U.S. military dominance to the impact of the information revolution and the all-volunteer military and to certain aspects of democracy that impact such efforts as the United States has pursued in Iraq, Dr. Schmierer conveys the enormous complexity that the Iraq issue embodies.

The diplomatic practitioners on Georgetown's campus, such as Dr. Schmierer, represent a unique and valuable resource for the

School of Foreign Service, whether through their teaching, their publications, and their public speaking or simply through their being available to consult with students and others. I am particularly pleased that Dr. Schmierer has made a conscious effort to incorporate into this work examples and anecdotes from his long diplomatic career—which has included nineteen years abroad, in Iraq, Saudi Arabia, and Germany—material that illustrates the real-life conduct of diplomacy, in particular in his area of specialization: public diplomacy. In this regard, this monograph renders a valuable service to students in Georgetown's School of Foreign Service by providing them with a window on the day-to-day world of a U.S. diplomat.

What you will find in Dr. Schmierer's in-depth treatment of the Iraq issue that follows is at times provocative, at times controversial, but always informed and insightful. As the Iraq conflict enters a new and possibly decisive phase in early 2007, Dr. Schmierer's concluding thoughts on the lessons of the Iraq experience and a possible path forward provide a hopeful note on which to close his discussion of this difficult and challenging topic. Dr. Schmierer himself describes this work as a primer on the Iraq issue. It is that, and much more. I commend Dr. Schmierer's study on Iraq for all who want to better understand this important and complex issue.

                          Casimir A. Yost
                          Director
                          Institute for the Study of Diplomacy

Introduction

Upon my return in late June of 2005 from a one-year assignment heading the Public Affairs Section of the U.S. embassy in Baghdad, I found myself frequently asked by family and friends to explain what "Iraq" is really all about and whether U.S. policy in Iraq is likely to succeed. I have been fortunate to have had an opportunity to witness, and to some extent participate from the inside in the evolution of U.S. Iraq policy for almost a decade, and from that experience I have drawn some personal conclusions about the U.S. approach to Iraq, the wisdom of this approach, its likelihood of success, and the factors that brought it about and will likely determine its outcome.

Over this period, I have had the good fortune to have participated in fora with some of the leading analysts on Iraq, on international security, on terrorism, and on the Arab world. I served as the head of the Public Affairs Section of the U.S. embassy in Riyadh, Saudi Arabia, from 1997 through 2000, then in the same position at the U.S. embassy in Berlin, Germany, from 2000 through 2004; and, as noted above, I headed the Public Affairs Office at the U.S. embassy in Baghdad, from the time the embassy reopened in June 2004 through June 2005. During these eight years, Iraq was the highest-priority foreign policy issue with which I dealt. This focus on Iraq led to my involvement in a host of activities with senior U.S. policymakers, as well as programs featuring the most influential U.S. commentators and analysts on foreign and security policy. Those whom I encountered during those eight years in Riyadh, Berlin, and Baghdad represented a Who's Who of U.S. experts, commentators, and pundits: President Emeritus of the Council on Foreign Relations (CFR) Leslie Gelb and CFR Senior Fellow Walter Russell Meade; Center for Strategic and International Studies expert Anthony Cordesman; *Newsweek*'s Fareed Zakaria; the Brookings Institution's Ken Pollack; the Heritage Foundation's Reuel Marc Gerecht; and Johns Hopkins University Middle East scholar Fouad Ajami, along with many others. Having the opportunity to listen to and engage such thinkers on various aspects of Iraq policy afforded me an unusually broad perspective on this complex issue.

In addition, during my year in Iraq I was in regular contact with the outstanding (and courageous) U.S. and international press corps that was reporting from Baghdad. The *New York Times'* John Burns, National Public Radio's Anne Garrels, the *Wall Street Journal's* Farnaz Fassili, the *Los Angeles Times'* Alissa Rubin, CBS's Kimberly Dozier—among many others—regularly filed insightful and perceptive dispatches on current developments in Iraq. I learned a great deal from speaking with them and from following their reporting.

My day-to-day interaction with the dedicated and talented senior leadership of U.S. forces in Iraq—including then Multi-National Forces-Iraq (MNF-I) Commanding General George Casey; General David Petraeus, who then headed the critical mission of training Iraqi security forces and is now the MNF-I commanding general; and my military public affairs counterparts General Erv Lessel, Admiral Greg Slavonic, and General Don Alston—was also invaluable to my understanding of developments in Iraq. Likewise, my interaction with members of the U.S. military at all levels—in Baghdad, Fallujah, Tikrit, Mosul, Kirkuk, and elsewhere around Iraq—was not only educational but also one of the most inspiring and uplifting experiences of my life.

During my year in Iraq, I also had the opportunity to visit and engage with fellow U.S. diplomats at the regional embassy offices in Basra, Hilla, Kirkuk, and Mosul and was impressed by their commitment and critical engagement with all elements of the regions and communities in which they operated. Similarly, I interacted with fellow diplomats from several countries—Britain, Italy, and Poland, among others—and with others from the international community, especially the UN elections team and a wide variety of nongovernmental organization (NGO) representatives, and developed a strong admiration for their involvement and personal commitment to the Iraq enterprise. The perspectives that I gleaned from my interaction with these focused and talented international players in Iraq were extremely useful to my own effort to understand and evaluate the unfolding dynamic of Iraq and its meaning in its broader international context.

I also had the good fortune to be in frequent contact with Iraqi interlocutors at all levels. The nature of my work led me to interact regularly with Iraqi government officials, journalists, academics, and

NGO leaders. While this engagement occurred most often in Baghdad, my travels around the country also brought me into contact with hundreds of Iraqis, from the far north to the far south of the country. On balance, I came away from this intense involvement with Iraqis with a deep admiration for the resilience and determination of these long-suffering people. This work is dedicated to them, with the hope that in some way it will contribute to the success of the historic struggle in which they are currently engaged.

However, perhaps the most valuable key to any insight that I might now claim on the issue of Iraq derives from my good fortune to be a member of what was undoubtedly the most impressive senior Foreign Service team ever assembled at a U.S. embassy—the senior staff that served under Ambassador John Negroponte in the period following the reopening of the U.S. embassy in Baghdad in late June 2004. This staff consisted of five individuals who had previously served in ambassadorial positions, an unprecedented circumstance for a U.S. embassy. Ambassador Negroponte, his deputy Jim Jeffrey, Political-Military Counselor Ron Neumann, and Political Counselor Robert Ford regularly briefed journalists, visiting U.S. government officials, and others on developments in Iraq, and my access to these sessions—sometimes several in a week—provided a unique vehicle for understanding the complexities of the Iraq issue, the developments on the ground in Iraq, and the evolution of U.S. policy to deal with these developments.

While I have been able to draw on exposure to this wealth of knowledge and talent in developing my own views concerning U.S. policy in Iraq, I would not impute to any of those mentioned above agreement with or support for any of the observations that I offer in this analysis. These conclusions are mine alone.

Following my return in late June of 2005 from my year in Iraq, I turned my focus to my next diplomatic assignment—as an associate at the Institute for the Study of Diplomacy in the School of Foreign Service at Georgetown University. There, over the coming two years, I would share my experience as an eyewitness to and participant in U.S. Iraq policy with the university community. In preparation for this task, I began to compile the material and collect the thoughts that I would draw on in presenting my assessment of the Iraq issue. My intention was to outline what I saw as the key elements related to this issue, elements that I felt in many cases were not sufficiently understood and appreciated. Specifically, while I saw that much had been reported—and was continuing to be reported—in the media and elsewhere on Iraq, I felt that the breadth of issues that are key to understanding the very complex Iraq story were not readily accessible in a comprehensive and succinct form. I thought that I could help address that shortcoming with a sort of primer on the Iraq issue, outlining the background to the Iraq crisis in the 1990s up to the Iraq War in the spring of 2003, and the factors at play in the aftermath of that war. This would be the material that I would use in teaching my seminars on Iraq at Georgetown University.

In compiling this material, which appears in this work, my approach has been to introduce as many issues as possible relevant to an understanding of the course of events that have taken place and that continue to unfold in Iraq, but not to attempt to lay out a comprehensive treatment of each such issue. There are primarily two reasons for this: My own level of expertise regarding many of the dozens of topics discussed in this work is limited, and these materials have been developed for use with supplemental, original-source readings in the context of my Iraq seminars at Georgetown University.

As it happened, in the months during which I was preparing such a primer in connection with my teaching activities at Georgetown, a number of publications appeared that provided much of the background and context needed to understand the Iraq issue. Perhaps the most comprehensive among these is *The New Yorker* magazine writer George Packer's *The Assassin's Gate*, which covers in depth and in context the most critical elements of the Iraq issue. Complementing Packer's work is the excellent human interest account of the Iraq conflict that Pulitzer Prize-winning journalist Anthony Shadid conveys in his moving volume *Night Draws Near*. Former Coalition Provisional Authority Administrator L. Paul Bremer III, in his book *My Year in Iraq*, also outlines many of the issues and challenges that need to be understood to adequately comprehend the Iraq issue and the U.S.' role in and efforts with regard to that country. The Iraq issue also received considerable, high-profile treatment in Bob Woodward's third installment in his "Bush at War" series, *State of Denial*. Two accounts of the Iraq War and its aftermath—first in *Cobra II*, by Michael R. Gordon and General Bernard E. Trainor (ret.), and then in *Fiasco*, by Tom Ricks—add key insight into the Iraq story from the military perspective. And two journalists with whom I worked while in Iraq—Rajiv Chandrasekaran, in *Imperial Life in the Emerald City*, and T. Christian Miller, in *Blood Money*—provide in-depth treatments of the Coalition Provisional Authority and U.S. reconstruction efforts in post-Saddam Iraq, respectively. I would recommend all of these publications to anyone who is seeking a thorough treatment of the Iraq issue. That said, in teaching seminars on the subject at Georgetown University, I have remained convinced of the value that a primer on the Iraq issue can bring to a discussion of this complex topic. It is such a treatment that I attempt to present in this work: a compendium that identifies and briefly treats the key elements that I believe need to be recognized and understood in order to be informed and conversant on the issue of Iraq.

In preparing this account of the Iraq issue, I have been mindful of an admonition that a journalist acquaintance of mine with extensive experience in post-war Iraq shared with me during a conversation in spring 2006: the resentment he heard expressed by some prominent Iraqis at those Americans who have used relatively brief periods of service in post-war Iraq to launch book-writing projects, and in so doing have, in the view of some Iraqis, compromised confidences that their Iraqi interlocutors shared with them. This realization has guided my own efforts in preparing this monograph, in which I have endeavored to use my own experience in Iraq to further understanding and support for the cause of Iraq and Iraqis while honoring the confidences with which my Iraqi counterparts and interlocutors entrusted me. For the record, I should perhaps note that, as a State Department Foreign Service Officer, I am precluded from realizing any financial gain from this or any other writing related to my professional activities.

Another development in the period since my return from Iraq also affected my approach during the research and writing phase of this monograph: my experience being back in Washington after eight consecutive years abroad, and in particular in the intellectually stimulating environment of Georgetown University. As the months went by, it became clear to me that, to fully understand all the moving parts involved in the Iraq issue, I needed much deeper insight into the discussion and debate within Washington academic and think tank circles on the Iraq issue, as well as into the domestic political and media climate in which the Iraq issue has unfolded.

Thus, I decided to devote considerable time and effort to participating in policy dialogues around Washington, attending numerous lectures by distinguished visiting speakers at Georgetown University, and using the opportunity afforded to me through an academic sojourn to immerse myself in the voluminous contemporary literature on Iraq. The result has led to a sobering assessment of the connection—as both cause and effect—between Iraq policy and the current domestic political climate, and the impact of this connection on the likely success or failure of our current Iraq policy, as well as, more generally, on the prospects of success for difficult foreign policy challenges in the future. This work encompasses my conclusions concerning this aspect of the Iraq issue as well.

My time at Georgetown University has led to another adjustment in my research and writing on Iraq—my decision to have this work more directly reflect my own experiences as a career diplomat, in particular as my own professional history relates to the Iraq issue. My inspiration for this pursuit has been my interaction with the bright and dedicated students in Georgetown University's School of Foreign Service. These students represent the next generation of U.S. (and, in many cases, non-U.S.) diplomats, and my experience in teaching them, discussing issues with them, and engaging with them in professional exercises related to diplomatic life has assured me that the future of diplomacy is in very capable hands. With their interests and curiosity in mind, I have sought to weave into the narrative that follows glimpses of diplomatic activity—in particular in my area of professional specialization, public diplomacy—and of foreign service life that will entice them to continue on the rigorous road of preparing to serve their countries as Foreign Service Officers.

In presenting the analysis that follows, I have endeavored to be objective, seeking to avoid judging U.S. policy or the U.S. approach to the Iraq issue. In a political and policy environment whose rancor is reflected in such titles of treatments of the Iraq issue as *Fiasco*, *Hubris*, and *State of Denial*, this approach may disappoint some. The analysis in the coming pages suggests, however, that where we are today with Iraq is the result of decades of developments and policy decisions spanning both Republican and Democratic administrations. Many, probably most, of these policy decisions could be second-guessed with the wisdom of hindsight. The purpose of this exercise is not to praise or criticize; rather, it is to attempt to identify and explain the factors that have played and are playing a role in Iraq and to analyze U.S. policies and actions involving that country, in order to leave the reader with a deeper understanding of these factors and the daunting complexity of the Iraq issue. I am pleased to leave to pundits—and perhaps historians—the task of judging the wisdom of U.S.

policy analyses and decisions concerning Iraq. Such an exercise in the current context would just distract from the purpose of this work.

The treatment that follows encompasses a number parameters that I view as inextricably linked to an understanding of the Iraq issue:

- the "end of history" thesis and the emergence of the United States as the sole superpower in the 1990s;
- the causes and consequences of the events of 9/11;
- the arrival of the Information Age—at a time of rapid population growth and economic and political stagnation—in the Arab world, and the impact of this development on the Arab street;
- sociocultural developments (secularism, multilateralism, demilitarization, pacifism), economic issues (social welfare, economic stagnation) and demographic trends (birth, dearth, aging population, Muslim immigration) affecting Europe and relationships between the United States and its European allies;
- religious, ethnic, economic, and cultural factors within Iraq and the Arab world that are affecting developments there; and,
- challenges to U.S. foreign policy efforts deriving from the interaction of democratic governance and the new international information environment.

In connection with these elements of the Iraq issue, I adopt certain perspectives to frame the treatment of Iraq—and the many broader international and foreign policy issues associated with Iraq—in what follows. I believe it is useful for the reader to be aware of these at the outset; they include the following:

- that the events of 9/11 ushered in a new era, what I call the post-Westphalian world, and that the international community (and international institutions) have yet to come to terms with the realities of this new era;
- that 9/11 revealed that western security interests necessitate that the political and economic dysfunction that afflicts

much of the Arab world be addressed in one form or another;

- that in the Information Age, basic elements of the democratic process and the nature of the information environment have created new challenges for liberal, democratic societies in confronting forces opposed to western democratic principles; and,

- that the unique position of the United States as the world's sole superpower at the point in history in which the international order passed from a Westphalian into a post-Westphalian world has had unexpected and very challenging consequences for the United States.

I appreciate the concurrence of my employer, the U.S. Department of State, in the publication of this monograph. However, the views expressed herein do not, of course, represent those of the U.S. government, the U.S. Department of State, Georgetown University, or the Institute for the Study of Diplomacy; they reflect my views alone.

Georgetown University
Washington, DC
February 2007

I
Iraq and 9/11

Much has been made of claims of a connection between the terrorist attacks of September 11, 2001, and Saddam Hussein's Iraq. Many who supported the U.S.-led coalition's action to remove Saddam from power in Iraq cite grounds for doing so in allegations that Saddam's Iraq was allied with the perpetrator of these attacks—al-Qaeda. Vociferous objections from those on the other side of the issue deride such claims of an alliance, citing among other factors the Iraq Baathists' secular nationalism as being anathema to the principles and aims of al-Qaeda. The 9/11 Commission looked closely into the issue of a possible connection between Iraq and al-Qaeda and, while noting credible reports that "describe friendly contacts and indicate some common themes in both sides' hatred of the United States," concluded that "we have seen no evidence that these or earlier contacts ever developed into a collaborative operational relationship. Nor have we seen evidence that Iraq cooperated with al Qaeda in developing or carrying out any attacks against the United States."[1] While among some the issue remains in dispute, for most Americans the matter of a direct, operational link between Iraq and al-Qaeda has been settled—there was none. I also hold this view.

However, while neither allied nor operationally linked, there was an important connection between the two. This first became clear to me more than four years before 9/11—in the summer of 1997, shortly after I arrived in Riyadh, Saudi Arabia, to take up my assignment as counselor for Public Affairs at the U.S. embassy there. Not long after returning to Saudi Arabia—for what would be my third time living in the kingdom over a period spanning more than two decades—it became clear to me that the ongoing conflict between the U.S. government and Saddam Hussein's Iraq had had a devastating effect on U.S.-Saudi relations in the years since the Gulf War of 1991.

Saddam, who had carte blanche in dealing with his own captive countrymen, used this power to pursue policies that required the United States to respond in ways that had an insidious effect on perceptions of and attitudes toward the United States in the region. Most devastating was his callous misuse of the resources made available to Iraq through the Oil-for-Food (OFF) program. Rather than apply these funds toward acquiring food, medicine, and other essentials for the Iraqi people—as the international community had anticipated would be done when OFF was conceived and launched—Saddam allowed the Iraqi people to suffer devastating shortages of these basic essentials while he built palaces, funded international bribery schemes,[2] and lavished luxury on himself, his family, and his cronies. The resulting suffering of the Iraqi people—including much-publicized child mortality—was widely and graphically reported throughout the Arab world largely due to the rapidly growing reach of satellite television in the region. The appearance in 1996 of the Qatar-based regional satellite broadcaster Al-Jazeera was a major milestone in this process, a development that will be considered in detail in chapter 3.

Of interest to those of us who were observing this from the vantage point of neighboring Saudi Arabia was that the wrath of the Arab world that was engendered by Saddam's mistreatment of his own countrymen was not directed at Saddam or the Iraqi leadership, but largely at the West in general, and the United States in particular, since it was the West—to some extent at U.S. insistence—that, in the view of the Arab street, was behind the UN sanctions on Iraq that made OFF necessary. The logic was that, while Saddam is a monster—we know that, and you know that—it is not this monster who is suffering under the sanctions, it is our fellow Arabs. In the case of Saudi Arabia, the level of personal identification with the suffering Iraqi people was intensified by the fact of many very close tribal and familial relations between Saudis and Iraqis. The long border between the two countries has for millennia been an open migratory route for the nomadic tribes of the Arabian Peninsula. Many Saudis can trace common ancestry to Iraqis going back only a generation or two.[3]

The suffering of the Iraqi people, conveyed visually in daily reporting by regional broadcasters, had a cumulative and strongly adverse impact on Arab attitudes toward the United States. It convinced many that, at their core, U.S. policies were anti-Arab and anti-Muslim and that at a human level the United States cared nothing for the lives and well-being of Arabs and Muslims. This situation was considerably aggravated by the fact that, by and large, Saudis and others in the Gulf dismissed Saddam as a current threat. Their analysis was that Saddam had been successfully declawed as a threat to other countries in the region, and thus—in the eyes of many—the continuation of the sanctions policy against Iraq was more a reflection of U.S. anti-Arab or anti-Muslim sentiments than it was a strategic security policy in the region. The longer this state of affairs continued, the worse would be its long-term effect on attitudes on the part of Arab populations toward the United States.

On more than one occasion during my time in Saudi Arabia in the late 1990s, I heard Saudi acquaintances and contacts make the claim that, on the basis of the observable evidence, the only logical conclusion to draw was that Saddam Hussein was actually an agent of the Central Intelligence Agency (CIA). In their eyes, his otherwise "illogical" actions only made sense when interpreted against this claim: He (alone) gave the United States a pretext for stationing large numbers of military forces in Saudi Arabia and elsewhere in the region, and his remaining in power (something "permitted" by U.S. actions at the end of the Gulf War) kept one of the potentially most powerful and influential Arab countries in a permanent state of weakness and decline. I have found such "conspiracy theories" as explanations for regional and international developments not uncommon in the Middle East; it is quite possible that a majority of man-on-the-street Saudis held this view of the situation concerning Iraq.

The second aspect of the situation during the latter years of the Saddam regime that convinced me that the status quo with Iraq was increasingly harmful to the United States was the impact that another aspect of U.S. (and UN) policy—the policy of containment against Saddam, requiring the enforcement of no-fly zones in both northern and southern Iraq—was having on Saudi Arabia itself. The maintenance of the southern no-fly zone was conducted largely using U.S. forces based in Saudi Arabia. The need to station five thousand U.S. military personnel in Saudi Arabia to enforce the southern no-fly zone was perhaps the single greatest factor in the growth of what was a small, obscure terrorist organization at the beginning of the 1990s—al-Qaeda—into an international actor capable of the attacks of 9/11. As noted in *The 9/11 Commission Report*, as early as 1992, "the al-Qaeda leadership issued a *fatwa* calling for *jihad* against the Western 'occupation' of Islamic lands."[4] This "occupation" was central to Osama bin Laden and his al-Qaeda organization in recruitment efforts, and the presence of so many U.S. military personnel in their country strongly (and adversely) affected the attitude of even many moderate Saudis toward the United States. As with the devastating impact of the UN sanctions on the Iraqi people, the longer U.S. forces remained in Saudi Arabia to enforce the southern no-fly zone in Iraq, the worse would become attitudes in the kingdom toward the United States and the stronger would grow support for expelling these forces—an action that lay at the heart of the agenda al-Qaeda promulgated.

The third impact of Saddam's policies that underscored to me the need for a change in the status quo in Iraq, while not as devastating to U.S. interests as the two cited above, was the Saddam regime's overt support for and encouragement of those who actively opposed any effort at finding a peaceful resolution to the Arab-Israeli conflict. The highly publicized policy of the Saddam government of providing payments to the families of Palestinian suicide bombers, and Iraq's public posture as the leader of the region's resistance to a peaceful resolution of the Arab-Israeli conflict and a normalization of relations between the Arab states and Israel, severely undermined what efforts there were to address this long-festering conflict. During all of this, the Arab street has proceeded to largely displace its anger, hostility, and frustration onto the United States, the one player whom they believed could solve the dispute, essentially by dictating to Israel terms favorable to the Palestinian side. The fact that this has never been a realistic option has not dissuaded its proponents from acting—often violently—on its premise. It was this sad and volatile state of affairs that the policies of the Saddam Hussein government were continuing to help fuel.

THE PARADIGM SHIFT

It has by now become a cliché to say that 9/11 changed everything: in the terminology popularized by science historian Thomas Kuhn in the 1970s, it is said to have entailed a "paradigm shift."[5] The failure of imagination alluded to in *The 9/11 Commission Report*, in this case the failure to anticipate the type of terrorist attacks carried out against the United States on September 11, 2001, derived from the fact that no one—not security or foreign policy experts, nor political leaders, no one—had the imagination to see 9/11 coming; but the events of that day forever changed the paradigm that governed security analyses.

Before the events of September 11, 2001, certain behaviors were assumed to be incompatible, such as combining the intelligence, rationality, and patience to plan attacks as sophisticated as those carried out on 9/11 with the "irrationality" of seeking to murder thousands, potentially tens of thousands of random, innocent people as they went about their daily lives, and to commit suicide in the act. The terrorist acts of 9/11 proved the fallacy of such thinking; it showed that a sufficient combination of rage, humiliation, fatalism, and religious fervor could trigger mass murder, potentially on an apocalyptic scale, and erased forever the bounds of the unthinkable.

It continues to be a challenge to rational planners with leadership or security responsibilities to anticipate the actions of extremists who have become all-consumed by hatred and a sense of outrage and humiliation. Perhaps nowhere has the level of such fanatical, suicidal activity ever been more evident than in post-Saddam Iraq. During the more than three years of the Iraqi insurgency, heinous acts committed by religiously inspired extremists have accounted for much of the tragedy and suffering that has befallen Iraqis, coalition forces, and others in Iraq. While our military and other planners continue to push the boundaries of the imaginable, it is likely that the terrorists will remain a step ahead of them.

THE WESTPHALIAN WORLD

Before looking at the U.S. response to this new, post-9/11 world, it is instructive to consider briefly the world that it replaced. The paradigm that has defined the international order for the past several centuries is often referred to as the "Westphalian world," after two treaties that ended the Thirty Years War in 1648 and that were negotiated in the Westphalian region of present-day Germany; together they are referred to as the Treaty of Westphalia. In the Westphalian world, individual nation-states have full sovereignty of action within their borders, and other nation-states are precluded—under international law—from interfering in matters that take place within the borders of another nation state. This system, which was originally designed for the nations of Europe in the seventeenth century essentially to settle religious disputes, evolved over the intervening centuries to define the global international order. Of course, there are many historical instances in which states have challenged, or even defied, the Westphalian principles. But such violations were always seen as aberrations, exceptions to the accepted system of inviolable national sovereignty. Article 2 of the UN Charter reflects perhaps the high point in the codification of the Westphalian principle of the territorial sovereignty of nation states when it states, in paragraph four, that "[A]ll Members shall refrain in their international relations from the threat or use of force against the territorial integrity or political independence of any state."[6]

Several international developments in recent years have challenged this system, especially the dangers posed by failed states and the proliferation of the know-how for producing weapons of mass destruction. While the United Nations, regional security bodies, the Group of Eight (G-8), and other international actors have, over the course of the past decade or two, studied the problem and mooted mechanisms to address these growing dangers, the events of 9/11 effectively ushered out the Westphalian era; however, the international community has yet formally to revise the international security architecture and international security principles to reflect this basic change in the international system. As British Prime Minister Tony Blair stated in a speech at Georgetown University on May 26, 2006: "There is a hopeless mismatch between the global challenges we face and the global institutions to confront them."[7] One casualty of the gap between current geopolitical reality and the inadequate international institutional infrastructure to deal with this reality is the international community's handling of the issue of Iraq.

THE (NEW) U.S. NATIONAL SECURITY STRATEGY

The U.S. National Security Strategy that President Bush announced on September 17, 2002, and updated in what has been characterized as a more "multilateral" version on March 16, 2006, explicitly acknowledged the changed circumstances that 9/11 wrought. "Enemies in the past needed great armies and great industrial capacities to endanger America," the document states, and then notes that "[n]ow, shadowy networks of individuals can bring great chaos and suffering to our shores for less than it costs to purchase a tank."[8] To deal with this new security environment the president announced that the United States

> "[w]ill disrupt and destroy terrorist organizations by . . . defending the United States, the American people, and our interests at home and abroad by identifying and destroying the threat before it reaches our borders. While the United States will constantly strive to enlist the support of the international community, we will not hesitate to act alone, if necessary, to exercise our right of self-defense by acting preemptively against such terrorists, to prevent them from doing harm against our people and our country."9

This new doctrine of preemption has provoked a great deal of discussion and controversy among the U.S.' friends and foes alike. The fact that the world's dominant power has explicitly announced such a policy of preemption has proven to be unsettling in many quarters.

THE GENEVA CONVENTIONS IN THE POST-WESTPHALIAN WORLD

Another element of the international system that has proven inadequate to deal with the new, post-9/11 reality is the body of international law referred to as the Geneva Conventions, the system of treaties and agreements that nation-states have codified as the laws of war. These legal principles and mechanisms were created to apply civilized standards to the conduct of conventional war between nation-states. The new reality of asymmetric, unconventional, armed conflict between nation-states and internationally organized and supported terrorists has left unclear how such combatants, when they are captured, are to be treated. While they purposefully violate the laws of war as defined in the Geneva Conventions—by employing such tactics as deliberately targeting civilians, executing prisoners, using human shields, and not distinguishing themselves from the general population by wearing uniforms or through other means; indeed, their basic war-fighting strategy is predicated upon the advantages that they gain by using such tactics—the nation-states at war with them are still bound by their own commitment to civilized norms to accord these combatants civilized treatment.

International law and the international community, however, have not yet addressed the basic challenges that the new reality presents in the area of international armed conflict, and it is the lack of consensus in this area that has sparked the intense international debate concerning such issues as the appropriate rules for interrogation and treatment of captured illegal combatants and terrorists, the proper processes for determining their guilt or innocence, the holding of such captives at facilities such as the U.S.'s Guantanamo Bay detention center or even at undisclosed locations, the policy of renditions, and so on. As the nation that has taken the lead in the post-9/11 effort to combat those aligned with the movement of international Islamic extremism behind the 9/11 attacks, the United States has borne the bulk of the responsibility for handling this new category of captured combatant. As the United States has improvised in this area, it has found itself subject to strong international criticism for its actions.

The challenges associated with the use of classified intelligence to identify such combatants, the treatment of illegal combatants who may only be in the planning stage for launching military or terrorist action, and the difficulty of meeting courtroom evidential standards in order to be able to prosecute such combatants reflect just some of the types of dilemmas that our troops and our system of justice face in the era of post-Westphalian warfare. Creating a system to address this new reality that is effective as well as seen as fair, and that is able to gain widespread international acceptance, is a task that is likely to involve world political leaders, diplomats, and the international human rights community for years to come.

URGENT U.S. POST-9/11 POLICY GOALS

Notwithstanding all the difficulties that have plagued Iraq in the more than three years since the U.S.-led coalition took military action to remove Saddam Hussein from power in the country, my conviction—first developed in Saudi Arabia in 1997—has not changed: that the United States had to adjust its policy approaches to the Middle East in three fundamental areas:

- It needed to remove the five thousand U.S. troops that were stationed in Saudi Arabia.

- It needed to see to it that the Iraqi people did not continue suffering under UN sanctions.

- It had to communicate in some manner to the people of the region that the United States would not support forever the status quo of authoritarian rule in the region but rather was on the side of those who sought measured political and economic reform.

The events of 9/11 confirmed that the need to take these actions had evolved into urgent matters of U.S. national security, and the policy course that the United States has followed toward Iraq and the Middle East since 9/11 has addressed all three imperatives.

WEAPONS OF MASS DESTRUCTION

As described above, the status quo in Iraq at the time of the Iraq War in 2003 was such that it was supporting the steady growth of Arab anger and antipathy toward the United States, fostering an increase in the capability and determination of al-Qaeda to continue its asymmetrical war with the United States, and undermining efforts to resolve the Arab-Israeli dispute, a conflict that has fueled anti-American sentiment in the Middle East for several decades. In using military means to remove Saddam Hussein and his government from power in Iraq, the American-led coalition effectively performed radical surgery on the entire Middle East region, concluding that the status quo was simply too dangerous to let stand.

While the *wisdom* of this action certainly deserves close scrutiny, the domestic and international debates on Iraq—especially in the period around the time that the coalition used force to remove Saddam from power—tended to focus heavily on its *legitimacy*. In fact, the legitimacy of coalition military action against the Baathist regime in Iraq rested on very solid ground. The question of its timing, its conduct—and the lessons learned from this action—should be debated and discussed, since the circumstances and elements that played into the Iraq issue are likely to become more, not less, prevalent in a world of increasing globalization, interconnection, and transparency. However, in the aftermath of coalition military action to remove Saddam Hussein's regime from power in Iraq, these crucial issues were overshadowed in the public debate on Iraq by the (largely non-)issue of the legitimacy of coalition military action against Saddam's regime.

As policymakers in the United States and elsewhere repeatedly pointed out in the months before the Iraq War, Saddam Hussein was in noncompliance with a series of UN Security Council resolutions that set the terms for the cease-fire that came into effect at the end of the Gulf War. His violation of the terms of that cease-fire was, in itself, grounds for the coalition to resume military activity against Iraq. Moreover, in November 2002 the UN Security Council unanimously passed Resolution 1441, which cited Iraq as being in "material breach" of the terms of the cease-fire agreement and threatened "serious consequences" if Iraq did not fulfill the cease-fire terms by documenting that it had disposed of its weapons of mass destruction. It also set a deadline of December 7, 2002, for Iraq to come into compliance. Iraq failed to do so, as Hans Blix, the head of UN Monitoring, Verification and Inspection Commission (UNMOVIC) announced on March 7, 2003.

As described above, the effects of the policies and actions of the Saddam Hussein government vis-à-vis the United States and the Middle East region following the Gulf War of 1991 led to a situation of considerable threat toward Americans. One could argue that this circumstance alone would justify the United States' taking action to remove that regime. But such action—solely on the basis of a theoretical analysis of the impact of another sovereign nation's policies on U.S. national interests and security—would truly represent a new chapter in international affairs. Concluding on the basis of a theoretical analysis that policies pursued by a sovereign government operating solely within its own borders and not overtly threatening any other sovereign state were inimical to your national security, and then taking action on that basis (alone) to remove that government by force, would entail a radically changed set of operating principles in the international arena. In a world of proliferating weapons of mass destruction (WMD) technology and extremists willing to conduct terrorism on an apocalyptic scale, it may be that such a development will occur at some time and that a country or coalition of countries will decide to take military action against another sovereign country solely on the basis of such a theoretical analysis. But this is not what happened in the case of Iraq.

Saddam Hussein's government, while successful in manipulating international opinion, oppressing its people, and frustrating the efforts of the international community to verify the contents of its weapons arsenal, had made one serious and lasting miscalculation, one that would ultimately prove to be its undoing—the invasion and occupation of Kuwait in 1990. The occupation of another sovereign state opened the Saddam regime to sanctions from the international community. The sanctions that the United Nations imposed included the requirement to undertake certain aspects of disarmament and, importantly, to verify such disarmament to the satisfaction of the international community. Here, as we have come to see, Saddam was caught in a trap.

While in hindsight we can see that world leaders and international arms experts misread Saddam, it is now clear that Saddam, after many years of gaming the weapons' inspection process, was in fact prepared to undertake the disarmament measures required by the international community, and that he actually did so. Thus, while there was essentially universal belief throughout the international community that Saddam continued to stockpile and produce weapons of mass destruction and other banned weapons right up to the time of the Iraq War in March 2003, the evidence that has come to light since Saddam's removal has contradicted this assessment. It is now generally accepted that Saddam had in fact destroyed his chemical and biological weapons—and had ceased pursuing nuclear weapons—by the late 1990s or the early part of the present decade. He seems to have crafted an alternate WMD strategy: to combine an effort—through bribery, economic incentives, and the manipulation of international opinion for the plight of the Iraqi people—to seek an end to UN sanctions against Iraq while continuing to maintain the human infrastructure required to reconstitute such weapons once sanctions were lifted. This, rather than actually maintaining stockpiles of such weapons, appears to have been Saddam's approach.

What ultimately baffled the international community—including, apparently, U.S. and other intelligence agencies—was Saddam's unwillingness to document credibly that he had destroyed his WMD, when such a course of action would have given his government a clean bill of health with the United Nations and almost certainly would have resulted in a lifting of sanctions against Iraq. The western miscalculation here seems to have been an inability from a western perspective to understand Saddam's need to maintain the fiction of retaining WMD and other weapons systems as a deterrent to domestic and regional adversaries. Such an admission of "weakness," he seems to have calculated, would have likely led to his overthrow from either internal or external actors.

Saddam's dilemma prevented him from fulfilling the disarmament conditions set out in the UN sanctions, and thus military action by an international coalition to enforce these sanctions—while arguably unwise or untimely—was legitimate under the UN sanctions resolutions in effect at the time against Iraq.

ALTERNATE SCENARIOS?

Military action to remove Saddam Hussein was, of course, not the only possible course to follow in dealing with the Iraqi dictator, and several others were contemplated or advocated. These included

- engineering a coup d'etat against Saddam,
- convincing or cajoling Saddam and others in the senior Iraqi leadership to go into exile,
- coming to an accommodation with Saddam, and,
- extending UN weapons inspections in Iraq.

These alternative scenarios vary, however, in the extent to which they would have addressed the three policy objectives whose urgency was revealed by the events of 9/11: (1) the lifting of the UN sanctions that were causing hardship and suffering for the people of Iraq, (2) the opportunity to remove the U.S. forces enforcing the southern no-fly zone in Iraq from Saudi Arabia, and (3) communicating to the people of the Middle East that the United States supported political reform in the region. The first two alternatives would achieve all three objectives; the second two—both of which allowed for leaving Saddam in power—would not. I look at each in turn below.

Coup d'etat

The literature on the possibility of a successful coup against Saddam in the period leading up to the Iraq War is considerable and uniform in its conclusion that through ruthlessness and multiple, overlapping security arrangements, Saddam had largely insulated himself from the possibility of being removed by a coup. As Bob Woodward notes in his book on the buildup to the Iraq War, *Plan of Attack*, as early as 1991 the U.S. government was secretly seeking to have Saddam removed from power. Woodward writes: "After the 1991 Gulf War, President George H.W. Bush signed a presidential finding authorizing the CIA to topple Saddam."[10] However, by the time of the runup to the Iraq War, the CIA had concluded, again according to Woodward's account, that "covert action is not going to remove Saddam."[11] As Woodward summarized the then-prevailing view: "The CIA had to face the reality that Saddam, in power since 1979, had erected a nearly perfect security apparatus to protect himself from a coup.... The only way to succeed was for the CIA to support a full military invasion of Iraq."[12] Writing more recently, Middle East scholar Fouad Ajami came to the same conclusion based on his many visits to Iraq in the post-Saddam period: "The Saddam regime would have lasted a thousand years had the Americans not come in and decapitated it. The system of control left nothing to chance: the capital was like a city under siege."[13]

Exile

With the prospect for achieving the stated U.S. policy of regime change in Iraq through a coup against Saddam essentially dismissed, the second scenario suggested above—the possibility of Saddam's regime going into exile—began to get an airing. In the months before military action was launched, senior voices in the U.S. leadership began to raise the issue of Saddam's "voluntary" departure from the country—i.e., his choosing exile over war. I recall, for example, being at the annual European Security Conference in Munich ("Wehrkunde") in early February 2003, supporting the participation of then Defense Secretary Donald Rumsfeld, where he engaged a largely skeptical audience of security officials and experts from Europe, a Europe that he had recently rhetorically divided into "old" and "new." While much of the discussion focused on the concern over weapons of mass destruction that were believed to be in the hands of Saddam Hussein, the secretary in his comments raised an interesting proposal, suggesting that military action could be avoided if Saddam Hussein were to relinquish power voluntarily and go into exile.

This appeal for Saddam and the senior Baathist leadership to depart Iraq as a means of avoiding war called to my mind an incident several years earlier, during one of my diplomatic tours in Saudi Arabia. I was in Jeddah, at the Saudi government's Conference Palace, when I glanced across the dining room and saw former Ugandan dictator Idi Amin sitting at a table with a small entourage. Recalling that that murderous dictator had lived in quiet and peaceful exile in Saudi Arabia for more than two decades following his flight from Uganda, the thought crossed my mind that such an outcome for Saddam might also be attainable.

Some weeks later, on the eve of the war, the issue of Saddam going into exile was raised by Secretary of State Colin Powell in an interview with Fox TV. Powell stated:

> If Saddam Hussein, his sons and a number of other top leaders were to leave and a more responsible leadership come in, a leadership that is determined to get rid of its weapons of mass destruction as they are supposed to and start to provide a better life for the Iraqi people, then war certainly could be averted."[14]

Woodward's treatment of the lead-up to the Iraq War also discusses in some detail the prospects of Saddam's exile as a solution to the Iraq crisis, noting some ambivalence on the part of President Bush to the idea but also citing efforts conveyed to him by the president that involved Saudi Arabia and Egypt actively pursuing such a step.[15]

On the very eve of hostilities—in his March 17 address to the nation concerning the Iraq crisis—President Bush included mention of the issue of Saddam's possible exile as a means of avoiding war:

> In recent days, some governments in the Middle East have been doing their part. They have delivered public and private messages urging the dictator to leave Iraq, so that disarmament can proceed peacefully.[16]

The U.S. leadership thus made it clear that the departure of the Saddam government from the country could lead to a peaceful resolution of the impasse. As the brinkmanship leading up to what eventually became hostilities intensified, there appears to have been a hope that a unified international front calling for such a departure from the country by Saddam and his senior associates—coupled with the threat from the massive international military presence that had been deployed to the region—would lead to a resolution of the crisis through diplomacy, not bloodshed, a peaceful outcome that would be favorable to the international community, the region, and—as it would spare them the brutality of a military invasion and violent overthrow of their government—an outcome especially beneficial to the long-suffering Iraqi people.

Evidence that has since come to light suggests, however, that certain parties active on the international diplomatic front at the time seemed more interested in pursuing other interests—largely financial in nature—than in helping bring about such an outcome, doing so at the expense of an international solidarity that might have forced Saddam's departure. Most observers have concluded that it was Saddam's perception that such dissension within the ranks of the international community would allow him both to remain in the leadership of Iraq and to avoid military action against him and his country.

Reconciliation

The third policy option noted above for dealing with the Saddam regime—the possibility of the United States and the international community reconciling with Saddam—seems to have had some support in the Arab world. I am aware of at least one instance in which an Arab leader, having come to the conclusion that Saddam's threat to the region and beyond had been neutralized and that Iraq was so weakened through the long years of UN sanctions, that he urged the United States to seek to "rehabilitate" Saddam and come to an accommodation with his regime that would leave Saddam in power but would address U.S., western and regional security concerns. As noted above, while such an approach might have been able to accomplish two of the three U.S. security policy imperatives revealed by the attacks of 9/11—removing U.S. forces from Saudi Arabia and lifting UN sanctions against Iraq—it would not have addressed the third and more fundamental one—the need for the United States and the West to be seen by those in the region as supporting political and economic reform in the Arab world. Aside from the very difficult question of how the United States and the West could strike a bargain with the notoriously brutal and belligerent Iraqi dictator that would satisfy their security concerns, an agreement that would have entailed supporting a continuation of a dictatorship by Saddam and the Sunni minority in Iraq that he represented would have reinforced the belief among those agitating for democratic reform in the region that the United States was opposed to such reform. Moreover, it would have further convinced the reformers that the al-Qaeda terrorists were the only viable conduit for confronting the region's autocrats and sparking the needed change in the Arab world.

One element that was likely at play among Sunni Arab leaders who countenanced accommodation with Saddam, not removing him, was the nature of the political course that the United States and its coalition allies were determined to promote in post-Saddam Iraq—democratic governance. Such a course would unavoidably result in political dominance within Iraq by the country's Shi'a majority. As war approached, and Saddam's demise seemed likely, Iraq's Sunni Arab neighbors may have come to have growing misgivings about the political implications for the region of a democratic Iraq under Shi'a political hegemony.

Extending WMD Inspections

A final alternative to initiating military action against Saddam's regime in March 2003 to consider would have been to allow the UN weapon inspection's process in Iraq to continue. This process had been taking place on and off since the end of the Gulf War twelve years earlier. Some might suggest that given the military pressure that was being brought to bear on Saddam at the time (some two hundred thousand coalition troops were already in place in the Persian Gulf area), and the clear determination of the U.S. president to bring the issue of Iraq's WMD to some final resolution, conditions were ripe for resolving this issue through inspections. Since that course was not chosen, its prospects for success will always be a matter of speculation. And, of course, even a successful inspection regime—however "success" was to be defined when the government of the country being inspected had failed for twelve years to be forthcoming with the inspectors—would also not have achieved regime change in Iraq.

As is well known, the dynamics at play at the time were such that those countries whose forces were poised to undertake military action against Iraq would have faced significant logistical, financial, and military (largely troop morale and readiness) challenges in keeping such forces in place indefinitely while additional inspections played out. The war-fighting capability of these forces—especially in a conflict in which coalition commanders foresaw the possibility of the use of chemical (and possibly biological) weapons against them, requiring the use of heat-trapping chem-bio suits—would steadily degrade as the heat of Iraq's summer approached. Meanwhile, those countries most insistent on allowing more time for inspections to go forward were not those with military personnel committed to the coalition. This very asymmetry undermined the dialogue and the prospects for agreement between the two camps on the issue of confronting Saddam by prolonging UN inspections, on the one hand, or, on the other, using military means to resolve the Iraq issue within the closing window during which those means could be employed.

THE POST-WESTPHALIAN CHALLENGE

As the history of the past few decades has made clear, in the case of Saddam Hussein's Iraq, the international community was faced with a rogue state that acquired—and used—weapons of mass destruction, both against a neighbor (Iran, in the Iran-Iraq War) and communities of its own citizens (the Kurds, in Halabja and possibly elsewhere). While such possession and use of WMD represented a clear threat to countries in the region, and possibly beyond, these actions by Saddam's regime did not in fact provoke international action to address this threat. It was only by invading and occupying a sovereign state—Kuwait—that Saddam violated a clear international principle—the Westphalian doctrine of inviolable national sovereignty—and thus triggered the response under international law that eventually led to his ouster by coalition forces acting in enforcement of UN Security Council resolutions from the post-Gulf War period in April 2003.

As difficult and divisive as the issue of handling Iraq proved to be to the international community, it did not involve the fundamental challenge that emerged from the events of 9/11. This new and elemental challenge is to construct a mechanism for reaching an international consensus to guide the post-Westphalian world in which catastrophic threats might emanate from states or actors within states that have not actually violated any of the acknowledged Westphalian norms and thus are not legitimate targets for the use of force under Westphalian principles. To date, more than five years after the events of September 11, 2001 alerted the world to this problem, little has been undertaken within the international community toward addressing this critical issue.

2

The End of the Cold War and the Emergence of a Unipolar World

Before considering the alternative rationale for the Iraq War that emerged after the intelligence on Saddam's WMD was found to have been incorrect—democracy promotion in the region—it is important to review what, in my view, are the two key megadevelopments whose consequences have largely defined the circumstances in which the current situation in Iraq is now playing itself out: the end of the Cold War in the late 1980s and early 1990s; and the dawn of the Information Age, as reflected in the spread of satellite television and Internet access into even the remotest corners of the globe starting around the mid-1990s. I look at the effects of the former occurrence in this chapter and the impact of the latter in the next.

During the period of the Cold War, the United States followed an acknowledged policy of "containment" toward our communist adversaries and a policy of selective "accommodation" with autocracies, monarchies, and other nondemocratic governments that were viewed as necessary strategic allies in the struggle against communism. This latter policy was followed with several Arab countries—from Egypt, to Jordan, to Saudi Arabia, to the Gulf states. The policy of accommodating nondemocratic governments was effectively acknowledged through its repudiation by President Bush in November 2003, in a speech at the National Endowment for Democracy. In his speech, the president reversed five decades of U.S. policy and announced that "the United States has adopted a new policy, a forward strategy of freedom in the Middle East." As the president noted:

> Sixty years of Western nations excusing and accommodating the lack of freedom in the Middle East did nothing to make us safe—because in the long run, stability cannot be purchased at the expense of liberty.[1]

In hindsight, this change in U.S. policy might be seen as having come some fourteen years too late. The fall of the Berlin Wall in 1989 signaled the end of the Cold War and removed any justification for a policy of accommodation with nondemocratic governments on the basis that such a compromise of U.S. principles was for the greater good of winning an existential ideological battle.[2] However, with the massive upheaval affecting the international community as a result of the ending of the Cold War, and the many challenges that this historic shift in the international order presented to the United States and the other western democracies, there was—not surprisingly—neither the will nor any perceived urgency to reassess and revise our approach to the "benign autocracies" of our allied governments in the Arab world. Although it would not be overtly stated until some fourteen years later, our policies at the time made it clear that stability trumped principle in our approach to these governments.

My own experience in the region involved considerable time spent living in the Kingdom of Saudi Arabia—two years in the late 1970s as a university professor, three years in the mid-1980s as a diplomat, and another three years in the late 1990s, again as a diplomat. My time in the kingdom gave me an opportunity to experience, and assess, the oft-cited "Saudi-American partnership," a relationship that has existed since the historic meeting between President Franklin D. Roosevelt and King Abdul Aziz Ibn Saud aboard the cruiser *USS Quincy* at Great Bitter Lake in Egypt on February 14, 1945, some seven years after U.S. geologists had discovered substantial oil deposits in the kingdom's Al-Hasa (today, Eastern) Province. The importance of this partnership grew with the increasing prominence of Saudi Arabia in international oil markets and the emergence of the kingdom as a moderating influence within the Organization of Petroleum Exporting Countries (OPEC) oil cartel. The partnership carried an implied U.S. commitment to the security of Saudi Arabia. In 1980, in response to the Soviet invasion of Afghanistan the previous year, President Jimmy Carter, in the Carter Doctrine, expanded and codified the policy of U.S. protection for the Gulf oil-producing states—of which Saudi Arabia is by far the largest—from outside intervention: "An attempt by any outside force to gain control of the Persian Gulf region will be regarded as an assault on the vital interests of the United States of America, and such an assault will be repelled by any means necessary, including military force."[3] By that time the Persian Gulf had become the most strategic locus of petroleum resources in the world, a position that it continues to occupy to this day.

During my assignment at the U.S. embassy in Riyadh from 1997 through 2000, the tension between support for the status quo ("stability") and advocacy for political reform ("principle") was ever present. I recall a meeting in Jeddah at which we brought together a number of opinion leaders—journalists, academics, and the like—to meet with a visiting senior State Department official. The animated discussion focused on the need for the United States to be seen as supporting political reform in the kingdom; there was growing anger, the Saudi interlocutors claimed, at the lack of freedom and opportunity in the country, and the large cohort of young Saudis (even today, more than 60 percent of Saudis are under the age of eighteen) was frustrated and becoming restless for reform.

However, despite a strong reporting message to the department on that evening's discussion, and the conviction on the part of the visiting Washington official that this phenomenon of growing rage among young Saudis needed to be taken into account in U.S. policy and public statements, no change in policy or rhetoric was forthcoming. Nonetheless, we in the mission's Public Diplomacy Section did continue to test the limits of speaker, cultural exchanges, and other programming that involved civil society, nongovernmental organizations and women's issues, on occasion with notable success, and on occasion engendering some push-back from Saudi authorities. One project that I personally lobbied long and hard for was a conference on civic education that we proposed to co-host with the Arab Bureau of Education for the Gulf States (ABEGS)—a consortium of the educational ministries of the six countries of the Cooperation Council of the Arab States of the Gulf (generally referred to as the Gulf Cooperation Council, or GCC). ABEGS has its headquarters in Riyadh, and over a several month period I called frequently on ABEGS officials there to promote the proposal. The concept was consistently viewed with interest, but despite repeated efforts on my part to get formal concurrence to proceed, such approval was always just beyond reach. I eventually concluded—no Arab would ever actually say no to such a proposal; that would be impolite, so one must develop a sixth sense as to when serial indecision in fact means "no"—that the project would never be approved, and I ceased my efforts to promote it.

In fact, the mission's center of gravity never swung toward the side of supporting reform at the risk of endangering stability. Saudi Arabia continued to be an important market for U.S. military and commercial products and, most importantly, has long held the world's largest proven oil reserves and for decades has been the world's largest oil exporter (at the time, the kingdom was also the number one supplier of oil imported into the United States); any attempt to raise with the kingdom's leadership the issue of opening the Saudi political sphere to increased public dialogue and accountability risked provoking a negative reaction.

In short, the tipping point for a change in approach had simply not been reached. There was no visible reason for upsetting the status quo, in which a reliable and stable ally—through its oil resources—played a key role in maintaining a healthy and prosperous international economy. There was little chance that an invisible, albeit smoldering anger on the part of many young Saudis toward the nature of their governance and their societal structure would cause U.S. policymakers to change the decades-long U.S. approach of cooperation with an undemocratic, but—arguably—largely benign Saudi government. This was in the late 1990s. When, on September 11, 2001, I learned that young Saudis from areas not far from Jeddah were involved in the terrorist attacks of that day, I immediately thought back to that evening in Jeddah several years earlier.

The tension in the U.S. approach to Saudi Arabia was also evident in another incident during my late 1990s tour of duty in Riyadh. In this case, we were staging a cultural performance at the residence of the U.S. ambassador and had invited an audience of several dozen prominent and influential Saudis from various walks of life. Shortly before the performance was to begin, a member of the Saudi royal family arrived, a grandson of the kingdom's founder, King Abdul Aziz Ibn Saud. Ever since Ibn Saud founded the Kingdom of Saudi Arabia in the 1930s, it has been ruled by the Al-Saud family, first by Ibn Saud himself and, following his death in the 1950s, sequentially by five of his (fifty-three) sons. However, Saudi Arabia now faces a generational challenge. The living sons of Ibn Saud are advancing in age, and within the next decade or so it is likely that the country will have to decide whether (and, if so, how) to maintain the tradition of rule by the Al-Saud family in the absence of a capable, first-generation male descendant of the kingdom's founder being available to ascend to the throne.

To return to the incident at the ambassador's residence, when the grandson of Ibn Saud arrived, he was immediately given obsequious attention by many present, including several of the U.S. diplomats on hand. Upon witnessing this scene, one Saudi friend who was at the event pulled me aside and commented that it was displays like this that undermined any home-grown effort to spark thinking about the need for political reform in the country. As he put it, while Saudis largely appreciate and accept the role of the Al-Saud in establishing their country and in providing stable rule for more than seven decades, there is a broad recognition among the now large and well-educated Saudi middle class that, as the country moves beyond rule by the direct offspring of Ibn Saud, a new approach needs to be taken to the governance role of the Al-Saud, and a process of political reform will need to accompany a reassessment of this role. In the words of my Saudi interlocutor: Saudis will not accept a continuation of complete political dominance by the Al-Saud family as the country transitions to the next generation of the royal family. He continued: There will still be an important role for the Al-Saud in the country's leadership, but the old formula of centralization of all political and economic power in the hands of the Al-Saud family will need to be revised. The international community, and especially the United States, needs to recognize this phenomenon and act accordingly, if it is not to play what would amount to a counterproductive role in Saudi Arabia's process of political evolution.

Our failure to recognize and respond to the impact of the end of the Cold War played out differently in Germany, where I served after my tour in Riyadh. There, this development—along with a host of other factors, which are explored in chapter 6—ultimately led to a state of affairs that sparked growing anti-Americanism, especially among young Germans.

The dissolution of the Cold War enemies of the Soviet Union and the Warsaw Pact resulted in a perceived unmooring of European security dependence from U.S. protection among many on the continent, which had two downsides. On the one hand, it allowed the transatlantic dialogue to become dominated by less existential issues—*trade disputes*: from "banana wars," to biotech crops, to aircraft subsidies; *treaty disagreements*: from the Kyoto Protocol, to the International Criminal Court, to the Landmine Treaty; to *"societal" values*: from capital punishment, to labor laws, to health insurance coverage. While I will look at this phenomenon of growing transatlantic estrangement in greater detail in chapter 6, suffice it to say here that, just as the fact that during the 1990s the end of the Cold War laid the groundwork in the Middle East for a rejection of the continued—but no longer strategically justified—U.S. support for a status quo in the region that increasingly failed to meet the needs and aspirations of the Arab people, the perceived uncoupling of the joint U.S.-European security imperative laid the groundwork for much of the transatlantic dispute that would affect the international community's attempt to deal with Saddam Hussein and his violation of UN Security Council resolutions.

THE UNIPOLAR WORLD

The post-Cold War emergence of the United States as the preeminent nation in several important areas—most particularly, with the disappearance of the Soviet Union, as the dominant military power—is a key development in understanding the world we entered post-9/11. During the 1990s, a period generally viewed as one of reduced international tension and void of any major, existential international threats, the U.S. mantra was reflected in the theme of Bill Clinton's 1992 presidential campaign—"It's the economy, stupid." The United States pursued a downsizing in its military, and foreign policy was relegated to a lower priority, behind trade and economic growth. Our allies—especially the wealthy nations of Western Europe—made even larger cuts in their defense spending and were largely content to leave responsibility for international stability to the United States. While this state of affairs did produce periodic expressions against unwarranted and unwelcome U.S. hegemony—French Foreign Secretary Hubert Vedrine's coining of the term *hyperpuissance* ("hyperpower") in 1998 to describe U.S. dominance is a case in point—there appeared to be general satisfaction with—and acceptance of—a (basically benign) U.S. "dominance" in international affairs. Germany's keenest America-watcher, *Die Zeit* editor Josef Joffe—summed up this state of affairs rather well in his analysis "Who's Afraid of Mr. Big" in *The National Interest* in summer 2001.[4] Joffe pointed out that the other wealthy nations of the world had the means to band together to balance the power and influence of the United States if they wished to, but they declined to do so. This, he suggested, was historically unprecedented and reflected a new reality of a dominant world power that was unthreatening to the international order and whose power did not elicit international anxiety and fear.

During this era of relative peace and prosperity, the world's leading nations took a largely passive, hands-off approach to the differing developmental trends that were taking place in various geographic regions: growing prosperity in Asia; expanding democratic governance in Central and Eastern Europe, the states of the former Soviet Union, and Latin America; festering conflict, poverty, and disease—especially HIV/AIDS—in Africa; and deepening economic and political malaise and stagnation in the Arab world. It was this last trend that contributed to the complex series of developments that eventually culminated in the attacks of September 11, 2001, and—in effect—ushered in the new era to which the international order is still adjusting.

The 1990s began with Saddam Hussein's occupation of and then ouster from Kuwait. The U.S.-led coalition that drove the Iraqi occupiers from Kuwait in a one hundred-hour offensive inflicted what was perceived as yet another humiliation by many in the Arab street, as the largely western coalition forces easily routed what was considered to be a very capable Iraqi military, with the third largest army in the world. Through the rest of the decade, and into the new century, Arab populations saw little economic advancement, gained essentially no political reform, and experienced a population boom with the highest birthrates of any region in the world.

The potential implications for western security and stability that these combined military, social, political, and economic developments produced were seriously underestimated by western intelligence, security, and diplomatic experts. Unnoticed by most observers was the fact that entrenched political leaders and elites in the Arab world sought to channel growing anger and frustration among their populations by deflecting such sentiments toward the United States—as the world's dominant country and sole superpower, a plausible puppeteer behind their malaise—using such regional sore spots as the suffering of the Palestinians at the hands of the Israelis or the suffering of the Iraqis under UN sanctions, with the responsibility for both ultimately laid at the doorstep of the Americans.

Parallel with such secular developments in the region, a growing Islamist sentiment in the Middle East sparked measures by Arab regimes to co-opt or otherwise neutralize the threat that such sentiments posed to their control. Particularly in Saudi Arabia—which was already under fire from Osama bin Laden and other Islamists for allowing the stationing of five thousand U.S. military personnel on

Saudi territory to enforce the southern no-fly zone in Iraq—the government sought to bolster its own religious credentials by providing increased financial support to the Wahhabist religious establishment with which it has de facto shared power through an alliance between the kingdom's founder, King Abdul Aziz Ibn Saud, and the spiritual descendants of the puritanical Islamic preacher Muhammed Ibn Abd Al-Wahhab.

The increasing anger, humiliation, and resentment among Arab populations caused a growing—albeit largely passive—toleration of Islam as a tool to force political reform in the region. Thus, while acceptance of the Islamic fundamentalists' agenda has always remained a phenomenon at the margins of Arab societies (even in Saudi Arabia, estimates of hard-core Islamist activists and sympathizers have never exceeded percentages in the teens), lack of alternative routes to achieve the kinds of political and economic reforms that were needed for the modernizing of Arab societies and to produce the jobs and economic growth needed to satisfy the aspirations of the large youth cohorts in these countries pushed large segments of Arab populations to abide, if not encourage, the Islamists in their midst. This development, paired with the impact in the Middle East of the burgeoning information revolution, set the stage for a series of al-Qaeda-sponsored terrorist incidents in the second half of the 1990s—including attacks on U.S. military personnel in the Khobar Towers in Saudi Arabia (1996), on the U.S. embassies in Nairobi and Dar es Salaam (1998), and on the *USS Cole* in Yemen's Aden harbor (2000)—culminating in the events of 9/11 and the transition of the international order from the relatively carefree period of the post-Cold War to what *New York Times* columnist Tom Friedman has called the "post-post-Cold War"[5]—the post-9/11 age of the threat of apocalyptic terrorism.

One aspect of this new reality has involved a discussion of the changed nature of foreign and security policy imperatives in the post-9/11 environment. This discussion has been reflected in the debate over *realism* and *idealism* in foreign policy.

THE REALISM VERSUS IDEALISM DEBATE

During the course of U.S. involvement in Iraq, a discussion has taken place in the U.S. foreign policy community regarding the distinction between two competing foreign policy doctrines: *realism* and *idealism*. This discussion intensified with the release of the revised U.S. National Security Strategy on March 16, 2006, and the launching of the Iraq Study Group in that same month. By that point, the rationale for U.S. actions in ousting Saddam, and the argument for continuing U.S. military involvement in Iraq, had largely come to be based on an idealistic view of foreign policy and U.S. interests—the promotion of U.S. values abroad, especially democracy promotion. The source of such an idealism-based foreign policy within the Bush administration was generally seen as coming from those associated with the Neoconservative school of thought. In light of the mounting costs and continuing difficulties of U.S. policy in Iraq, voices from the opposing foreign policy camp—the realists, who argue that national interests, not values, should drive foreign policy—have gained increased prominence in the U.S. foreign policy debate. The report of the Iraq Study Group, treated in chapter 4, has been touted by some as realism's revenge against the supposed idealism of some Bush administration officials.

In May 2006, I had an opportunity to address this issue in delivering remarks at Tufts University's Fletcher School of Law and Diplomacy while accepting the school's annual Edward R. Murrow Award for excellence in public diplomacy. My own analysis of the Iraq issue, as laid out in detail in this monograph, led me to express my take on the realism–idealism debate as follows:

> One element of today's discussion relates to the concepts of realism and idealism in foreign policy. My conclusion is that, viewed through the prism of 9/11, and its causes, idealism is, in fact, the new realism. In an increasingly globalized world, a world of almost unlimited information access and networking, foreign policy "idealism"—seeking to make the world freer and fairer, striving to empower citizens and to foster accountability in governments—represents, in my view, the only viable path to a more secure, more stable and more prosperous future for us all. There will be honest and at times heated debate on how to achieve such goals—as Murrow himself famously stated, when he was confronting the demagoguery of Senator McCarthy: "We must not confuse dissent with disloyalty"—but the principles which America pursues in using its influence in the world—from individual freedom, to human rights, to rule of law, to representative government—must be clear and uncompromising.

In this time of enormous transition in international engagement and interaction, and with America occupying a unique position of influence on the world stage, it should not surprise us that the change sweeping through societies and economies around the world is unsettling to many, and the anxiety which this rapid change can engender is sometimes displaced onto the one actor who is viewed by many to be all-powerful—the United States. This can be discouraging to those of us involved in public diplomacy on behalf of the U.S. government—just look at the current favorability ratings towards the U.S. on the part of many foreign publics—but I believe that time is our ally and that energetic promotion of our principles will prove to be a wise and winning strategy in this age of the new idealism.

Terrorists and fascists might attempt to hijack processes of political transition or reform, foreign publics might initially be skeptical about statements of high principle behind American policies, and foreign leaders and elites whose positions of power are threatened by our promotion of such principles might be able to distract or mislead their publics in the short run, but I am confident that over time the attractiveness and correctness of the principles at the heart of our current foreign policy agenda will cause these principles to prevail.[6]

The following week, British Prime Minister Tony Blair delivered a speech at Georgetown University in which he also addressed the realism-idealism debate. Sitting in the audience as he gave his take on this issue, I was gratified to hear that he shared a very similar conclusion to mine concerning the realism-idealism dichotomy in the post-9/11 world:

[T]he rule book of international politics has been torn up. Interdependence—the fact of a crisis somewhere becoming a crisis everywhere—makes a mockery of traditional views of national interest. You can't have a coherent view of national interest today without a coherent view of the international community. . . . [T]o meet effectively the challenge that faces us, we must fashion an international community that both embodies, and acts in pursuit of global values: liberty, democracy, tolerance, justice. These are the values we believe in. These are the values universally accepted across all nations, faiths and races, though not by all elements within them.

[I]n my nine years as Prime Minister I have not become more cynical about idealism. I have simply become more persuaded that the distinction between a foreign policy driven by values and one driven by interests, is obviously wrong. Globalisation begets interdependence. Interdependence begets the necessity of a common value system to make it work. In other words, the idealism becomes the real politik.[7]

3
The Arab World and the Information Revolution

The second of the two megatrends that sparked increased anti-Americanism in the Middle East region—the rapid expansion of international broadcast media and the Internet—can perhaps best be viewed through the lens of the appearance of the Qatar-based, regional satellite TV broadcaster Al-Jazeera in 1996. The phenomenon of Al-Jazeera fundamentally altered the information landscape in the region, ending what had been essentially a limitation on information sources available to the people of the region to those controlled by governments and supportive of their authority and their policies. While CNN had made some inroads into the region during the period of the Gulf War, and the spread of the Internet had allowed small, wealthy segments of the societies in the region to access "uncontrolled" information sources through connecting to the Internet abroad, the appearance of an Arabic language, "local" satellite broadcaster that offered unscripted discussions of current issues affecting the Arab world was revolutionary.

The immediate and longer-term substantive impact of Al-Jazeera's appearance in the region was the daily presence of images of Arab suffering—especially in Iraq and the Palestinian territories—in Arab living rooms across the Middle East and emotional ventings of the anger and frustration of Arab publics concerning the social, economic, and political conditions in the region. In response to this new phenomenon, regimes in the region reacted in various ways. First, they loosened programming restrictions on their own government-controlled media. I noticed with some surprise after my arrival in Riyadh to begin my three-year tour there in 1997 when Saudi Arabian television introduced unrehearsed discussion and call-in programming, something that would have been unthinkable even a few years earlier. Some governments in the region also reacted "officially" to the "provocation" represented by Al-Jazeera by lobbying the Qatari government to cease its financial support for Al-Jazeera and shut down the broadcaster.

Al-Jazeera regularly broke the unwritten taboo against broadcasters in the region criticizing Arab regimes. The station found itself in the precarious balancing act of fostering open, real-time international dialogue on the issues (and about the rulers) of the region while shying away from any controversial coverage or criticism of the regime in its host-country, Qatar. This state of affairs did not, of course, sit well with the other Arab countries, and over time Al-Jazeera found its operations either banned or restricted in Jordan, Bahrain, Tunisia, Saudi Arabia, and the Palestinian territories (and, while I was serving in Baghdad, a ban on Al-Jazeera's operations was also imposed in Iraq).

The picture of suffering and malaise in the Arab world that emerged from Al-Jazeera and eventually other new media and information sources available to the people in the region, however, challenged the region's entrenched regimes and elites. One strategy that these actors used to deal with this new development and the challenge to their authority and privilege that it represented was to attempt to deflect the anger of the Arab street off of themselves and onto the "West" in general and the United States in particular. In the face of the information revolution, the backwardness that characterized most aspects of the social, economic, and political dynamics of the region could no longer be hidden or denied; because addressing these problems would entail a fundamental change in the status quo in the region—and lead to the loss of their favored status by the elites—these elites worked to transfer in the minds of the public responsibility for these failures to hegemonic forces dominating the region, most particularly the United States. U.S. support for Israel, U.S. "anti-Arab" policies as reflected in its policy toward Iraq, etc.—rather than the policies of Arab regimes—were, as the Arab street heard from the Arab elite, the causes of the Arab world's stagnation and decline.

The anti-U.S. impact of the information revolution in the Arab world continued to deepen in the years between the appearance of Al-Jazeera television and the attacks of 9/11. The pervasive tendency of the Arab public to buy into conspiracy theories to explain and understand events taking place around them provided fertile ground for agenda-driven regional media that sought to portray the United

States (and the West) as the sources of all problems in the region (and the world). Biased, fictional, and selective reporting, together with less-than-professional sourcing and verification standards for news coverage by the emerging media in the region, left gullible, unsophisticated Arab publics open to manipulation and misinformation. To some extent, as in the West during this period, media audiences in the Arab world began to splinter along ideological lines, more "hard-liners" choosing to get their news from a station such as Al-Jazeera, more "moderate" viewers choosing a broadcaster such at the Dubai-based regional satellite station Al-Arabiya (opened in 2003). As in the West, such trends tended to be self-reinforcing, with the various broadcasters molding their news reporting to fit the assumed biases of their viewers. This phenomenon has had a significant effect in the region in the aftermath of the Iraq War.

The impact of the information revolution in the region was also felt through the now well-documented fact that, in the Internet age, the reliability of information has been turned on its head. Before the emergence of the Internet, "mass media" was largely limited to published or broadcast media that included internal reliability controls—through editors, who at least attempted to apply accuracy standards to what was being disseminated. With the Internet, everyone can be a publisher, and with the essentially cost-free access to Internet-based information (as compared with the usual need to pay to gain access to traditional media), we now operate in a world in which the most unreliable information is also the most available. This fact has also taken its toll on Arab attitudes and perceptions, as has been seen, for example, in connection with the events of 9/11. With the widespread dissemination on the Internet of conspiracy theories about the 9/11 attacks, majorities of publics in many Arab countries state that they believe that these events were the work of Israeli or U.S. government agents, not Arab terrorists operating on behalf of al-Qaeda.

These effects of the information revolution in the Arab world combined to contribute to an amorphous sense of anger and frustration on the part of broad elements of the Arab street toward the United States. The specific impact of any one of these elements would be hard to assess independently, but taken together it is clear that within the Arab countries during the 1990s there was a growing awareness that—in socioeconomic terms—the Arab world was falling farther and farther behind the developed world. The bitterness that this recognition engendered was coupled with a growing recognition that to change this situation would require radical action. The one actor in the region that seemed to have a capability and a program for such radical action was al-Qaeda. To use Reuel Marc Gerecht's poetic formulation: "Correctly understood, bin Laden is an ugly expression of protest against the region's rot."[1] Thus, while certainly broad segments of Arab publics rejected the specific political agenda of al-Qaeda—the reestablishment of an Islamic Caliphate under a tyrannical brand of fundamental Islam based on the Saudi Wahhabist sect—they saw in al-Qaeda the only existing mechanism for fostering the type of radical change needed in the Arab world in the face of support by the world's sole superpower—the United States—for the maintenance of an oppressive status quo. Arab publics were prepared to passively accept escalating al-Qaeda violence against the United States in the hope that the "pain" would eventually cause the United States to rethink its policy of support for Arab autocracies. In the aftermath of 9/11, they got what they were wishing for.

ASYMMETRIC PROPAGANDA

One of the phenomena that resulted from the information revolution in the region was the new-found ability of those with agendas opposed to that of the United States to create and widely disseminate any kind of claims concerning events in the region or U.S. motives for its actions. As the goal was generally to provoke an immediate "emotional" response among their target audience, long-term credibility has not been a factor in their information efforts. As a result of such information activities, the United States would find itself on the defensive, trying to "prove a negative" or "prove" its motives. In addition to simply false information—often resulting from regional media with agenda-driven reporting and that neglected basic journalistic standards for sourcing and verification of news reports—claims that such issues as oil, anti-Muslim (or anti-Arab) bias, or interest in establishing permanent military bases were and continue to be cited as purported "motives" for U.S. actions in the region.

Some reporting from the Bahrain-based daily *Ahkbar Al-Khaleej* ("News of the Gulf") provides a good case study of this challenge to the efforts of U.S. diplomats involved in public diplomacy in the region. In late March 2005, Ambassador William Monroe, the U.S. envoy to Bahrain, contacted my office in Baghdad seeking to coordinate with us on a written interview that the paper had requested. There were two questions in particular on which Ambassador Monroe was requesting our input:

> During the early days of Baghdad's occupation, U.S. forces stood by and watched libraries, museums, and galleries looted. The military did not raise a finger while Iraq's wealth and culture was plundered. Any occupier has a moral responsibility to protect these. What is the difference between you and what the Nazis did in occupied Europe?
>
> What about the future of Iraq? It is devastated. Tens of thousands have been killed, with no security or no reform apart from elections. What exactly is America's vision for the future of Iraq at a time when not a single school, hospital, health center or road has been rebuilt? Money has only been spent on securing oil supplies.

As is evident, there is nothing neutral about these questions. They reflect the biases and agendas of many in neighboring Arab countries. Drawing from recent opinion polling and reports on reconstruction efforts from that time, we developed the following responses:

> There are many factors which contributed to the disorder which followed the liberation of Iraq. These include the release of tens of thousands of hardened criminals from Iraqi prisons by the former regime just prior to its fall, the anger on the part of many Iraqis towards the former regime and the institutions which represented it, and the speed of the Coalition military victory in liberating the country. These events took place almost two years ago, and there has been a great deal of progress during these two years, both in Iraq's political development and in efforts to reconstruct the country. The U.S. alone is providing more than $20 billion in reconstruction aid, and other nations have together pledged billions more in assistance. What is important now is that the international community continue its support for Iraq as it progresses in developing a free and democratic society. The courage of Iraqis in the historic vote of January 30, and the political dialog of compromise and inclusion which has characterized the period since the elections, strongly suggest that Iraqis are determined to succeed in this effort.
>
> The Iraqi people have a very optimistic view of the future of their country. In an opinion poll taken earlier this month, more than

90% of those polled said that they are hopeful for the future, almost the same number said that they believe life in Iraqi will slowly improve, and more than 60% indicated that their lives today are better than before the war. And there are good reasons for this. To date more than 3,000 schools have been fully rehabilitated, and more than 800 are currently being renovated. 20 hospitals and almost 250 primary health care facilities have either been renovated or are currently in the process of rehabilitation. Hundreds of kilometers of roads have been paved. Cell phone and Internet usage, which were almost non-existent in Iraq before its liberation, have become commonplace. The U.S. has spent almost $4 billion to date on such projects, and has more than $11 billion currently committed to more than 2,000 on-going reconstruction projects in these areas.

The political reform in Iraq has also been remarkable. Opinion polling indicates that 70% of Iraqis feel that the results of the January 30 elections reflect the will of the Iraqi people. And the Shi'a-affiliated political majority which emerged from the elections has demonstrated goodwill in reaching out to all Iraqi communities to seek inclusion and consensus in creating the Iraqi Transitional Government which will oversee the writing of a new, democratic constitution for Iraq. Such political dialog among various religious and ethnic communities could well serve as a model for other states in the region.

The deaths which have occurred in Iraq since its liberation have been tragic, and in reaction to the mounting toll of terrorist-related killing Iraqis themselves have become more vocal against the terrorism which is being exported from other Arab countries to Iraq. This week the respected, independent Iraqi newspaper *Al-Mada* ran a commentary which stated that "during the period right after Saddam's fall from power, the Iraqis have not seen anything positive from the Arabs. The Arabs only brought their car bombs into Iraq. . . ." There is an historic opportunity for the countries of the region to support the Iraqi people in this time of transition. As Iraq reestablishes its proper political, economic and intellectual role in the region, it will contribute to stability, security and prosperity throughout the Middle East. The countries of the region have a large stake in Iraq's success.

These answers served not only to correct the record concerning the false claims made in the questions, but also had woven into them several comments aimed at Iraq's Arab neighbors—such as those in Bahrain—concerning their attitudes, behavior, and responsibility toward the situation in Iraq. To be frank, we were not terribly optimistic that the paper would print such comments and thus were pleasantly surprised when it did so and even more pleased when we found that a regional wire service had picked up the interview and disseminated it to media around the region and beyond; we welcomed this as a small victory in our efforts to address the largely antagonistic and misleading regional media environment.

Our experience with *Akhbar Al-Khaleej* did not end there, however. Two months later—in June 2005, not long before I was to conclude my tour in Iraq—another item from the paper came to our attention, a front-page story that ran on June 17, with a Baghdad dateline:

> Sources in the Iraqi Sunni Awqaf Endowment stated that occupation forces demolished by heavy artillery 215 mosques located in the Western part of Iraq where resistance operations are escalating. A report issued by the Sunni Awqaf Endowment on June 11 revealed that occupation forces raided during the past two years 1,900 mosques claiming that they were searching for wanted insurgents. The raids were conducted in different times of the day without taking in consideration the timing of prayers. The report also indicated that 71 religious scholars (mosque Imams) were either killed or tortured or disappeared, among them 20 Sunni Muftis. Additionally, 111 Sunni religious scholars were arrested by occupation forces, some of them are still in detention without allowing their families to see them or even know their fate till this moment!
>
> A source in the Iraqi Ministry of Planning revealed that the occupation authority is planning to build the largest church in Iraq if not in the entire Middle East. Sources indicated that the church will be built close to the shrine of Al-Jenaidi Al-Baghdadi, a leading Sufi figure in Baghdad. The church will have a capacity to receive 5,000 visitors and will be built by American funds!
>
> On a different note, the Iraqi Turkmen Front in Kirkuk revealed that three Israeli officials will visit Kurdistan Province in the next few weeks! Sources in the Turkmen Front said that the Turkish government facilitated the entrance of the three Israeli officials from the tourism sector to Mosul to visit the ancient Jewish sites in Kurdistan and Mosul!

This egregious piece of "reporting"—containing no semblance of truth whatsoever—led us to look further into the source of the

U.S. Marines resting in a damaged mosque in Fallujah (November 2004).

item. Our research revealed that the journalist who filed the report—who, it turned out, was also reporting for influential newspapers in Jordan (*Al-Ghad*) and Saudi Arabia (*Al-Jazeera*), as well as for the Baghdad-daily *Al-Mashreq*—had gotten his information not from actual sources but from an anti-American Web site—iraqpatrol.net. We engaged the journalist and set the record straight on the issues on which he had reported, but the incident once again brought home the Sisyphean effort in which we were involved in our Iraq-related media efforts.

THE BLOGOSPHERE

The discovery that an obscure, anti-American Web site was the source for a report—widely disseminated in mainstream Arab media—that contained a provocative but completely false account of U.S. actions in Iraq underscored the challenge we faced in our public diplomacy efforts in the new information environment. The Iraq conflict is perhaps the first such international undertaking whose information environment has been fundamentally affected by the Internet—and in particular the blogosphere. It was challenging enough for us to try to keep up with the Iraq coverage of the print and broadcast media in Iraq, the region, and internationally in our effort to be current on—and, where appropriate, address—the issues and perspectives concerning Iraq that were being provided to the worldwide audiences of the traditional media. It was impossible to do so with the blogosphere. The amount of Iraq-related material generated on the Internet certainly amounted to several thousand pages each day. And, as with the blogosphere more generally, Iraq-related information on the Internet was usually targeted at—and read by—self-selecting audiences whose sympathies and points of view essentially determined what was written and read.

The Fallujah offensive of November 2004 was in itself probably the single most misreported occurrence of the Iraq conflict to date. The insurgents—especially the al-Qaeda element of the insurgency, which had the largest stake in Fallujah—pulled out all stops in their quite sophisticated information effort. Those in control in (preliberated) Fallujah provided "sources" to sympathetic media, who made wildly exaggerated claims of huge civilian casualties, destruction of mosques, hospitals, housing and other infrastructure, and alleged atrocities—including a claim of the use of nuclear weapons—by U.S. forces. Keeping up with—and refuting—these was more than a full-time job.[2] These reports then, typically, took on a life of their own, first gaining widespread repetition in sympathetic media around the region and beyond, and then morphing into urban legends in the blogosphere.

The unintended consequences of the ability to use the Internet to find, replicate, and disseminate information and images worldwide at essentially no cost, with the need for little technical skill, using simple, inexpensive equipment, and at lightning speed turned up in some surprising ways. As we were dealing with Fallujah-related issues, we came across a photo—obviously taken by someone in the U.S. military as a personal memento, and probably e-mailed to family and friends—that we learned was circulating widely on Muslim and Arab Web sites—a photo of a group of U.S. Marines resting in a mosque in Fallujah. The photo was eventually published by some newspapers in the region, in one case bearing the caption "Get Your Dirty Feet Out of Our Mosque." The widespread appearance of such a photo in the Middle East and the Muslim world provided a major propaganda boon to those who sought to portray U.S. and coalition actions in Iraq as a war against Islam.

This "souvenir photo" was, of course, not the most damaging example of the new information environment (negatively) affecting the efforts of the United States and its coalition partners in Iraq. The most prominent (and troublesome) such incident by far was the appearance of photos of prisoner abuse at Baghdad's Abu Ghraib prison in early 2004. In that case, a group of ill-trained and inadequately supervised military reservists not only subjected Iraqi detainees under their control to inappropriate treatment, but also documented and then effectively put into the public domain this documentation of such abusive treatment. Thus, the abhorrent (but extremely aberrant and unrepresentative) behavior by U.S. forces that took place at Abu Ghraib became, through the medium of technologies that had never previously been available to military personnel during war time—inexpensive and routinely accessible digital photography, and the Internet—a defining element of the public perception of U.S. actions and motives in Iraq.

In the real world, in which a military action involves hundreds of thousands of personnel, it is unfortunate but almost certainly unavoidable that some inappropriate behavior will take place among the troops. The United States has, of course, shown its commitment to holding those who demonstrate such behavior legally accountable for their actions. Nonetheless, legal sanction applied months after the fact does little to counter the perceptions (and emotions) in the minds of Iraqis, other Arabs, and the global public in general that result from such emotionally charged images as those that emerged from the Abu Ghraib prison scandal.

Although occurring with less high visibility and largely outside the attention of the mass media, a steady stream of "souvenir" U.S. military videoclips from Iraq also makes its way to widely viewed Internet sites such as "YouTube," where such scenes as U.S. soldiers "playfully" leading unwitting Iraqi boys in an obscene chant about their country or teasing young Iraqis with bottles of water provide grist for Arab perceptions that the U.S. presence in Iraq serves to humiliate Iraqis, and Arabs in general.

In the new world of instant and indelible images defining perceptions of policies and intentions, perhaps one of the most unhelpful images to coalition efforts in Iraq was that of the fleeting instance of a U.S. flag being draped over the statue of Saddam Hussein in Firdos Square in Baghdad moments before the statue was toppled. Although the flag was in place for just a brief moment, it was captured on film and instantly transmitted worldwide (this action also stunned the onlooking crowd into silence). Thus, what was undertaken by the

United States and its coalition partners as the liberation of Iraq from the tyranny of Saddam and his Baathist henchmen for the benefit of the Iraqi people was, through the widespread circulation of this signal photo, conveyed to many as a U.S. conquest of an Arab nation, with all of the psychological impact that such a message entails. In short, the new information environment in which all activity—including military activity—now takes place presents a major new challenge to nations (and their militaries) in conducting war-related operations that are inherently unpredictable and imperfect.

PROVING MOTIVES

As alluded to above, probably the biggest challenge—and largest cause of the decline of the U.S. image in the Arab world in connection with the Iraq War—is the discrepancy between stated U.S. motives for its actions in Iraq and the beliefs concerning these motives on the part of Arab publics. The issue of ascribed motives for U.S. actions is certainly the most challenging aspect of the work of those of us involved in U.S. public diplomacy. This derives not only from the essential impossibility of "disproving" attributed motives, but also from the subtle way in which such ascribed motives affect discourse concerning U.S. policies. An oft-cited Pew Global Attitudes Survey, for example, concluded that "antipathy toward the United States is shaped more by what it *does* in the international arena than by what it *stands for* politically and economically."[3] Such a statement misses the important point that it is not U.S. actions per se that determine attitudes toward the United States by foreign publics, but rather it is how these actions are *interpreted*, i.e., what their motivation and goals are taken by these foreign publics to be.

The media worldwide and the Internet have carried claims, debates, and conspiracy theories addressing why the United States *really* sought to topple the Saddam regime. U.S. claims concerning its motivations have been largely dismissed in the region on the basis of the Arab publics' perceptions of U.S. policies toward the region and developments there in recent decades. As mentioned earlier, there is a widely shared mindset—conspiracy theory—in the region that both the actions of the United States and of Saddam Hussein in the 1980s and 1990s can only be understood within a paradigm in which Saddam was actually acting as an agent of the United States. This belief, along with the common view that Saddam's Iraq was a spent military force and posed no security threat to the region—let alone the United States—undermined the motive stated by the United States for its leading a coalition to remove Saddam from power: that he possessed weapons of mass destruction that represented a dire threat in themselves and, in the post-9/11 world, an even greater threat through the possibility of their falling into the hands of international terrorists.

Added to this was the fact that, while the United States was also espousing as a motive for its actions in Iraq support for—indeed, an urgent need for—political reform and democratic development in the Arab world, the experience of Arab populations living in politically and economically stagnant autocracies whose leaderships have enjoyed U.S. support for the past several decades largely precluded their acceptance of this as a real motive for U.S. actions. In short, historical developments involving the United States, Saddam, and the region undermined acceptance of the U.S. message that it was acting in the post-9/11 world to forestall, in the first instance, the emergence of a "nexus of WMD and international terrorism," and, in the second instance, to address political and economic failure in the Arab world as the root cause of the rage that led to the attacks of 9/11.

Indeed, in the case of the toppling of the Saddam regime, the "action" itself can be interpreted in many ways. One interpretation would be that it supports the stated U.S. goal of promoting democratic reform in the region, a goal that Arab publics would overwhelmingly support, if they believed it. The claim that this is a goal of the United States in its actions in Iraq, however, is largely dismissed by those in the region, both because it represents a new U.S. approach to the Middle East (and thus the historical record of U.S. policies and actions in the region runs counter to such a policy) and because—given the complexity of the issue—there are many other interpretations of U.S. actions in Iraq that are available to be promoted as the true motives behind U.S. actions in Iraq by those opposed to the U.S. policy of political reform in the Arab world. Several such motives have been widely cited; five are examined below.

Oil

Probably the most widespread motive cited for U.S. policy in Iraq has been "oil." To understand this claim, however, requires understanding what is meant by "oil" as a motive behind U.S. actions. There is no denying the fact that because Iraq sits atop one of the largest proven oil reserves in the world it is a country of great strategic importance to the United States, and to the world. The international community has a large stake in ensuring that world oil markets continue to function based on economics, not politics or strategic influence. Thus, while concern for a possible attempt by the Saddam regime to gain leverage over the immense oil reserves of the Gulf has played a role in U.S. policy toward the region for decades, the claim—either stated or implied—that the U.S.-led toppling of the Saddam regime in 2003 was motivated by a desire to "control," "steal," or otherwise exploit Iraq's oil resources has been debunked by the events that have unfolded since. With the price of a barrel of crude oil spiking to above $75 in the summer of 2006, as compared to a price in the mid-twenty-dollar range at the time of the Iraq War, and with the Iraqi government the sole beneficiary of this higher price for the oil that Iraq exports, the facts refute the claim that U.S. actions were prompted by a desire to steal Iraq's oil.

There are those who still cite "oil" as *the* factor that has driven U.S. policy in Iraq, but these critics generally conflate the legitimate consideration of preventing the oil resources of the Persian Gulf from being seized and used for political purposes (by Saddam Hussein or anyone else)—which has been a cornerstone of U.S. policy in the region since the 1970s—with a claim that U.S. action in Iraq is for the purpose of gaining "favorable" access to Iraqi oil. The fact is that oil, including Iraqi oil, now sells on the world market at near-record prices, and the United States pays this price for every barrel of oil, from whatever source, that it imports.

Military Bases

The suggestion that an interest in establishing permanent military bases in the country is what has driven U.S. policy is likewise often presented in an oversimplified and, thus, misleading manner. There is no question that the United States has strategic interests in the Middle East, and for this reason we have long had military installations in various countries in the Gulf. However, the claim that such a U.S. presence in the region—and a U.S. presence in post-Saddam Iraq—is a one-sided, U.S.-driven-and-directed state of affairs, is untenable. The security situation in the Gulf region is delicate in many regards. These countries are small, with fairly small citizenries and relatively large foreign populations, with hereditary governments and with limited military capabilities of their own, but possessing the tremendous wealth associated with their substantial oil reserves, which collectively account for some 70 percent of worldwide proven reserves. That the United States, given its power and role in the world and a corresponding responsibility to help ensure that these states not be vulnerable to intervention or coercion by hostile outside powers, would offer security assurances to these countries is understandable. That these countries would accept such assurances, even including the presence of U.S. military personnel on their territory, is likewise reasonable.

The situation regarding Iraq, moreover, presents yet an additional complexity. Given the Iraqis' recent history, especially under the Sunni-minority-dominated Baath Party during the past several decades, the Iraqis' level of distrust of a central government holding a complete monopoly on force within the country's borders is high. The majority Shi'a community suffered terribly at the hands of Saddam following its aborted uprising after the Gulf War. The Kurds likewise were the victims of genocidal campaigns directed against them under Saddam's orders. Even the Sunnis, who, in view of their political dominance since the founding of the country have not suffered at the hands of an all-powerful central government, are aware of what such power might mean for them as a minority community in a post-Saddam Iraq characterized by Shi'a political hegemony. Thus, all of the major players in the new Iraq have legitimate concerns regarding prospects of a future Iraqi government misusing any absolute monopoly on the use of force it might enjoy within the country.

The situation in Iraq is, in this respect, not terribly different from that in Germany since World War II. What was interesting to me to observe during the twelve years I have spent in diplomatic service in the country—spanning the period from 1980 to 2004—is the recognition by Germans of the positive, stabilizing role that the continuing U.S. military presence has played in the country and the desire of large numbers of Germans to see that role continue. While serving in Bonn in the mid-1990s, during a time when U.S. troop levels in Germany were being significantly reduced, what I found most surprising concerning the German reaction to this development was the unease of many that a reduced U.S. presence might lessen the largely subliminal, but real, effect that this presence has had in reassuring Germans and Germany's neighbors. In Iraq today, the presence of large numbers of coalition forces is essential for reassuring those who are casting their lot with the new, free, and representative Iraq that this effort will not be allowed to be defeated by the violent opposition of the terrorists and fascists waging the current insurgency. In discussions in Iraqi Kurdistan, I was even told that a guarantee of continued U.S. military presence in the country—preferably in Iraqi Kurdistan itself—was a prerequisite for the Kurds to remain in a unified Iraq. Such sentiments are increasingly expressed by the most unlikely of all of the communities in Iraq, Iraqi Sunnis, who have begun to call for U.S. troops to remain in the country as protection for them from rogue elements of Iraq's Shi'a majority community. Indeed, this reassurance—through the continued presence of a much-reduced contingent of U.S. and other foreign military personnel in Iraq for an indefinite period—is likely to be an important factor for Iraq's ethnic and sectarian communities in gaining their buy-in to the political, social, and economic transition currently being attempted in the country.

Israel

Another claim that has been made as being the reason behind the U.S.-led toppling of the Saddam regime is the assertion that this policy was for the benefit of Israel. It is certainly the case that the widely accepted view that the removal of the Saddam regime would be a plus for Israeli interests helped empower a pro-Israeli administration (operating within a pro-Israeli domestic U.S. political climate) to take the course it did, but I have seen no convincing evidence to suggest that Israeli interests were the overriding (or even an important) consideration in the president's decision to undertake military action against Iraq.

This claim, however, is essentially impossible to rebut directly, since Israel effectively has the same strategic interests in the region as the United States. In pursing our interests in the Middle East—neutralizing those who seek to dominate or destabilize the region through military force or threats, and seeking to encourage political reform and economic development in order to allay the anger and frustration of Arab populations resulting from the steadily worsening prospects that they and their children face under current political and economic conditions—the United States is attempting to shake up the status quo, a status quo that has kept the Israeli-Palestinian conflict as the region's central international focus and allowed political leaders and elites to use it as a convenient excuse for the political repression and economic malaise that has characterized the Arab world for the past half century. A successful Iraq will undoubtedly represent a positive change for Israel, just as it will for the United States, the international community, and the people of the Middle East, since it will embody a model that is likely to foster indigenous efforts to push through much-needed economic and political reform in the region.

The academic and media discussion during 2006 of a provocative essay by Professor Stephen Walt of Harvard's Kennedy School and University of Chicago Professor John Mearsheimer in the *London Review of Books* entitled "The Israel Lobby" added a new dimension to the Israel-as-motive claim concerning the U.S. decision to oust Saddam Hussein from power. One thesis in the Walt-Mearsheimer essay is the claim that the power of the pro-Israel lobby in the United States extends to the point that it can cause the United States to pursue policies that—while promoting Israel's foreign policy objectives—are actually counter to U.S. national interests. As Walt and Mearsheimer put it:

> Other special-interest groups have managed to skew foreign policy, but no lobby has managed to divert it as far from what the national interest would suggest, while simultaneously convincing Americans that US interests and those of the other country—in this case, Israel—are essentially identical.[4]

Pursuing this line of reasoning, the two academics suggest that such was the case with respect to U.S. Iraq policy:

> Pressure from Israel and the Lobby was not the only factor behind the decision to attack Iraq in March 2003, but it was critical. Some Americans believe that this was a war for oil, but there is hardly any direct evidence to support this claim. Instead, the war was motivated in good part by a desire to make Israel more secure. According to Philip Zelikow, a former member of the president's Foreign Intelligence Advisory Board, the executive director of the 9/11 Commission, and now a counselor to Condoleezza Rice [Note: Zelikow left this position in mid-2006], the "real threat" from Iraq was not a threat to the United States. The "unstated threat" was the "threat against Israel," Zelikow told an audience at the University of Virginia in September 2002. "The American government," he added, "doesn't want to lean too hard on it rhetorically, because it is not a popular sell."[5]

Walt and Mearsheimer do make a strong case that the pro-Israel punditocracy was lined up in support of military action to remove Saddam Hussein from power. This fact in itself, however, falls far short of showing a cause-and-effect relationship between voices from the pro-Israeli community calling for such action and a decision by the president to pursue such a policy.

Islam

A fourth element cited by some as being behind the U.S. decision to remove Saddam Hussein's government from power is a purported desire to convey to the world's Muslim community that the United States is a force to be feared, that attacks on the United States—such as those of 9/11—will be dealt with harshly, and that in delivering its response the United States will attribute responsibility for such attacks broadly to communities from which they arise. Such a position is generally espoused at the margins of mainstream debate on U.S. Iraq policy; nonetheless, it deserves mention, even if only due to the fact that it mirrors a claim often made by al-Qaeda and others who purport to speak and act in the name of Islam. From the U.S. perspective, the very process of explicitly formulating this thesis—as is done above—essentially shows it to be untenable: such a policy would undermine—not promote—U.S. security and other interests.

In seeking to refute the claim that a general American anti-Islam bias exists and was a contributing factor in the decision by the Bush administration to topple the Saddam regime, one historical reference that is generally cited is the fact that it was the United States that led the international effort to intervene on behalf of the Muslim populations in Bosnia and Kosovo in the 1990s. Such actions by the United States, so the reasoning goes, should have strongly established the view with Muslims worldwide that the United States has no animus against them or their religion. In this instance, however, we again observe a disconnect between western views and those of most Muslims: for the United States and the West in general, the operative fact is that the West—led by the United States—intervened to stop ethnic cleansing (and worse) being conducted against Muslim populations in the Balkans; for Muslims, the operative fact is that this action by the West came only after tens of thousands of Muslims had been slaughtered and many more driven from their homes. Thus, what we in the West view as a positive demonstration of concern for Muslims, the world's Muslim community views largely as a reflection of U.S. and western willingness to stand by while Muslim populations were being decimated in full view of the international community.

The Muslim community itself is in the throes of a struggle between the forces of moderation and modernity, on the one hand, and those of extremism and regression, on the other. While some U.S. and international critics translate a broad rejection of the Bush administration and its policies into a conviction that the administration's Iraq policy stems from a misguided sense of *machismo*, the claim by such critics that U.S. Iraq policy derives from a desire by the administration to "teach a lesson to" the international Muslim community fails to take into account basic U.S. interests; the fact that this argument is actually a mainstay of America's enemies within the Muslim world itself suggests its lack of credibility as a true motive behind U.S. policy in Iraq.

Unfinished Business / Revenge

Finally, a claim that has been alluded to as a putative motive for the Iraq policy pursued by the George W. Bush administration is the desire of the current administration to "finish" the unfinished business of the Gulf War of 1991 by removing the Iraqi dictator who was expected to fall shortly after his humiliating defeat at the hands of coalition forces. According to this scenario, Saddam's unexpected longevity in and of itself represented an affront to the United States, and especially to the president's father, whose decision to terminate U.S. military activity after just one hundred hours in the Gulf War had been second-guessed for more than a decade. A corollary of this line of reasoning is the view that President George W. Bush felt compelled to avenge the attempt on the life of his father in Kuwait in April 1993 at the hands of Saddam's agents. Those who focus on this alleged motive for the president's decision to launch military action against Iraq often cite a comment made by President Bush on September 26, 2002 at a political fund-raising event in Houston. After listing a number of charges against Saddam, Bush added: "After all, this is a guy who tried to kill my dad at one time."[6] While both of these claims make for interesting parlor room discussion, there is nothing to support them beyond speculation and conjecture. Perhaps when George W. Bush writes his memoirs, he will provide some insight into these two purported motivations for his decision to oust Saddam Hussein from power, but, at present, there is absolutely no evidence to support them.

4
Democracy and its Discontents

It is difficult politically for democracies to take action that is controversial or costly, or that requires sacrifice on the part of the people; democratic political systems act in the interests of their citizens—not to fulfill sometimes misguided ambitions by their leaders—and thus are largely precluded from being adventuresome. In light of this attribute of democratic societies, it can take an event like 9/11 to create a domestic political environment that would allow taking decisive and costly action to address a long-term threat such as that which the status quo in the Arab world posed to U.S. security and the contribution to that dangerous status quo that derived from Saddam Hussein's remaining in power. In this chapter, I treat aspects of democratic governance that I see as affecting the kind of foreign policy challenge represented by Saddam's Iraq.

DEMOCRATIC GRIDLOCK

It is an axiom of U.S. civics that, in our democratic system—with its checks and balances, separation of powers, and an elected executive—the founding fathers deliberately made it difficult for the government to take action. The normal state of affairs is supposed to be a sort of benign political paralysis, with the threshold for political action being hard to reach. We are reminded almost daily of such intractable national issues as illegal immigration, health care coverage, and oil imports, all of which have been crying out for political action for decades; and yet little or nothing has been done, because none has reached the point at which failure to take political action is seen as being more painful than the pain that would be associated with actually addressing the issue politically (although with all three of the above issues there are signs that that may be changing). As a resident of the District of Columbia, I am acutely aware of my not even having voting representation in Congress, an obvious flaw in our democracy; yet the idea of extending such representation to me and my fellow DC residents barely registers on the national political radar screen.

What trip-wire is needed to cause political leaders in a democracy to take action that is likely to be costly, painful, and controversial in order to address a looming security, economic, or other serious threat to the national interest? To answer this question, it is instructive to look at a case study of such a circumstance described in the report of the "National Commission on Terrorist Attacks upon the United States" (The 9/11 Commission): its analysis of the growing threat of al-Qaeda through the 1990s. The commission asked, "When [did] the U.S. [have] reasonable opportunities to mobilize the country for major action against al Qaeda in its Afghan sanctuary [?]," and proceeds to the observation that "officials in both the Clinton and Bush administrations regarded a full U.S. invasion of Afghanistan as practically inconceivable before 9/11."[1] The 9/11 Commission then concludes:

> Since we believe that both President Clinton and President Bush were genuinely concerned about the danger posed by al Qaeda, approaches involving more direct intervention against the sanctuary in Afghanistan apparently must have seemed—if they were considered at all—to be disproportionate to the threat.[2]

The commission might have added that such action as a full-scale invasion of Afghanistan—with the cost in blood and treasure that it would have entailed—would not have been politically sustainable on the basis of the terror attacks attributed to al-Qaeda between 1995 and 2000: the Saudi Arabian National Guard building in Riyadh in 1995 (five U.S. civilian contractors killed); Khobar Towers in eastern Saudi Arabia in 1996 (nineteen U.S. service members killed); the U.S. embassies in Nairobi and Dar es Salaam in 1998 (eight Americans and more than seventy non-Americans killed); and the *USS Cole* in the Yemeni port of Aden in 2000 (seventeen U.S. sailors killed). The sober lesson that the commission drew from its analysis was that "[I]t is hardest to mount a major effort while a problem still seems minor. Once the danger has fully materialized, evident to all, mobilizing action is easier—but it then may be too late."[3]

Opinion columnist Robert J. Samuelson, writing in the *Washington Post* in the immediate aftermath of Hurricane Katrina, wondered why governments did not adequately prepare for such foreseeable disasters. He suggested a "Catch-22 of national disasters":

> We cannot address serious national problems until they are conclusively shown to be serious, but the required proof is usually the very crisis that we are trying to avoid. In a democracy, it's necessary to mobilize public opinion to undertake unpleasant or expensive actions, but public opinion mobilizes only after the fact.[4]

Why is it that democracies are typically constrained in dealing with challenges to their well-being and threats to their security?

First, the public discussion of policy options to deal with a challenge or threat rarely includes serious discussion or analysis of taking no action at all. Thus, to return to the issue of al-Qaeda pre-9/11, with the exception of limited Cruise missile attacks against Sudan and Afghanistan in 1999, the entire decade saw only inaction in mounting a military confrontation in response to the growing threat and escalating actions of this terrorist organization. Such inaction was essentially noncontroversial to both the general public and the opinion elite, especially as compared to the outcry that followed those occasions in which only what was essentially "symbolic" military action—action that did not even rise to the threshold of putting U.S. personnel into harm's way—was taken. While there are always the occasional instances of "crying wolf" by the chattering classes about "looming crises"—such as with illegal immigration, health care, or dependence on imported oil, the critical but heretofore largely ignored policy issues mentioned above—these almost invariably stay below the attention level of the general public.

Second, choosing a course of action to confront an impending danger almost always entails choosing from among unappealing options. There is nothing good about a decision to go to war, for example; invariably such a decision will lead to hardship, suffering, and death. At the same time, in the face of evidence that there are those who seek to inflict death and destruction on your country—9/11 comes to mind—responsible leadership requires taking some action to address this threat. Whatever action is decided upon will then be open to second-guessing, without the wisdom of knowing what would have happened if a different course of action had been followed, or if no action at all had been taken. Inevitably mistakes or misjudgments will come to light, and these will provide fodder for criticism of the policy decision without any means for balancing this criticism against "what might have been." In the course of the national discussion of the Iraq issue since the coalition launched military action against Saddam's regime in March 2003, the focus has centered—as is to be expected in democratic debate—on the difficulties that have been encountered in Iraq and on policy "mistakes" that are claimed to have caused or contributed to these difficulties.

So how does a democracy shake off inaction in the face of a threat or a challenge? Heretofore, the pattern has been to wait until a cataclysmic event—Pearl Harbor, 9/11—occurs and then use that devastating event to mobilize the public to support the sacrifice and pain that will be needed to deal with the threat. Here, however, is where the 9/11 paradigm shift comes in. In the past, when foreign threats emanated from nation-states, and mechanisms had been crafted to evaluate and address such threats—containment, mutually assured destruction, etc.—political and military leaders generally found policies such as deterrence, "survivability," and "credible response" sufficient to render such threats tolerable. But in a post-9/11 world of international terrorists with no self-imposed limits on the level of atrocity they are willing to commit, and proliferating international capabilities to produce chemical, biological, radiological, and even nuclear weapons, the threshold for "threat tolerance" has been considerably lowered.

A MUSHROOM CLOUD AS "SMOKING GUN"

Then National Security Advisor Condoleezza Rice's now famous comment in September 2002, in alluding to uncertainty concerning the Saddam Hussein regime's possible possession of or access to a nuclear weapon, that "We don't want the smoking gun to be a mushroom cloud,"[5] vividly captures this post 9/11 perspective, one that is treated by author Ron Suskind in his book, *The One Percent Doctrine*. The book's title is drawn from a quote attributed to Vice President Dick Cheney, to the effect that "If there's a one percent chance [that WMDs have been given to terrorists] we have to treat it as a certainty in terms of our response."[6] In his book, Suskind takes a critical view of such a policy approach. However, whether one accepts or rejects such a cautious / preemptive / aggressive approach (characterize it as you will) to potential threats in the world, the fact remains that, with 9/11, the rules changed—and the Iraq War happened under the new rules. As suggested above, in the post-Westphalian world that emerged from the events of 9/11, the international community remains far from agreed on a blueprint for legitimizing action against possible or potential threats before such threats become manifest through the "smoking gun" of a biological or chemical attack, or perhaps, as Condoleezza Rice once ominously suggested, even a mushroom cloud.

HARD POWER AND SOFT POWER

As those of us involved in U.S. public diplomacy in Europe in the period up to and after the Iraq War in spring 2003 witnessed repeatedly, many Europeans had by that time developed a conviction that the U.S. approach to the world had evolved into one of "might makes right." The overwhelming superiority of U.S. military capability—a capability that had actually served Europe well in the 1990s in addressing crises in several areas of the former Yugoslavia—was, in the view of many, more to be feared than it was to be welcomed as a force for maintaining international peace and stability. This perception was reflected in several well-publicized opinion polls, which showed that more Europeans viewed the United States as a threat to international peace than held such a view of Saddam Hussein.

In 1990, Harvard Professor Joseph Nye Jr. coined the phrase "soft power" to describe the ability of a country to achieve its foreign policy goals through attraction rather than coercion. During the 1990s, and especially in the first half of the current decade, as the pace of globalization quickened and the information revolution spread into all corners of the earth, the concept of soft power came to be viewed as an increasingly important tool of foreign policy, in the eyes of some even eclipsing hard power in its importance. Such aspects of a nation's attractiveness as educational excellence, cultural creativity, entrepreneurship, and economic success—elements of soft power—are, especially in today's globalized world, now seen as key to a nation's influence on the world stage and its ability to attain its international objectives. One lament of many U.S. professionals involved in international affairs in recent years has been a decline in the influence of the U.S.' soft power as a result of U.S. actions since 9/11, in particular the decision to use military means to remove the Saddam Hussein regime from power.

Distinctions in attitudes toward soft power and hard power are perhaps nowhere reflected more strongly than in Europe, in particular among the original Western European founders of the European Union (EU). As a region that has overcome centuries of conflict and animosity largely through soft power activities—educational exchange; travel, tourism, trade, and investment; cultural interaction; athletic competition; etc.—members of the EU have heavily invested in their soft power while reducing their hard power. This state of affairs has produced a division of labor that has increasingly entailed instances of U.S.-dominated military intervention followed by EU-led peacekeeping and nation-building. Neither side seems satisfied with this arrangement, and as the transatlantic relationship has recovered from its depths of estrangement in the spring of 2003 both sides have been working to rectify this imbalance.

An inspiring example of the impact of soft power occurred in Germany in the lead-up to the Iraq War in the spring of 2003. On February 14, 2003, Hans-Ulrich Klose—a member of the SPD [Social Democratic Party] faction in the German Bundestag, the faction headed by then Chancellor Gerhard Schroeder—published an op-ed in Germany's leading national daily, the *Frankfurter Allgemeine Zeitung*, under the headline "In the Off-Sides Trap." The title makes reference to a soccer strategy in which a team falls victim to getting trapped off-sides (the use of a soccer analogy probably assures that the symbolism is lost on most U.S. readers). In the article, Klose takes Chancellor Schroeder to task for his stance in opposing military intervention against Saddam Hussein under all circumstances. In characterizing this policy position by Schroeder, Klose comments that "the foreign policy damage was and is enormous, since it did not take into consideration how our partner [the U.S.] would react, and since American interests and sensibilities were either not noticed or consciously ignored. . . . When the Chancellor says he is fighting for a peaceful solution, that sounds good, but is in truth empty rhetoric, which is more in reaction to the state of opinion of the [German] population than to the actual threat. And it is just this rhetoric, which requires responsibility but which does not actually accept responsibility, which has maneuvered us into the off-sides."

Klose's obvious empathy for U.S. "interests and sensibilities" has very firm roots: As a teenager in the 1950s, he spent a high school exchange year in the American Midwest, living with a U.S. family with which he has remained in close contact ever since. That formative experience has clearly had a life-long impact and has fostered a level of empathy and understanding toward the United States that expressed itself in his remarkable act of political courage and statesmanship at a time when German-American relations had reached what was perhaps their lowest point since World War II. In my diplomatic career, I have never seen a more striking example of the value and impact of "soft power."

DEMOCRATIC DEBATE

Another aspect of the Iraq issue that relates to the concept of democracy is the inherent element of public discussion, debate, and (usually) disagreement on policy issues, and the issue of Iraq has been no exception to this normal course of the democratic process by U.S. politicians, media, and the public at large. Such public treatment of critical national policies is an essential element to the functioning of a democratic system; in fact, it is a necessary "corrective" to ensure that policy decisions are sound and supportable. James Madison addressed this issue in his Federalist Paper #10, when contemplating the issue of "faction" in the body politic. He postulated as a "first remedy" for the "removal of faction" "destroying the liberty which is essential to its existence"—and then famously concluded that "it could never be more truly said than of the first remedy, that it was worse than the disease."[7]

Two outcomes of this fundamental aspect of democratic systems, however, need to be factored into policy decisions at the outset, since these directly affect the likelihood of the success of such policies: (1) the fact that—in a democracy—respected, mainstream voices from leaders and others in the political opposition can be expected publicly to question and criticize the policy being pursued; and (2) the fact that the free press in a democracy will almost certainly ensure that prominent public and media figures will do the same. The result is that a large body of public discourse will emerge in the United States that questions the motives, efficacy, and wisdom of U.S. policies and effectively provides argumentation that often mirrors that of our adversaries concerning the policy at hand. This has, of course, occurred with respect to Iraq policy, and especially in the period of the post-war insurgency. The point is not that such public discussion should therefore not take place: it is an essential element to the proper functioning of a democracy. Rather, the point is that this fact needs to be considered in determining from the outset the feasibility of the success of a given policy, and the policy implementation process needs to take it into consideration.

One unintended consequence of such discussion, however, is its impact in a region—in this case, the Middle East—that has little experience with public discussion, and especially public criticism, of government policies. Thus, either through selective use of information arising through such public discourse, or simply a naiveté concerning the nature and purpose of such debate, the replaying of U.S. voices of disagreement or dissent on U.S. policy in Iraq into the volatile environment in Iraq and the region has a direct impact on the prospects for the success of the policy itself. While such public debate on foreign policy has been a feature of the U.S. landscape since the founding of the republic, it intensified in the highly charged partisan climate that has characterized the U.S. political atmosphere during the period of the Iraq War and its aftermath.

To the extent that those Iraqis who are risking their lives to build a free and democratic Iraq are confronted with doubts about the U.S.' commitment to support their efforts until the new Iraq can stand on its own, these doubts undermine the very effort itself. Similarly, those who oppose the evolution of Iraq into a free and democratic country will not cease to exploit any disagreement or debate among U.S. leaders concerning the legitimacy, wisdom, or sustainability of U.S. policy on Iraq. This is not to say that such debate can or should be stifled or silenced; as noted above, such public airing of debate on policy issues—especially on an issue such as Iraq, involving U.S. casualties and massive financial outlays—is essential to the process of policy decisionmaking and course-correction in democratic societies. The point to draw here is simply to recognize that such debate, because it affects the very prospects for the success of the policy, must be taken into account in developing and executing the policy itself.

A corollary of the public discussion aspect of foreign policy initiatives is the fact that the nature of a democracy also generally entails a distinction between domestic messaging for a policy and the message concerning such a policy directed at foreign audiences. In a given case, the appropriate approach to take in the domestic promotion of a certain policy might actually undermine the ability to gain support for that policy abroad. Iraq offers some cases in point. As President Bush himself has commented, his use of such phrases as "bring 'em on" (with respect to the insurgency in Iraq) and "dead or alive" (concerning Osama bin Laden)[8]—while perhaps helpful for rallying Americans on the home front—may have reflected a tone at odds with the need to gain support among foreign publics for our policy in Iraq. Likewise, the president's use of the phrase "axis of evil" to refer to Iraq, Iran, and North Korea in his 2002 State of the Union Address, while effective in conveying to Americans the threat that he saw such countries posing to the United States in a post-9/11 world, had the opposite effect on some foreign publics, who generally saw the phrase as bellicose in tone and, in parts of Europe at least, it eroded the goodwill that European publics had extended toward the United States in the aftermath of the events of 9/11.

The dichotomy between domestic and foreign message targeting in pursuit of foreign policy objectives can take on unanticipated complexity on other ways as well. In an exchange I had in April 2006 with an Arab journalist in Washington, DC, for example, he stated that—while he understood that domestic support in the United States for the administration's democracy promotion agenda in the Middle East necessarily required that Americans be told, and be convinced, that this agenda was being pursued for U.S. interests—this very message, to the extent that it carried over into the Arab world, would actually undermine the potential for the success of the policy itself. It is imperative, in the view of this Arab journalist, that the United States convey to the Arab street that U.S. policies in support of political and economic reform in the Arab world are being undertaken for the benefit of Arabs, not Americans. Of course, this entails essentially a Catch-22 situation, since governments, especially democratic governments are, by definition, supposed to act on behalf of their citizens, not foreign publics.

POLITICS AS POLICY

An additional aspect of democratic debate that typically comes into play regarding major national issues such as war and peace is the claim that "political calculations" are playing a role in a particular policy decision. In connection with the Iraq issue, to the extent that being at war (or at least being perceived as "dealing with a crisis") is seen to convey political advantage to an incumbent politician in terms of approval ratings, reelectability, etc., any decision to go to war will be invariably second-guessed and criticized within the domestic political debate as being based on such political calculations, rather than on the stated basis for the decision to wage war. This is the now well-known *wag the dog* phenomenon, a factor that has frequently been raised in the public discussion of the Iraq issue in the United States.

An interesting variant on the politics-as-policy hypothesis embodied in the wag-the-dog concept is the delay-defeat-in-order-to-avoid-blame claim being made by some politicians and pundits in connection with President Bush's early 2007 decision to send more troops to Baghdad and Al-Anbar Province in Iraq. In both cases, analysis and evaluation of policy choices are obfuscated by ascribed political calculations deriving from the nature of our democratic system.

STAYING POWER

It seems clear that the United States continues to pay a high price for a policy course in recent decades that has signaled to America's enemies that the United States has little staying power in its foreign engagements. The record has led those who oppose us overseas to embrace the notion that the United States will abandon its efforts as soon as its policies start generating "costs." The conventional wisdom has been that one simply needs to cause the United States to suffer a few casualties in a given location, and its engagement in that location will quickly come to an end. Osama bin Laden himself has taunted the United States with this claim in several of his *fatwas* and other messages. Iraq has showcased just how difficult it is to change such perceptions. Even well over three years into the conflict, those who oppose U.S. policy there—and the kind of free and representative Iraq that most Iraqis seek—are still betting on the United States withdrawing before the task is complete. As the Brussels-based International Crisis Group (ICG) noted in February 2006, those involved in the Iraqi insurgency have become ever more confident of the success of their efforts. In the ICG's words:

Today, the prospect of an outright victory and a swift withdrawal of foreign forces has crystallized, bolstered by the US's perceived loss of legitimacy and apparent vacillation, its periodic announcement of troop redeployments, the precipitous decline in domestic support for the war and the heightened calls by prominent politicians for a rapid withdrawal."[9]

The consequences that our reputation of not being willing to take casualties has engendered in Iraq have been twofold. On the one hand, it has convinced those who oppose U.S. goals in Iraq to press on with their violent opposition, believing that it is just a matter of time before they will break the U.S.' will. On the other hand, and just as devastatingly, it has kept the bulk of the Iraqi people sitting on the fence, unwilling to publicly demonstrate their support for the new course underway in the country, despite the fact that the Iraqi people overwhelmingly support exactly the type of outcome in Iraq that the United States is striving for. As President Bush has commented, describing the dilemma faced by Iraqis: "You badly want to believe the Coalition forces can really help you out, but three decades of Saddam's brutal rule have taught you a lesson: Don't stick your neck out for anybody."[10]

The importance of this factor vis-à-vis Iraq cannot be overstated: The essential struggle in Iraq is not primarily a military one, but rather it is a psychological battle for the allegiance of the Iraq people to the cause of a free and democratic society. The initial reaction of the Iraqi people to the liberation of their country from Saddam's iron fist, and all opinion polling conducted in the country since that time has shown that the Iraqi people overwhelmingly support the creation of the kind of society envisioned by the United States and its coalition allies. However, the facts on the ground—including violence, insecurity, and ethnic and sectarian tension—have caused them to hedge on any overt commitment to such a society.

GOVERNANCE AND POLITICS

There was a vast gap between the eighth-grade level of some public statements and the graduate-school level of private White House conversations. It was about this time that a bewildered newcomer to the Bush administration interrupted an interview to ask me why

> I thought there was such a big difference between the probing and realistic President Bush he would see in the Oval Office, and the pat and repetitive Bush he would see at press conferences and on TV.[11]
>
> David Brooks, *New York Times,* December 4, 2005

The above quote suggests a dichotomy that has emerged in the media portrayal and public perception of the current U.S. political leadership—in particular of President Bush—in the period since 9/11 and especially in connection with the administration's Iraq policy. The portrait conveyed of an engaged and astute President Bush in such writings as Bob Woodward's *Plan of Attack* or L. Paul Bremer III's *My Year in Iraq* could not contrast more sharply with the description of the president and many senior administration officials contained in much of the mass media. While this disconnect certainly has many causes—running the gamut from the personal histories of the officials themselves, to the political orientation of the Bush administration, even to body language issues—one factor at play is the gap between the attributes involved in successful governance and those central to success in politics, a gap that in the new, all-pervasive information environment seems to be growing.

New York Times commentator Tom Friedman, in the runup to the 2004 presidential election, specifically took President Bush to task for, in Friedman's view, positioning himself more as a political candidate than a political leader.[12] What is missing from Friedman's analysis, however, is acknowledgment that unless one can be a successful candidate, one will not have the opportunity to become or remain a political leader. This basic element of democratic governance is probably the one that leads to the greatest criticism of politicians and the political process. In today's context, one simply needs to look at the media treatment of such 2008 presidential hopefuls as John McCain and Hillary Clinton as they have undertaken outreach to prominent political personalities and key party constituencies from whom they have previously maintained their distance. This aspect of the democratic political process probably alienates more citizens from politics and politicians than any other; in fact, however, it is both inherent in and essential to democracy.

It is in connection with the dichotomy between governance and politics that another important issue—admitting policy errors, or correcting the policy course—arises. Once a difficult and divisive policy—such as taking military action in Iraq—has been decided upon and implemented, political calculations come to play a key role in the public discussion of such a policy. In this connection, the highly partisan atmosphere of the current U.S. political arena largely precludes either side from allowing even a brief sound bite to emerge that would provide electoral ammunition to its opponents in a future political campaign.

The level of partisanship that has emerged in Washington over the past decade has, unfortunately, affected the realm of U.S. foreign policy as well. With respect to Iraq, for example, an administration official overtly acknowledging "mistakes" in U.S. Iraq policy, or a Democratic politician suggesting that some good has (or even might) come from the U.S. intervention in the country, would likely result in a sound bite that would almost certainly be exploited by the other side in its political campaigning in future electoral seasons. As a result, a moderate, candid public discussion among political leaders concerning our policy toward Iraq, and where that policy should be headed, becomes difficult if not impossible. The reality that David Brooks describes above is, unfortunately, a direct consequence of the political and media climates in present-day America and the factors underlying them.

Another outcome of the partisanship that colored all aspects of policy discussion during the period leading up to the Iraq War in March 2003 concerned the willingness to have a national discussion on—and appropriately plan for—the likely costs of undertaking regime change in Iraq through military intervention, especially during the period of reconstruction and political rehabilitation in Iraq that would necessarily follow a military victory over Saddam's forces. George Packer, in *The Assassin's Gate*, quotes a Defense Department official as saying the following: "The senior leadership at the Pentagon was very worried about the realities of the post-conflict being known, because if you are [Douglas] Feith (Undersecretary for Policy) or if you are [Paul] Wolfowitz (Deputy Secretary) your primary concern is to achieve the war."[13] The implication of such a statement is that a candid airing of the costs and needed contingency planning for an undertaking as ambitious and uncertain as *Operation Iraqi Freedom* might have led, not to a sober assessment of the resources needed to achieve what were considered to be important U.S. policy goals related to Iraq, but rather to partisan posturing and bickering, thereby undermining the ability to implement the policy itself, something not uncommon in politically charged Washington.

Some analysts of the partisanship factor as it relates to U.S. Iraq policy suggest a negative effect of "one-party-rule"—i.e., having the presidency and both houses of Congress in the hands of one political party—during the lead-in to and conduct of current Iraq policy. Such a circumstance is a relatively rare occurrence (in the modern era, such a situation has obtained for only ten years since 1969), but the fact that this was the case from 2002 until the Democrats retook both the House and Senate in the November 2006 elections has been suggested as a contributing factor to the partisanship that has affected U.S. Iraq policy. Brookings Institution scholar Jonathan Rauch, for example, writing in *The National Interest* on the eve of the 2006 election, commented:

> In a complicated world, good policy is usually bound to be eclectic; in an unpredictable world, successful policy-making depends on correcting errors. Eclecticism comes from compromise, error-correction from coherent criticism. One-party rule seems to short-circuit both mechanisms. Politicians compromise because they have to, not because they like to. Divided government forces them to compromise as a fact of daily life. . . . Two-party rule also helps to marginalize partisan extremists and curb ideological excess. . . . One-party rule, by contrast, impelled the Republicans to govern from the center of their party, instead of the center of the country. . . . Coherent criticism comes from a coherent opposition, and one-party rule undermined that, too. Without any institutional stake in the government's policies, Democrats have been free to surf the wave of Republican unpopularity, offering little—too little, in any case—by way of ideas and agenda. Control of part of the government would have forced them into the game."[14]

The November 2006 election, of course, changed this situation, giving the Democrats control of both houses of Congress for the final two years of George W. Bush's presidency; it remains to be seen what effect this new circumstance will have on the level of political partisanship affecting U.S. Iraq policy.

One instructive exception to the general reluctance that the democratic process instills in politicians to acknowledge policy errors is a book on contemporary politics and the current political climate in the United States by former (Republican) Secretary of State James A. Baker III, who found new public prominence in connection with his co-chairing (with former Democratic Congressman Lee Hamilton) of the Iraq Study Group. In the work, published in October 2006, entitled *Work Hard, Study, . . . and Keep Out of Politics!* Baker cites four aspects of Iraq policy that he sees as having been flawed. In his words: "The Defense Department made a number of costly mistakes, including disbanding the Iraqi army, outlawing the Baath Party, failing to secure weapons depots, and perhaps never having committed enough troops to successfully pacify the country."[15]

This seems to be the most succinct cataloging to date by a senior Republican political figure of specific actions or policy decisions that may have harmed the prospects for the success of U.S. goals in Iraq. The first two actions—which amounted in the first case to sending tens of thousands of trained Iraqi military personnel onto Iraq's streets with no income and little prospect for employment, and the second resulting in a purging of thousands Baath Party members from government positions—have received considerable discussion among politicians and pundits.

While it is essentially indisputable that the effect of these policy decisions was to provide thousands of potential recruits for the Sunni-led insurgency, as Coalition Provisional Authority (CPA) Administrator L. Paul Bremer III noted in his account of the considerations that led to these decisions, at the time they were made there was a need to ensure Shi'a and Kurd buy-in to the CPA and coalition agenda. One factor in gaining such support was to convince these two communities—which had suffered mercilessly at the hands of the Baath Party and Iraqi army—that these two organizations would never again be able to inflict violence upon them. Bremer cites an exchange with Kurdish leader Massoud Barzani, who, upon being told by Bremer "some were encouraging us to reconstitute a smaller version of Saddam's army," replied, "That would have been a big mistake. . . . We Kurds would have left Iraq, seceded."[16] In *Fiasco*, Tom Ricks cites former Central Command (CENTCOM) Commander Anthony Zinni as imputing responsibility for this decision to Ahmed Chalabi, a secular Shi'a Iraqi expatriate who at one point enjoyed considerable access and influence in certain quarters in the Pentagon; in Zinni's words: "I think the de-Baathification and dissolution of the army was at Chalabi's insistence."[17] Thus, what are increasingly in hindsight seen as errors in the early stage of the coalition occupation of Iraq may in fact have represented what at the time was a Faustian bargain to gain the acquiescence of 80 percent of Iraqis—the Shi'a and Kurds—in proceeding with the political rehabilitation of the country along democratic lines. Clearly, this is an issue that historians will debate for years to come.

The other two areas in which former Secretary Baker cites policy errors—failure to secure weapons depots, and deploying insufficient troops to establish security in the country—are also today largely accepted as conventional wisdom. The former does seem to have been an avoidable and costly mistake—that Iraq had massive amounts of weapons and ordnance was well known. However, even here, as Tom Ricks notes in his treatment of the U.S. military campaign in Iraq in *Fiasco*, the belief at the time of the invasion and march to Baghdad was that Iraq harbored biological and chemical weapons, and this caused military commanders to forgo destroying any weapons stockpiles that they came across for fear that such action might expose their troops to chemical or biological agents in those stockpiles: "In bunkers across Iraq there were tens of thousands of conventional weaponry—mortar shells, RPGs, rifle ammunition, explosives, and so on. . . . Yet U.S. commanders rolling into Iraq refrained from detonating those bunkers for fear that they also contained stockpiles of poison gas or other weaponry that might be blown into the air and kill U.S. soldiers or Iraqi civilians."[18] In retrospect, this assumption is now seen to have been wrong, and these intact munitions depots have clearly been a major source of weapons and materiel for insurgents in Iraq; at the time, however, U.S. commanders were making prudent decisions based on the best information they had.

The fourth area of policy raised by Secretary Baker—the level of coalition forces committed to the military campaign in Iraq—is discussed in detail elsewhere in this monograph, and while differing arguments can be made for what impact a higher level of troops might have had on various aspects of the invasion and on postinvasion developments, as concluded in that treatment of the issue the one area in which more troops would likely have made a significant, positive impact would have been in sealing Iraq's borders against the influx from Iraq's Arab neighbors of foreign fighters, weapons, and financial resources in support of the insurgency, as well as efforts by Iranian-linked elements to influence and meddle in the emerging Shi'a political hegemony in the country. However, as also discussed elsewhere in this work, in the prewar public and policy discussions of the likely consequences of the removal of the Saddam regime from power by outside military force, no one foresaw countering either of these prospective developments as urgent postliberation priorities.

THE BUREAUCRACY: EVEN PARANOIDS HAVE ENEMIES

> The first job of any Republican administration is to figure out how to use government agencies, which are staffed by people who may be liberals, but who are also professionals. The tightly controlled Bush White House has not successfully done that.[19]
> David Brooks, *New York Times*, May 14, 2006

As Brooks' comment above suggests, the famous quip by the late Israeli Prime Minister Golda Meir to then Secretary of State Henry Kissinger as he was pressuring her to make concessions in the 1972 Sinai talks that "even paranoids have enemies" may be pertinent to the issue of U.S. Iraq policy as it has been affected by relationships within the Bush administration and between policymakers and the career bureaucracy: some elements of the administration's prewar policy deliberation and planning process do suggest a degree of mistrust, or at least questioning of motives and commitment, on the part of some policymakers toward other policy players as well as toward the civilian and military bureaucracies that have been involved in developing and executing Iraq policy.

In conversations with colleagues involved in or witness to planning and deliberations at high levels relating to the administration's Iraq policy, I have heard comments reflecting wariness by high-level State Department officials toward their counterparts at the Pentagon, and by high-level Pentagon and National Security Council (NSC) officials toward their counterparts at State. Such a lack of mutual confidence was displayed in many now well-documented instances involving interactions between policy-level officials and the career bureaucracy as well. A statement by Army Chief of Staff General Eric Shinseki, for example, to the effect that historical parallels dictated that an occupation of Iraq would necessitate the use of "several hundred thousand troops"[20]—while it may well have been an honest attempt by Shinseki to ensure proper planning and execution of military action and postwar stabilization and occupation in Iraq—may at the same time have conveyed to political leaders a message that the Pentagon brass did not support war with Iraq; military expert Andrew Bacevich, writing in *The American Conservative*, was one who drew such a conclusion: "Given that the requisite additional troops simply did not exist, Shinseki was implicitly arguing that the U.S. armed services were inadequate for the enterprise."[21] The treatment then afforded to General Shinseki left no doubt that such (perceived) lack of support would not be tolerated.

The issue of posturing by careerists as a means of swaying policymakers in their decisions arose again in the Senate confirmation hearings for Secretary of Defense Robert Gates in December 2006. During the hearing Senator Hillary Clinton cited a comment by Gates contained in a Public Broadcasting System (PBS) *Frontline* program on the 1991 Gulf War that, typically, the military "exaggerate[s] the level of forces required to accomplish a specific objective." In fact, on the *Frontline* program, Gates commented that "contrary to mythology, the biggest doves in Washington wear uniforms," and went on to explain: "I think that they [the military] try, perhaps even unconsciously, not only to exaggerate the level of forces that will be required to accomplish a specific objective, but the casualties as well, in the hope of forcing a sanity check on the politicians or on the civilian experts who have no concept of what it is like to sit there and watch a young soldier bleed and die." At his Senate confirmation hearing, in response to Senator Clinton's question, Gates described what in his view is a broader bureaucratic tendency to skew policy advice on the basis of institutional perspective: "It was always my experience that, contrary to the conventional wisdom, it was the State Department that most often wanted to use force; and the Department of Defense that most often wanted to use diplomacy; and the CIA never wanted to use covert action. Everybody wanted everybody else . . . to take action."[22]

With respect to aspects of the CIA's role in the lead-up to the Iraq War, there now appears, in fact, to have been considerable uncertainty within the intelligence community concerning the status of Saddam's WMD, with reporting available to suggest that these weapons had been discarded or destroyed, and conflicting evidence suggesting that Saddam still had such weapons on hand or at least had the capability to produce them quickly.

As Paul Pillar, now a Georgetown University colleague but from 2000 through 2005 the CIA's national intelligence officer responsible for the Middle East, has written:

> [I]intelligence on Iraqi weapons program did not drive [the White House] decision to go to war . . . its decision to topple Saddam was driven by other factors—namely, the desire to shake up the sclerotic power structures of the Middle East and hasten the spread of more liberal politics and economics in the region. . . . If the entire body of official intelligence analysis on Iraq had a policy implication, it was to avoid war—or, if war was going to be launched, to prepare for a messy aftermath.23

Pillar (in my view, correctly) perceived that President Bush had concluded that U.S. policy needed to address the "sclerotic" status quo in the Middle East; his account, however, does not indicate that the intelligence community ever sought to develop information or analysis relevant to the successful implementation of such a policy. The White House and the intelligence community seem to have been working at cross purposes: The former was seeking an Iraq policy to employ as a potential instrument in addressing a root cause of the 9/11 attacks; the latter was approaching Iraq policy from the vantage point of how best to mitigate any threat emanating from Saddam Hussein's weapons arsenal.

The well-publicized case of Richard Clarke, a career official on the staff of the National Security Council in the Clinton and first George W. Bush administrations who held the position of chairman of the Counter-terrorism Security Group on the NSC at the time of the 9/11 attacks, suggests that a disconnect also existed between Bush administration policymakers and at least some elements of the career NSC bureaucracy. Clarke's 2004 book, *Against All Enemies: Inside America's War on Terror*, which he wrote following his retirement from government service in 2003, is critical of many of the Bush administration's actions following the 9/11 attacks, including the decision to use force to remove Saddam Hussein. Clarke, in a 2004 interview with *salon.com*, described his exchanges with administration officials on Iraq as follows:

> I started saying on September 11 and September 12 that their [certain officials in the Bush administration] idea of responding to the

terrorists attacks by going to war with Iraq was not only misplaced but counterproductive. . . . I made it very clear to Condi Rice . . . that I thought going into Iraq was a mistake. And I thought that if you did have to go in—if the President was determined to do that—then it had to be done within the United Nations context."[24]

Here, too, there is no indication of an understanding that the president's approach to Iraq derived from a broader strategic assessment of the impact of Saddam's Iraq on U.S. security interests rather than from a tactical concern about how best to ensure that Saddam gave up his WMD.

The State Department was not immune from such disconnects. One Iraq-related, State-led initiative was the Future of Iraq project, an attempt to engage Iraqi expatriates and U.S. subject-matter experts from government, NGOs, and the private sector in planning for a post-Saddam Iraq. The project, which grew out of the 1998 Iraq Liberation Act, came to encompass seventeen working groups to study and plan for all aspects of a post-Saddam transition in Iraq. However, shortly before the start of hostilities, when the Department of Defense (DOD) created its own organization to deal with the aftermath of Saddam's removal (the Office of Reconstruction and Humanitarian Affairs [ORHA]), the work of the Future of Iraq project was largely shunted aside. In some retrospective analyses, the decision to shelve the Future of Iraq project is ascribed to a turf war between the State and Defense Departments, to some extent based on perceptions concerning the views of some of its participants. Published accounts suggest that two of the State officials associated with the project, Tom Warrick and Meghan O'Sullivan, were blocked at a high level in the Bush administration from participating in DOD's post-Saddam planning efforts.[25] *The Atlantic Monthly*'s James Fallows, in *Blind into Baghdad*, relates the following concerning Warrick's involvement with the Future of Iraq project:

> Contemplating postwar plans posed a problem for those who, like many in the State Department, were skeptical of the need for war. Were they making war more likely if they prepared for its aftermath? Thomas Warrick, the State Department official who directed the Future of Iraq Project, was considered to be in the antiwar camp."[26]

In analyzing the postwar challenges that the United States and its coalition partners have faced, many have suggested that the shelving of the Future of Iraq project was a fundamental error, that it would have provided the detailed blueprint needed for the postwar effort in Iraq. Independent experts, however, have generally dismissed such a claim. In *Cobra II*, for example, Gordon and Trainor review the background to the Future of Iraq project issue and cite comments by David Kay (a security expert who worked briefly with ORHA and then headed the Iraq Survey Group that searched for WMD in post-Saddam Iraq), who dismissed the project as not having been a viable postwar plan. Their account is as follows:

> The decision [to shelve the project] typified the ill will between the State and Defense Departments, but was not in itself a crippling blow. After the war, it was commonly held that failure to rely on the "Future of Iraq Study" had deprived [ORHA Director Gen. (ret.) Jay] Garner and his team of a vital blueprint at a critical moment. The more than 1,000-page study was the product of seventeen working groups and was of uneven quality. It offered a useful way to bring Iraqi exiles together to discuss the problems of a new Iraq and propose some good ideas but it was far short of a viable plan. Kay, who read the study, summed it up: "It was unimplementable. It was a series of essays to describe what the future could be. It was not a plan to hand to a task force and say 'go implement.' If it had been carried out it would have made no difference."[27]

Taken as a whole, the situation that obtained in the lead-up to the Iraq War embodied, at least to some degree, the kind of circumstance described in a comment attributed to former Secretary of State Henry Kissinger to the effect that policy papers presented to him for decision always contained three options: "nuclear war, surrender, and the position the bureaucracy wanted me to sign off on." That is, the career bureaucracy had its views on which policy choices should be made and used the bureaucratic process to attempt to steer policy decisions accordingly. To the extent that policymakers perceived this to be the case in their efforts to deal with Saddam, it was an unhelpful element in the process of developing policies, policy options, and policy implementation plans for addressing the challenge that Saddam's Iraq posed.

INSTITUTIONAL DYSFUNCTION

In commenting on the debacle that was the Dubai ports deal, *New York Times* columnist Tom Friedman frustratingly suggested that "[I]f you had any doubts before, have none now: 9/11 has made us stupid."[28] I believe a more accurate reading of that incident would lead to a somewhat different version of Friedman's statement: "If you had any doubts before, have none now: 9/11 has made us dysfunctional."

In my view, a systematic dysfunction that had been building during the 1990s tightened its grip on government institutions in the wake of the 9/11 attacks. This dysfunction manifests itself in a mind-set of extreme risk-avoidance at the level of individual responsibility and decisionmaking. This then produces collective outcomes that are actually counter to the very aims of the United States and the interests of the American people.

GOVERNMENT BY ACCOUNTABILITY REVIEW BOARD

I refer to this phenomenon as an "Accountability Review Board" (ARB) mentality, a mind-set that strengthened in response to the terrorist incidents of the 1990s.[29] In connection with each of al-Qaeda's terrorist attacks against U.S. interests during that decade—the bombing of the Saudi Arabian National Guard offices in Riyadh in 1995; the bombing of the Khobar Towers in eastern Saudi Arabia in 1996; the bombings of the U.S. embassies in Nairobi and Dar es Salaam in 1998; and the attack on the *USS Cole* in Aden harbor in Yemen in 2000—Accountability Review Boards were convened to identify shortcomings and needed improvements in security planning and implementation, seek "lessons learned," and—implicitly, if not overtly—assign blame. In each succeeding case, the threshold of expectations about the length to which those in charge should be expected to go to ensure security against possible terrorist attack was raised.

By the end of the decade, the prevailing atmosphere was unambiguous: no possible security measure could be considered too extreme or harsh, no matter what the collateral damage to U.S. interests that such measures might inflict; all other U.S. interests were to be subordinated to security considerations. It was this ratcheting up of the primacy of security over mission that led to a military in which "force protection" became the dominant mission; on the civilian side of the government, a similar attitude of subordinating all other aspects of an agency's mission to security has had a likewise negative impact on the pursuit of agency goals.

In connection with the events of 9/11, one element of criticism that I found particularly troubling was that attributed to the visa adjudication process that led to the issuance of visas to the nineteen 9/11 hijackers. As it happened, at the time of 9/11 I was serving in Germany (where ringleader Mohammad Atta's visa was issued) and I had just completed a three-year tour of duty in Saudi Arabia (where fifteen of the hijackers had obtained their visas) in June 2000. Thus, I was familiar with visa adjudication procedures in both countries and knew how off-the-mark the public discussion—and attributed blame—on this score actually was.

In particular, some claims that the visa applications of most of the hijackers who were issued their visas in Saudi Arabia were "improperly completed"—and thus should have been denied—were misplaced at best, especially any claims that these Saudi applicants should have been denied visas because they were "intending immigrants." Saudi Arabian nationals are probably that group of foreign visitors to the United States who are *least likely* to remain in the United States illegally or to seek immigrant status. The fact is that Saudi visitors to the United States embody that rare combination of being both affluent and unlikely to remain illegally in the United States. If, before 9/11, consular officers in Saudi Arabia had routinely denied visas to otherwise qualified Saudi visa applicants based on poorly completed visa applications, the already considerable amount of correspondence from U.S. politicians, U.S. schools, and U.S. tourist agencies that the embassy typically received whenever a Saudi visa application was delayed or denied would likely have increased significantly. In the course of one day—September 11, 2001—this situation was turned on its head. As it happened, visitors from Saudi Arabia to the United States dropped from 72,891 in 1999 to 18,573 in 2004, the latest year for which figures are available, with significant economic consequences for some U.S. educational institutions and several U.S. tourist destinations.

During my assignment in Riyadh in the late 1990s, we took pride in telling visiting U.S. officials that the Saudi Arabian cabinet had more Ph.D.-holders from U.S. universities than did the U.S.

cabinet, this a result of the large number of Saudis sent to study in the United States in the 1970s and 1980s. The personal connections and mutual understanding that arose out of such intensive educational exchange formed one of the core elements of the Saudi-American relationship. The greatly increased numbers of foreign students in the United States in recent decades has been an invaluable element in engendering increased mutual understanding between Americans and foreigners. This aspect of the relationship has been severely damaged in the years since 9/11. Fortunately, both the U.S. and Saudi Arabian governments have recognized this fact, and both are taking steps to reverse the growing recent estrangement at the personal level between our two countries.

The value and importance of international interaction and person-to-person experience are well documented. In connection with the attitudinal impact on foreigners of personal exposure to the United States, the "Discover America Partnership"—a consortium that advocates for policies that promote foreign tourism in the United States—cites research from 2005 showing "a 16% increase in favorable opinion of the U.S. among those who have visited the country compared to those who haven't," and notes that "72% of people who have visited the country have a positive opinion of Americans."[30] The U.S. government has long recognized the value of such international interaction. The world's premier academic exchange program—the Fulbright Program—was conceived by Senator J. William Fulbright as a contribution to increasing international understanding in the aftermath of the devastation of World War II. In the sixty years since its inception in 1946, the Fulbright Program has supported some fifty thousand Americans for study and research abroad and almost one hundred fifty thousand foreigners for such activities in the United States. While serving as chairman of the German-American Fulbright Commission during my 2000–04 assignment as minister-counselor for Public Affairs at the U.S. embassy in Berlin, I saw first-hand how this German-American program—one of the largest in the world—help maintain a foundation for U.S.-German understanding and dialogue even during times of heated bilateral disagreement on policy issues.

Appreciation of the value of the Fulbright Program is reflected in the fact that reestablishing this program in post-Saddam Iraq was one of the earliest activities that the Coalition Provisional Authority undertook. During my year in the country, I was profoundly impressed and inspired by stories that Iraqi Fulbright applicants told me of the risks they would endure in an effort to participate in the program. They would explain how they used subterfuge (and disguise) to travel to Baghdad to pursue their applications, and they were all well aware of the fact that simply applying to participate in the Fulbright Program entailed the risk of violent retribution by insurgents. Most Iraqi participants in the Fulbright Program were unable to share the fact of their participation in the program beyond their immediate family members, for fear that they and their families would become targets of the insurgents.

A recognition of the value of first-hand exposure to the United States on the part of foreigners is also a pillar of what has arguably been the most effective U.S. government long-term investment in fostering support for U.S. international interests and policies—the International Visitor Leadership Program (IV Program). Like the Fulbright Program, the IV Program is a State Department-supported exchange program.[31] This program seeks to identify future leaders in foreign countries—from among government officials, academics and educators, businesspeople, media professionals, and other opinion elite—and invite them to visit the United States for an intensive professional and cultural program in order to acquaint them with the United States and the American people. There are some five thousand IV Program participants each year; more than two hundred current and former heads of state, one thousand five hundred cabinet-level ministers, and many other distinguished leaders in government and the private sector have participated in the IV program. As with the Fulbright Program, one of our highest public diplomacy priorities in Iraq was to implement a robust IV Program; during my year in the country, we sent more than eighty Iraqis from around the country on this key program.

These, and other government-supported programs in international exchange notwithstanding, by far the greatest amount of exposure by foreigners to America and Americans comes through the millions of such encounters that arise from privately funded business travel, tourism, educational exchange, and other types of activities. It is due to this fact that I share the concerns that officials, educators and others have expressed at the possible long-term impact that many post-9/11 procedures may have on this aspect of America's engagement with the world. Since 9/11, the United States has fallen from the first to the sixth most popular foreign tourist destination in the world, a troubling development that has triggered efforts by government officials and the travel and tourist industries to reverse this trend.

Our post-9/11 experience in Berlin offers an informative case study of unintended (and unhelpful) consequences of changes arising in the post-9/11 security climate. Following 9/11, at the U.S. embassy in Berlin, where I was assigned at the time, the embassy—and the German police units responsible for protection of embassy facilities—scrutinized very closely the embassy's physical security and its operations to ensure that there were no unseen or unaddressed vulnerabilities. Certain enhancements to the embassy's physical setback and new security barriers were put in place. While not attractive or "welcoming," these security upgrades were necessary and were largely received with understanding and acceptance by those who lived and worked in the neighborhood surrounding the embassy and were therefore affected by their implementation.

Operational changes were also made to enhance security. Screening of visitors and their belongings was moved from the lobby inside the embassy building itself to a small guard booth a few dozen meters outside the embassy's front door. Visitors would now line up at that guard booth to go through a metal detector and check their cell phones, cameras, and other electronic equipment before proceeding into the embassy. When individual visitors were being processed, the system worked perfectly well. However, at the embassy we often hosted groups—exchange students, school classes, business delegations, etc.—who came for briefings. In these cases, the visitors were required to line up outside the guard booth and proceed one at a time into the booth for screening. For a group of thirty or so visitors, this could mean a wait outside in the rain, snow, or summer heat of Berlin for a half hour or more, as compared with the pre-9/11 procedure of having all visitors in a group enter the shelter of the embassy lobby together to be individually screened in the (secure) lobby before they proceeded into embassy briefing or work areas proper. While, in light of the events of 9/11, there was understanding on the part of these visitors for the discomfort and inconvenience of these new security screening procedures, these new arrangements resulted in many a visitor to the U.S. embassy being in a less-than-pleasant mood by the time he or she completed the entry screening process.

The situation at the embassy's office in the neighborhood of Dahlem on Berlin's outskirts was even more problematic. It was there that the embassy's consular operation was located, and consular services—comprising visas and U.S. citizen services—received dozens, sometimes hundreds—of clients each day. Post-9/11 enhanced security procedures were put in place in Dahlem as well, and these included screening in a guard booth out in front of the building and admission of only a limited number of clients into the Consular Section at a time. This resulted in frequent long lines of consular clients outside the embassy dealing with the elements of Berlin's often harsh Central European climate.

To compound matters, due to the volume of clients, and the potential risk involved, Consular Section clients were not permitted to take bags or other materials into the embassy with them, and—again for security reasons—the embassy guards were not allowed to take and store these items for the clients who came for consular services. This Catch-22 put the clients in the position of having to leave items sitting on the sidewalk outside while they conducted their business in the consular section. As it happened, an enterprising fast food merchant in the subway station located across the street from the embassy's Dahlem location recognized the opportunity this situation provided and began a lucrative side business of holding personal items for embassy Consular Section clients for the fee of one euro. A journalist from the German national weekly *Die Zeit*, having come one day to apply for a U.S. visa and having witnessed this spectacle outside the embassy building, was moved to write a tongue-in-cheek article on the "entrepreneurial spirit" unleashed by the embassy's inscrutable security procedures.

Of course, a maximalist security posture vis-à-vis the large number of visitors to the embassy Consular Section required just the procedures described above. Anything less—such as allowing more people into the consular waiting room, or checking personal items for consular clients—would have entailed taking avoidable risks, and should such more considerate procedures have been adopted, and should a security incident have taken place, the person responsible for such a "lapse" would have been held accountable. In such an environment, at the individual level no one is prepared (or, in fact, should be expected) to accept responsibility for a less-than-maximal position regarding security arrangements. Thus, policies are put in place that work against the broader interests of the U.S. government and the American people, in this case alienating hundreds of persons each day who have business with the embassy.

The point is not to excoriate individuals, or particular decisions or procedures. In fact, the State Department, while necessarily implementing new post-9/11 procedures that have been legislated for the visa system, has coupled this with a renewed effort to encourage our consular staff to be as helpful and forthcoming as possible to prospective foreign visitors to the United States. Through determination and effort, in cooperation with the Department of Homeland Security and other government agencies, the State Department has now reached the important milestone of surpassing the number of student and exchange visitor visas issued before 9/11, after what had been several years of decline. The problem, clearly, is not with the professionals who organize and implement the nation's visa process from the inside, nor with the very capable professionals who oversee security procedures at U.S. diplomatic missions. Rather, the problem is systematic: a mind-set of extreme risk avoidance, one-size-fits-all procedural directives, and apprehension about after-the-fact scapegoating when a terrorist incident does take place.

Fortunately, there does exist one mechanism at all U.S. diplomatic missions that already plays a useful role in helping balance security considerations with mission goals—the Emergency Action Committee (EAC). Each U.S. diplomatic post has an EAC, usually comprised of the senior officers whose function it is to provide the chief of mission with its collected, professional advice in dealing with security threats. While ultimate responsibility for whatever operational decisions are made still rests with the chief of mission, the "collective responsibility" embodied in the recommendations of the EAC to the chief of mission does provide a helpful united front for decisions that might, in hindsight, be criticized or second-guessed in the event that a worst-case scenario plays out. Greater use of the EAC mechanism for deciding on procedures and precautions to be implemented locally, based on the circumstances in a given host country—in place of universally mandated, worldwide policies—could potentially help address some of the adverse effects on U.S. interests that have arisen through our post-9/11 security posture.

THE CASE OF TARIQ RAMADAN

In August 2004, while heading the Public Diplomacy Office at the U.S. embassy in Baghdad, I was contacted by the Swiss Muslim scholar Professor Tariq Ramadan, whom I had met the previous January at a conference that my office—at that time I was serving in Berlin—had supported: "The Arab-Western Summit of Skills." Prof. Ramadan, a well-known and respected European Muslim scholar, delivered the keynote address at the Berlin conference. His appearance at the event was enthusiastically received by the several dozen Arabs in attendance, and in my perception—as an observer of the proceedings—it was noteworthy in the thoughtful, moderate message calling for "engagement" by Muslims—with the European societies in which many were now living, and with the West in general—that Ramadan conveyed to his listeners.32 Equally significant, in my view, was the dichotomy in the audience's reaction—with the older generation of Arabs in attendance generally challenging such "accommodation" and arguing for greater "militancy" in dealing with the West, while the younger group largely supported Ramadan's position. The exchanges during the discussion session at times became quite heated, and Ramadan proved himself to be both unflappable and persuasive in arguing his position.

Following his conference session, he and I had a chance to talk informally over coffee, and he mentioned that he had been invited to the United States to teach at Notre Dame University during the 2004–05 academic year. I congratulated him and told him that I thought this would be very beneficial, both to him for the positive experiences I was sure he would have in America and to the many Americans he would engage during his time teaching at Notre Dame who would get to hear a very articulate advocate of Muslim-western understanding. I also offered to be of assistance, if there was anything I could do on his behalf.

As I was sitting in Baghdad in August 2004, Prof. Ramadan took me up on that offer. As I learned from the e-mail that he sent me, the U.S. government bureaucracy had, unfortunately, managed to offend and alienate this influential Muslim scholar. The course of events is well described in an article by Scott Smallwood in the August 25, 2004, issue of the *Chronicle of Higher Education,* under the headline: "U.S. State Department Revokes Visa of Muslim Scholar Who Was to Teach at Notre Dame":33

> A Muslim scholar who had accepted a position at the University of Notre Dame had his visa revoked earlier this month at the request of the U.S. Department of Homeland Security.

Tariq Ramadan had been scheduled to begin teaching Monday, but he learned earlier this month that his previously approved work visa had been taken away, according to Matthew V. Storin, a Notre Dame spokesman. Mr. Ramadan, a Swiss citizen who had been teaching in Geneva, had planned to arrive with his family in South Bend, Ind., last week. His furniture is already there and his children are registered for school, Mr. Storin said.

Kelly G. Shannon, a spokeswoman for the State Department's Bureau of Consular Affairs, told the Associated Press that the visa had been revoked at the request of the Department of Homeland Security. She cited a section of immigration law that was changed by the USA Patriot Act, but she did not clarify how the law applied to Mr. Ramadan.

Mr. Ramadan has been accused by some Jewish groups of being an anti-Semite and possibly connected to terrorist groups. He has denied such allegations. He is the grandson of Hassan al-Banna, founder of the Muslim Brotherhood, a conservative Islamist political organization that was created in Egypt in 1928.

Earlier this year *Time* magazine named Mr. Ramadan one of the world's 100 most influential people. The author of several books, he encourages Muslims to integrate into Europe without betraying their religious values. In February, Notre Dame announced it had hired him for a full-time, tenured post at the Kroc Institute for International Peace Studies.

As a Swiss citizen, Mr. Ramadan had been able to travel freely to the United States in the past without a visa. But to work in the country, he needed the approval of the U.S. State Department.

Mr. Storin said university officials learned a few weeks ago that the visa had been revoked. At first, they thought it might have been a bureaucratic mix-up. But after checking into the matter, they realized it was not. "This was something that was done with a certain deliberateness," Mr. Storin said.

"We're very disappointed and we're very concerned, both for him and for the Kroc Institute," Mr. Storin said. "It also raises broader issues regarding academic freedom."

Scott Appleby, the director of the Kroc Institute, said the university is asking federal officials to reconsider, or at least explain the reasons behind their decision.

In the spring, Mr. Ramadan went through a thorough security clearance and was granted a visa, Mr. Appleby said.

"We're not the CIA at this university, but we had also done our own vetting and found him free of any of the charges that have been made against him," Mr. Appleby said.

Mr. Appleby said Mr. Ramadan remains in Geneva and is not commenting to the media at the moment.

© 2004 Chronicle of Higher Education; reprinted by permission.

Over the subsequent weeks, I engaged my State Department colleagues in Washington from afar, and considerable effort was made within the department to seek a positive outcome in Ramadan's case. I also spoke with my embassy Baghdad colleague from the Department of Homeland Security, vouching for Ramadan's bona fides as someone whose engagement in the United States would help contribute to the range of Muslim outreach efforts that had become so important in the wake of 9/11. However, in the end the visa impasse could not be overcome, and Ramadan resigned his appointment at Notre Dame, with considerable bitterness.

I cannot, of course, judge the validity of the reasons for which the Department of Homeland Security revoked the visa that had earlier been approved for Ramadan and his family, since I am not privy to this information. I do, however, view this very unfortunate incident as another instance of bureaucratic dysfunction born of a post-9/11 risk aversion that, ironically, actually serves to exacerbate the very causes of the 9/11 attacks themselves.

PARTISANSHIP AND THE WATER'S EDGE

In my own case, my appreciation for the tension between domestic policy disputes and the discussion of controversial U.S. policies in a foreign context goes back to my first experience abroad, as an undergraduate exchange student in Bonn, Germany, in 1972. As a typical liberal, anti-Vietnam-War college student of the time—a veteran of the 1971 March on Washington, a Woodstock alumnus, and a regular antiwar leafleteer in Bethlehem, Pennsylvania, where I was a student—I yielded to no one in my belief that U.S. policy in Vietnam was misguided. However, upon arriving in Bonn, I was completely unprepared for the mindless, overblown anti-Americanism I experienced on the Bonn University campus. While I was opposed to U.S. policy in Vietnam, I did not view that policy as emanating from a country that was, at its core, evil, as clearly did the most vociferous antiwar voices that harangued Bonn University's students over lunch each day in the university *Mensa* (dining hall).

My epiphany in Germany—the realization that criticizing the United States or its policies in the context of a foreign country is fundamentally different from doing so in the United States—is, in my experience, almost universal among Americans who spend any extended period of time overseas. I recall an incident in the late 1970s in Saudi Arabia in which I ran into an African-American colleague from King Faisal University in Dammam, where we were both teaching at the time, at the Dhahran International Airport. We had both been living in Saudi Arabia for almost two years; my colleague had completed his contract at the university and was preparing to fly back to the United States. I recall him telling me that, at the time he left the United States for Saudi Arabia almost two years earlier he had been a fairly radicalized African-American, angry at continued racism in the United States and generally critical of his country. As he prepared to depart Saudi Arabia, he explained that, having lived in the Middle East for almost two years—his first extended time spent abroad—and having visited several countries in the region, his attitudes toward his own country had changed drastically.

As he understood, America—for all its faults—was committed to creating a just society, even if the path to such a society was uneven and painfully slow. His anger at his country had not been based on the country's principles, but rather on the chasm he saw between those principles and the everyday reality that many Americans experienced, in his case most pointedly by the African-American community. However, his experience abroad had shown him that in very many cases foreigners viewed America's shortcomings as fundamental flaws in U.S. principles. To his considerable irritation, he found his country being unfairly criticized on "first principles" by those who—given obvious shortcomings in their own political, social, and cultural systems—were in no position to find fault with America. As we concluded our conversation, he commented that, much to his own great surprise, he would want to kiss the ground when he landed the next day back in the United States.

Those without the perspective gained from having spent time immersed in societies overseas are not in a position to adequately appreciate the effect that being abroad has in terms of tempering political bias and criticism. However vehement and politically divisive the domestic political discussion of an issue might be, the dynamics change completely when the American discussion of that issue moves overseas. This fact may not be well understood by those who have not lived abroad for a significant period of time, and this may be at the bottom of some claims of "partisanship" in a State Department program—the U.S. Speakers Program—that sends U.S. experts on lecture tours abroad. In spring 2006, Senator Joseph Biden asked the State Department inspector general to review the program, after reading claims that "potential participants were vetted—via Internet searches, for example—for any comments or writings that criticized administration policies, particularly its approach to Iraq."[34]

Such a policy would, of course, not only be misguided, but counterproductive. Participants in the U.S. Speakers Program are effective only to the extent that foreign audiences perceive them to be credible. In Iraq, we programmed a number of U.S. Speakers, and these included such prominent foreign and security policy experts as Dr. Anthony Cordesman of the Center for Strategic and International Studies and Dr. Leslie Gelb, president emeritus of the Council on Foreign Relations. Both have been critical of aspects of the current administration's policies on Iraq, both before and after their speaking tours in Iraq. Their contribution to our dialogue with Iraqis, however, was outstanding. They enabled us to engage Iraqi political and opinion leaders of all points of view and from all communities; they conveyed key aspects (as well as the complexity) of the discussion of Iraq policy taking place in the United States; and they were able to inform their subsequent writing and speaking on Iraq through the first-hand encounters and exchanges that they experienced in the country. Whether it was in a packed auditorium at the Iraqi foreign ministry in Baghdad, at a meeting with local politicians and political leaders in al-Hilla or Kirkuk, or a during roundtable with academics and officials in Erbil, the kinds of dialogue that ensue from speaker programs of this nature—with speakers from across the U.S. political and policy spectrum—are indispensable to the communication needed to credibly engage foreign opinion leaders and publics.

In my more than quarter-century of Foreign Service experience, I have never seen a participant in this program—and I have programmed hundreds of such speakers—take a partisan stance in engaging a foreign audience or interlocutor. Those who participate in this program are sufficiently experienced and knowledgeable to appreciate the need to present a balanced, contextualized treatment of the issues they are addressing to their foreign audiences. Furthermore, as these scholars represent mainstream points of view, they invariably couch their presentations on policy issues within mainstream parameters of the domestic discussion of the policy at issue. By no means do they all argue for the current policies of any particular administration. However, in presenting the diversity of mainstream U.S. thought on a policy or policy area, these experts consistently convey the best of America's commitment to civil discussion of even the most controversial of issues, and our ability to agree to disagree and to settle policy disagreements through the electoral process and peacefully abide by the results. Although second nature to us in the United States, this message is still a source of wonder (and envy) to peoples in many parts of the world.

ELECTIONS

As we continue to observe the development of the democratic process inside Iraq, it is important to keep in mind the distinction between the theory and the practice of democracy. Democracy is, in theory, about self-government—government selected by and accountable to the people. Whatever political structures are chosen to implement this concept, at its core democracy entails providing those to be governed with a free choice among competing candidates in choosing those who are to govern.

As we have seen in Iraq, the enthusiasm among the Iraqi people for choosing their leaders is palpable. However, the structures available to Iraqis to demonstrate their political preferences have been limited and in key respects flawed. In the first national elections—in January 2005—the short time frame to prepare, the lack of adequate census information, and the fact of out-of-country voting all necessitated that the balloting be by a nationwide electoral district with consolidated political lists of candidates, which essentially precluded any fine-tuning in the options available to the Iraqi electorate. In the most recent election—in December 2005—the system was improved upon slightly by setting the electoral districts at the provincial level. Thus, rather than a single national list, parties wishing to contest the election had to field candidate lists in each of Iraq's eighteen provinces in which they wished to run.

Here it is important to note that one legacy of Iraq's recent political history is the fact that political parties are held in very low esteem by the Iraqi public. This lack of trust of or identification with particular political parties, together with the broad geographical basis on which parliamentary seats were being contested—nationwide in January, provincewide in December—led to the predictable result that, when voters were forced to cast a single vote for a single political list, they largely fell back on their ethnic or sectarian identity in choosing how to cast their ballot. This outcome, in turn, has inhibited the ability of Iraq's various communities, regions, and other natural interest groups to compromise and coalesce around constitutional structures and national policies that will foster unity and reconciliation and promote Iraq's political and economic recovery from the trauma of more than three decades of brutal Baathist misrule.

In August 2006, I had an opportunity to discuss with an Iraqi acquaintance who was in Washington, DC, at the time his take on the Iraqi government that ultimately emerged from Iraq's December 2005 election. This Iraqi—a secular Shi'a from Iraq's Shi'a-dominated south-central region—was disappointed and discouraged by the course that the electoral process had taken in his country. In his view, political candidates had misused religious factors—most prominently, had misrepresented themselves as having the backing of Grand Ayatollah Ali al-Sistani—in seeking electoral advantage, leading to an electoral outcome in which an Islamist minority among Iraq's Shi'a gained political dominance at the expense of Iraq's secular Shi'a majority. A similar pattern of voting under the influence of religious sway has been observed elsewhere in the region, most recently in elections in Kuwait and Saudi Arabia, and conveys a cautionary message about the path that the process of democratization may take in the region.

The challenge of weakness in the democratic infrastructure in the Middle East as an impediment to successful democracy promotion in the region is reflected as well in the oft-cited strategy of some Arab leaders to game the system by ensuring that the only choice available to their populations in electoral contests is that between themselves—i.e., the autocratic leadership in power—and an Islamist opposition. What these entrenched leaders and their supporters will not allow is the emergence of a vibrant civil society that would produce the kind of democratic infrastructure needed for successful transition to functioning and sustainable democratic governance. U.S. policy has, rightly, been to expose and criticize such efforts to thwart needed democratic evolution in the region.

THE IRAQ STUDY GROUP

One tack that democracies sometimes resort to in order to address divisive or controversial issues for which politicians wish to deflect accountability is to create bipartisan or non-partisan task forces, commissions, or study groups. The Base Closings Commission that Congress created in the 1990s under the Base Closure and Realignment Act to make decisions concerning the politically and economically contentious issue of military base closings is one example, as are the various independent commissions that have been convened to study Social Security and make recommendations for reform.

In spring 2006, Congress and the Bush administration agreed on the creation of such a group to look at all aspects of the Iraq issue—the Iraq Study Group (ISG). The ISG consisted of ten distinguished former public servants, balanced between five Republicans and five Democrats, under the co-chairmanship of (Republican) former Secretary of State James A. Baker III, and former Democratic Congressman Lee Hamilton. While the group started its work well below the Washington radar screen, by the time it published its report on December 6, 2006, speculation, leaks, and expectations concerning its recommendations had become almost a national obsession.

At a June 2006 conference at the U.S. Military Academy at West Point, I had an opportunity to discuss the work of the Iraq Study Group with Ambassador Edward Djerejian, an accomplished career Foreign Service Officer (now retired) and Director of the James A. Baker III Institute for Public Policy at Rice University. Amb. Djerejian served as a senior advisor to the ISG and is credited with authoring much of the group's final report. Before his work with the ISG, Djerejian most recently came to prominence following the Iraq War and the plummeting of attitudes among Arab publics toward the United States when he chaired the Advisory Group on Public Diplomacy in the Arab and Muslim World, whose report—entitled "Changing Minds, Winning Peace"—was issued on October 1, 2003; the report examined U.S. government public diplomacy efforts aimed at Arab and Muslim populations and urged significant changes in and increased funding for those efforts.[35]

Ambassador Djerejian delivered the opening address at the West Point conference, convened under the theme "Public Diplomacy: Message, Process, Outcomes." Because the conference operated under Chatham House Rules (i.e., deep background, no attribution), participants were precluded from divulging the content of speakers' remarks or attributing comments to them. However, following the formal session, Amb. Djerejian joined a small group of us gathered at the postdinner reception and discussed several of the fundamentals that lie at the root of international opinion toward the United States and its foreign policies, in particular its Iraq policy. These included many of the factors discussed previously in this monograph—from the emergence of the United States as the sole superpower, to the impact of the information revolution, to continued political and economic stagnation in the Middle East.

The release of the ISG report was timed to come after the 2006 electoral season but before positioning for the 2008 presidential campaign shifted into high gear, and its high-level, bipartisan nature was intended to allow the group to succeed in developing a cohesive strategy for the United States to continue to pursue its important security goals in the Middle East. At the same time, its bipartisan nature was supposed to temper the role of Iraq in contributing to the rancor and divisiveness that has defined the political atmosphere in the country since the costs and casualties of the Iraq War started to mount in the months after the overthrow of the Saddam regime.

To some observers, the ISG report was seen as a return to a doctrine of foreign policy realism, reflecting Secretary Baker's well-established realist credentials and proposing such courses of action as direct diplomatic engagement with Iran and Syria in an attempt to gain their support for defusing the violence in Iraq, and a renewed effort to resolve the Arab-Israeli conflict as a means of addressing a broader Arab sense of grievance that is affecting the situation in Iraq. The first sentence of the executive summary—"The situation in Iraq is grave and deteriorating"[36]—set the report's tone.

Among those who have most strenuously criticized the report are Iraqi officials and leaders from the various communities in Iraq. To some extent this is understandable, since the ISG mandate was to determine what course in Iraq would be in the best interests of the United States. Thus, the linking of a continued U.S. security commitment to Iraq with Iraqi progress in such areas as interethnic and intercommunal reconciliation, demobilizing sectarian militias, amending the constitution, etc., has been interpreted by many in Iraq as unwarranted U.S. meddling in internal Iraqi affairs. Interestingly, one Iraqi acquaintance confided to me even well before the ISG report was issued that the fact of Secretary Baker's history—his involvement in the George H.W. Bush administration's decision not to come to the aid of Iraqi Kurds and Shi'a when they rose up against Saddam following the 1991 Gulf War, and thus (in their view) his complicity in the slaughter that Saddam inflicted on these two communities in putting down the uprising—already tainted most Iraqi's views toward the ISG's efforts.

On the U.S. side, the reaction has been equally reserved on the part of both Republicans and Democrats. The Republicans largely rejected the report's suggested timeline of early 2008 for the withdrawal of most U.S. forces from patrol, policing, and combat duties in Iraq, while the Democrats generally saw the suggested early 2008 timeline for such U.S. withdrawal as too drawn out. The ISG's efforts also sparked a broader Bush administration review of its overall approach to Iraq and the wider policy goals pursued through our efforts there, which are discussed at the end of chapter 11.

5
Iraq and the U.S. Military

This chapter considers issues related to the U.S. military, its role in Iraq, its place in U.S. society, and the consequences of the growing international military dominance of the United States and the increasing gap between U.S. military capabilities and those of our allies. Among these consequences is the fact of the increasing reluctance of our allies to join in military activities, since through their own actions in defense planning and resource allocation many have severely limited their ability to apply military action as a means for addressing international challenges. In addition, our allies are aware that their contribution to a military undertaking is generally not essential to the effort, because—from a strictly military point of view—the United States has the resources to accomplish its military objectives on its own anywhere in the world. Additionally, there is the inevitable resentment and unease toward a country that is as dominant militarily as the United States, especially in a post-9/11 environment in which "preventive" military action might be undertaken. Finally, there is the fact that the U.S.' ability to apply overwhelming force has caused our adversaries to largely forgo conventional military resistance and instead use insurgency as a countermeasure to U.S. military might.

Since the end of the Cold War, U.S. defense resources and expenditures have increasingly outpaced those of our major allies. This disparity in approach toward military funding has reached the oft-cited point where the United States now devotes as much money to military and defense-related outlays as the next several dozen nations of the world combined (by some calculations, by the rest of the entire world combined).[1] In the early years of this trend, the United States encouraged, and sought to cajole, its allies to increase their defense expenditures, or at least not to continue to reduce them, but these efforts had little effect. Thus, over the course of the past decade-and-a-half, this divergence in approach to defense has played itself out, and from today's perspective can be seen to have had a number of unexpected and unintended consequences. Several of these consequences have been brought into sharp focus during the lead-up to the launching of the Iraq War in 2003 and in the period since. Three of the most critical relate to (1) international attitudes toward and expectations of the United States, (2) the division of labor (or lack thereof) in addressing instability or conflict in the world, and (3) the inevitability of asymmetric warfare when U.S. forces intervene.

ATTITUDES TOWARD THE UNITED STATES

> Big powers have been respected and feared but not loved for good reasons—even if benevolent, tactful, and on their best behavior, they were threatening simply because of their very existence.
>
> Walter Laqueur, *"The Terrorism to Come"*[2]

As this quote from security expert Walter Laqueur suggests, the simple fact of the U.S.' role and power in the world has become a cause of some degree of anti-Americanism. Political scientist Michael Mandelbaum, in his 2005 work, *The Case for Goliath*, describes the context of attitudes abroad toward the United States as follows:

> anti-American sentiment . . . stems not only from what the American government does but also from what the United States is. What the United States is, first and foremost, is powerful. . . . The powerful can be dangerous. They can bully, dominate, and, if they choose, crush those who are weaker. In a world in which all other countries are weak by comparison, beneath the dislike and disapproval of the United States that public demonstrations manifest and opinion polls record lies another, more potent feeling: fear.[3]

As those of us involved in U.S. public diplomacy in Europe in the period up to and after the Iraq War in spring 2003 witnessed repeatedly, many Europeans had by that time developed a conviction that the U.S. approach to the world had evolved into one of "might makes right." The superiority of U.S. military capability—a capability that had actually served Europe well in the 1990s in addressing crises in the Balkans—was, in the view of many, more to be feared than to be welcomed as a force for maintaining international peace and stability. This perception was reflected in several well-publicized opinion polls that showed that more Europeans viewed the United States as a threat to international peace than held such a view of Saddam Hussein. Europeans, by contrast, emphasized diplomacy and "soft power" as preferred alternatives to the use of force in addressing misbehavior or aggression in the international arena.

Given its significant military superiority, the United States is largely viewed as having the power to resolve every problem of every aggrieved community anywhere in the world. Moreover, even those who have the wealth to develop the capability to address problems in the world but choose not to do so still see the United States as having the "moral obligation" to confront and defeat morally repugnant activities—such as genocide and ethnic cleansing—taking place in the world. In the age of ubiquitous, instant worldwide communications, atrocities taking place anywhere in the world are beamed instantly to a worldwide audience. In the face of such information, the world's morally righteous "demand" that such crimes be brought to an end. In a world in which only one country—the United States—has the capability (or, more precisely, is universally seen to have the capability) to intervene in such circumstances, either the U.S. takes action (leading in many quarters to condemnation for interfering in the internal affairs of others, often with accompanying theories concerning America's "real" motives for its action), or the United States takes no action, leading to criticism of the United States for its failure to use its unique power to confront obvious violations of basic human rights.

Overwhelming U.S. military superiority also leads to an international scenario in which the United States gets to do the fighting, alone. The perception—essentially true—that based on strictly military considerations the United States is able to undertake military action anywhere in the world without the involvement of its traditional allies leads to a dynamic that undermines the willingness of our allies to join us in military action. This is not to say that there are no other nations that are willing to join us militarily in addressing international security challenges: The North Atlantic Treaty Organization's (NATO's) involvement in *Operation Enduring Freedom* in Afghanistan, and the coalition of more than three dozen countries that has participated in *Operation Iraqi Freedom*, demonstrates that others do become involved. However, such involvement more and more comes with limiting caveats. The course of events that unfolded in connection with *Operation Iraqi Freedom* is instructive in understanding the new security dynamic that has emerged in the era of overwhelming U.S. military superiority.

THE ROLES IN IRAQ

In Iraq, it is the U.S. military, not the troops of America's coalition partners, that has borne the brunt of the fighting from the outset. The contribution of the other members of the coalition, while important and laudable, has—with the exception of considerable British military engagement in the early days of the conflict—largely been restricted to peacekeeping and occupation duties; war-fighting has been the business almost exclusively of U.S. forces. Tom Ricks, in his account of the Iraq War in *Fiasco*, for example, describes the participation of coalition forces in Iraq as follows: "Countries sent soldiers to Iraq as a political favor to the U.S. government, and except for the British contingent, that good turn didn't extend to getting them into combat."[4]

During my time in Iraq, I saw that when Fallujah was to be retaken from the insurgents in November 2004, British forces were moved from the (fairly quiet) south to relieve U.S. forces in the Baghdad area so those U.S. forces could participate in the retaking of Fallujah. This phenomenon—that it is the Americans who get to fight—is a second, unexpected result of the U.S.' emergence as a military power far more capable than any other: Those who might be expected to put their citizens in harm's way abroad in support of clear security, humanitarian, or moral ends can today largely avoid doing so if they wish to, since the United States has the capability to execute such missions on its own. As my Georgetown University colleague Robert Lieber has written: "The power disparity also contributes to a free rider problem . . . there is a temptation to evade responsibility because participants know that the United States is likely to pay the cost of dealing with potential threats . . . whether or not they contribute."[5] In a democracy, one of the most difficult and controversial decisions a leader can make is the decision to place its military forces in harm's way. Given the current international military order, leaders of our allied countries faced with such a decision now have an "out": They can leave that burden to the United States. Clearly, this is an unwelcome and unintended outcome of America's unassailable international military dominance.

One object lesson of the consequence of U.S. military dominance can be found in the role of Germany and its response to the Iraq crisis. As described in the next chapter, in the period leading up to the Iraq War a number of social, political, and other factors internal to German society came together in a "perfect storm" scenario to mitigate against German support for or participation in the military action that the United States spearheaded against Saddam's Iraq. A cycle of national catharsis emerged to align all elements of German society—the young as well as the old, the opinion elite as well as the man in the street, the political leadership, the media, the educational system, and other key elements of German society—behind rejection of a military solution to the Iraq crisis. As a result, Germany stayed out of the fray.

Or did it? Even while frustrated at the political climate and posturing that were dominating Germany's public response to the Iraq crisis in early 2003, we in the embassy in Berlin at the time were busy reminding our Washington colleagues that, while politically Germany was playing the role of a vociferous opponent of using military force against Saddam, tactically Germany was providing key elements of assistance to the U.S.-led war preparation effort. At the time of the Iraq War, the United States had some seventy thousand troops stationed on bases in Germany, and many of these troops—and much of their equipment—would need to be transported to locations abroad to stage the military effort to topple the Saddam regime. This meant relying on Germany's excellent rail and road systems: There was no opposition—either politically or from the German public—to such use of the German infrastructure to this end. More directly, the U.S. personnel stationed in Germany who were normally used to provide force protection for the many U.S. bases in the country would be needed for the action in Iraq. Germany stepped in and sent its soldiers to guard U.S. bases in the country, allowing the U.S. military personnel they were relieving to depart for the fight in Iraq. Germany also left important military hardware in Kuwait, including tanks and unique troop carriers that were secure against chemical-biological-radiological attack and that would be essential should Saddam use such weapons against coalition forces. Accounts have also now been published to suggest that German intelligence even provided assistance to U.S. military planners in connection with the campaign against Saddam's Iraq.[6]

In short, the evidence indicates that Germany's leaders and professional security apparatus understood and appreciated the consequences that were at stake in Iraq and decided that—within limits—they could act as helpful, responsible allies in the Iraq effort. However, the fact that the United States—on its own—had the might to effect the military operation in Iraq without the need for German troops allowed Germany to avoid sending its own forces into harm's way. The astute German journalist and commentator Josef Joffe actually suggested (in the prestigious national German weekly *Die Zeit*) that, in the matter of the campaign to liberate Iraq, the Germans "were the most important allies of the United States, except for the British."[7] What allowed them to be so, while avoiding the prospects of casualties to German soldiers, was the overwhelming nature of U.S. military might.

PREEMPTIVE CAPITULATION AND INSURGENCY

> The United States possesses overwhelming conventional military superiority. This capability has pushed its enemies to fight U.S. Forces unconventionally, mixing modern technology with ancient techniques of insurgency and terrorism. Most enemies either do not try to defeat the United States with conventional operations or do not limit themselves to purely military means. They know they cannot compete with U.S. Forces on those terms. Instead they try to exhaust U.S. National will, aiming to win by undermining and outlasting public support.
>
> Army Counterinsurgency Field Manual[8]

A third unintended consequence of the dominance of the U.S. military is the fact that, when a crisis reaches the point of military action, our enemies will largely avoid direct military engagement. As we saw in Iraq, when a small expeditionary force of U.S. Marines probed Baghdad's defenses in early April 2003, they met very light military resistance. At a time when this small force was still the only U.S. military presence in the city, widespread looting broke out, dealing a severe blow to the prospects for Iraq's quick recovery in the post-Saddam era.

Was this development a preplanned aspect of Saddam's military strategy to counter overwhelming U.S. military superiority? Retrospective analyses of this turn of events have come to different conclusions about whether there was an Iraqi strategy of preemptive capitulation coupled with postconflict insurgency. One of the earliest such analyses, by Rutgers University Middle East expert Professor Eric Davis, was published by the Philadelphia-based Foreign Policy Research Institute on June 30, 2004. It concluded:

> A widespread insurgency was planned by the Baathist regime prior to its being overthrown in March 2003. Knowing that the Iraqi army would be unable to confront U.S. military superiority, Saddam's regime organized a resistance movement that would fight American forces after the war ended. Large caches of arms and money were planted throughout Iraq, especially in the rural towns and villages of the so-called Sunni Arab triangle northwest of Baghdad. These resources were to be used in escalating attacks on American military units intended to sap the U.S. forces' resolve and force them from Iraq.

In *The Assassin's Gate*, published in 2005, George Packer cites the view of the Iraq Survey Group that also concluded that leaders in Saddam's government understood that they would need to counter overwhelming coalition military might not with direct resistance but with guerrilla tactics.

> But the report also found that guerrilla war had been the enemy's plan all along. "Saddam believed that the Iraqi people would not stand to be occupied or conquered by the United States and would resist—leading to an insurgency."[9]

Gordon and Trainor, in *Cobra II* (published in 2006) came to a similar conclusion (although they excluded Saddam from being involved in such planning):

> While there are indications that Iraq's intelligence service and other diehards prepared to battle after the regime was toppled, there is no convincing evidence that Saddam anticipated and planned a guerrilla campaign.[10]

Tom Ricks, in *Fiasco* (also published in 2006), while arguing that U.S. and coalition policies and actions in the early stages of the occupation "helped spur the insurgency and made it broader than it might have been," nonetheless noted that:

> There is some evidence that Saddam Hussein's government knew it couldn't prevail conventionally, and some captured documents indicate that it may have intended some sort of subversion campaign against the occupation. The distribution of arms caches, the revolutionary roots of the Baathist Party, and the movement of money and people to Syria either before or during the war all argue for some advance planning for an insurgency."[11]

The U.S. military's own study of this issue, however, downplays the idea of a pre-planned insurgency:

> Much of the debate on the origins of the postwar insurgency in Iraq has centered on the question of whether Saddam's regime placed munitions around the country to support future guerrilla war against an external foe. There is no significant documentary evidence to suggest it did so.[12]

It is clear, however, that the motivation, organizational capability, and tools for such a strategy were at hand after Saddam's regime fell, and we have seen the devastating impact of this capability in the post-Saddam era. The events and circumstances internal to Iraq that have contributed to the level of violence and lawlessness in the country—the insurgency in its broadest definition—include the following:

- the availability of weapons caches and financial resources at locations—especially in the Sunni triangle, as well as, evidence now suggests, across the border in Syria—that have been used to support post-Saddam insurgent activity;

- the destruction of the governmental and essential services infrastructure of Baghdad and other major cities in the country—immediately upon the fall of the Saddam government—that seriously undermined the capacity for effective governance and state functioning from the beginning of the post-Saddam era;[13] and

- the emptying of Iraq's prisons of hard-core criminals before the conflict began, letting them loose on the streets to ensure that coalition forces would have a major criminal element to handle.

To return to the passage from the Army Counterinsurgency Manual cited at the outset of this discussion, it makes clear that the view that America's adversaries cannot stand up to U.S. military force but rather, when faced with such force, will resort to insurgency and other elements of asymmetric warfare is now explicitly recognized in U.S. military doctrine.

INSUFFICIENT TROOPS

One of the most heated debates about the conduct of the Iraq War has involved the issue of U.S. troop levels in Iraq. In my view, it is accurate to state that in the period since the war it has become conventional wisdom that troop levels were too low for an effective, postwar occupation and that more troops would have fundamentally altered (in a positive way) the developments we have witnessed in Iraq since the fall of the Saddam regime. A strong argument can be made for this point of view. Perhaps the most detailed treatment in support of this position appears in Tom Ricks' account of the Iraq War and the subsequent occupation, *Fiasco*.

The key line of argument in favor of a larger occupation force was typically stated as the need to intimidate—even physically prevent—any individuals or group that might seek to disrupt public order or challenge the coalition's authority. As James Fallows put it in *Blind into Baghdad*: "This was the shock and awe which really mattered, in the army's view: the ability to make clear who was in charge."[14]

Notwithstanding the strength of the case that can be made for having used more coalition occupation troops in the period following the fall of the Saddam regime, there are a number of considerations that open up to question whether the presence of additional troops would have been decisive in enabling the coalition to counter the unique and unprecedented circumstances that arose in post-Saddam Iraq.

First, additional troops would not have prevented the disbursement of materiel and funds around the country to support a postliberation insurgency (such prepositioning had already taken place before the war), and once those assets were in place, the level and lethality of the coming insurgency were largely assured. Second, even if more troops had been on hand in Iraq, there would have been no plan to have those additional troops in place in Baghdad in time to prevent the destruction of much of the city's infrastructure in the immediate aftermath of the unexpectedly quick collapse of the capital's defense. Once that had happened, although it was not known at the time, the die was probably cast for a very difficult occupation and a long and violent insurgency.

Under such circumstances, the presence of two or three times the number of U.S. troops in Iraq—from around 150,000 to what is usually suggested as a needed 450,000—would have had two undesirable effects. First, it would have significantly increased the exposure of U.S. forces, since there simply would have been very many more targets for the insurgents to attack. Thus, while the conventional wisdom holds that significantly higher troop levels would have held insurgent violence in check, resulting in much lower U.S. and coalition military casualties, a possible alternate scenario is that, in view of the extensive weapons arsenal that was already in the hands of determined insurgents, higher troop levels could have increased the already tragic level of U.S. casualties in Iraq.

Second, the friction that results from the presence of U.S. forces among Iraqi civilians would likely also have increased. As it is, during my year in Iraq I witnessed too many instances of unpleasant (or worse) interaction between U.S. personnel (military and civilian, like me, with our heavily armed personal security details) and Iraqis simply driving down a street or otherwise going about their daily routines. These incidents in and of themselves caused significant anger and animosity toward the U.S. presence in Iraq. As one example that occurred during my time in Iraq, an incident involving coalition troops entering the campus of Baghdad's Al-Mustansriyah University[15] to arrest a suspected insurgent supporter there caused a major uproar among the students. This was only defused by a call that I and a senior U.S. military commander made on the university rector to soothe the situation (and to donate a collection of books and computer equipment as a goodwill gesture). What the impact would have been on the collective attitude of Iraqis toward the U.S. military and civilian personnel of multiplying the frequency of these occurrences by a factor of three can only be guessed.

Iraq and the U.S. Military 103

In comparing the situation in post-Saddam Iraq with historical postwar military occupations, several differences become apparent:

- The money, materiel, and determination of a fanatical minority to undertake a postwar insurgency that were in place in Iraq did not exist in recent postconflict situations. In an environment in which massive amounts of weapons and other war-fighting materiel are available to a large number who are committed to attacking coalition forces, Iraqis cooperating with the new Iraqi government, and the country's basic infrastructure for essential services, simply increasing the number of security forces would not necessarily eliminate their ability to undertake such actions.

- The information and communications infrastructure that is essential to the current insurgency in Iraq also did not exist during other recent periods of occupation. Thus, it is not clear that the number of troops, per se, would have had the same effect in the current Iraqi environment that it had in a pre-Internet / pre-cell phone world. Insurgents are not reliant on physical interaction and coordination—as they would have been in earlier times—in order to plan and carry out their activities. Thus, this element of the impact from an increased physical presence by security forces—an increased ability to identify and intercept efforts to plan and implement insurgent activities—would likely be less successful than historical parallels would suggest.

- As has often been noted, Iraqis bristle at being occupied. They are a proud people, and while most have accepted the need for a foreign military presence in their country under current circumstances, they do not like it. Doubling or tripling that presence would not have helped in this regard.

- The role and attitude of the Iraq people with respect to the Iraqi government that the coalition removed are markedly different from those of the populations of other recently occupied countries toward their respective governments. In Germany and Japan, for example, the governments that were defeated enjoyed the support of the majority of the German and Japanese people, respectively. When these governments were defeated, their populations accepted this as a defeat for them as well. In Iraq, except for elements of the Sunni community, the great majority of Iraqis see themselves as very much victims of the former regime. This undoubtedly contributes somewhat to their attitudes toward being occupied, and a significant increase in the visibility of that occupation would certainly not improve the situation.

The fact is it is impossible to know with certainty whether the deployment of a higher level of coalition troops into Iraq after the toppling of the Saddam regime would have been the panacea that, in hindsight, is imputed to it. Interestingly, it may be that the person who is most associated with the issue of postconflict troops levels and held most directly responsible for the alleged failure to deploy sufficient troops to secure Iraq during Phase IV operations—former Secretary of Defense Donald Rumsfeld—has provided the most reasoned assessment of this issue. Bob Woodward, in *State of Denial*, cites an interview with then-Secretary Rumsfeld in the summer of 2006 in which he commented on the issue of troop levels in Iraq:

> It's entirely possible that there were too many at some point and too few at some point, because no one's perfect. All of us that were trying our best to make these judgments were doing it in a context of concern about having enough to get the job done, and enable a process, political and economic process, to go forward, and not so many that it persuaded people that we were there to steal their oil and occupy their country and disrupt and cause disturbances in the neighboring countries that cause the overthrow of some of those other regimes. And so we made the best judgment we could. In retrospect I have not seen or heard anything from other opiners that suggests to me that they have any reason to believe that they were right and we were wrong. Nor can I prove we were right and they were wrong.[16]

By the end of 2006, however, as violence continued unabated in Iraq and the Iraqi government showed no ability to move its agenda of sectarian reconciliation and economic and infrastructure development forward in the reigning climate of insecurity and fear, President Bush reviewed his overall Iraq strategy and decided that, in fact, some additional troops were needed. A fact sheet released by the White House at the time, explaining this decision, noted that "the situation in Baghdad determines nation-wide trends; its stabilization has been seen as key to a unified Iraq" and then stated that "force levels in Baghdad have been inadequate to stabilize a city of its size."[17]

THE IMPACT OF FOREIGN JIHADISTS AND ESCAPED BAATHISTS

The above notwithstanding, there is one aspect in which the immediate availability and use of additional coalition forces very likely could have measurably helped, and this would have been in making every effort to secure Iraq's borders once the Saddam regime fell. As discussed in detail later in this monograph, the opposition that the neighboring Arab Sunni majority countries would come to display toward a free and democratic Iraq, an Iraq in which its 60 percent Shi'a population has gained political hegemony in the country, was overlooked (or at a minimum underestimated) before the war. We also did not anticipate what now seems to have become a strategy that Iraq's defeated Baathists adopted: to retreat into neighboring Syria with the resources—military, financial, and logistical—to wage a rearguard action against the coalition, the new Iraqi government, and Iraq's Shi'a community. As a result, cross-border infiltration from the territory of these countries by al-Qaeda operatives and recruits, and apparent insurgent planning and support by former Iraqi regime elements operating from Syria, introduced two potent additional elements to the cauldron of violence within the country arrayed against the course of Iraq's democratic political evolution.

In the case of the jihadists, while their numbers are generally viewed as being relatively limited—most analysts ascribe to "foreign fighters" no more than about 10 percent of the insurgency's active participants—the viciousness and lethality of this element of Iraq's insurgency have been having a far greater impact on the country than their numbers by themselves would suggest. A majority of suicide bombers, and the perpetrators of the most heinous acts against innocent Iraqis and against any innocent foreigners who came into their capture, appear to have come from this group. As for the other group fueling, possibly even orchestrating, insurgent activity from abroad—escaped Iraqi Baathists—most observers have concluded that they have formed the backbone of the insurgency from the beginning. It seems likely that the impact of both groups could have been greatly circumscribed had the coalition taken effective measures to secure Iraq's borders at the time of Saddam's removal from power.

THE ABSENCE OF A NORTHERN FRONT

One element related to the capability to wage a robust insurgency that emerged after the fall of the Saddam regime was the unexpected absence of a northern front in the military campaign to remove Saddam. Turkey's decision not to allow its territory to be used as a transit and staging ground for an attack on Iraq from the north seems to have allowed Saddam's partisans to more effectively disperse and conceal resources for supporting the postconflict insurgency in the Sunni triangle area to the north and west of Baghdad. It is quite likely that, once elements of the Baathist leadership whose power bases were located in the Sunni triangle saw that no forces would be descending upon the country from the north, they were able to deploy materiel and financial assets to this area earlier and more effectively than they otherwise might have been capable of doing. The fact that, absent a northern front, Al-Anbar Province—the center of Iraq's Sunni stronghold—was the last area of the country to fall to the coalition also facilitated the escape of senior Baathists across the province's long border with Syria, from where they have been orchestrating an insurgency against the coalition and the Iraqi government.

THE U.S. MILITARY THROUGH OTHERS' EYES

During my recent diplomatic service in Germany, I came to know prominent German journalist Claus Kleber quite well, first during his service as the Washington correspondent for Germany's public broadcasting network ARD and then in his role as evening news anchor on the national public TV network ZDF, Europe's largest television broadcaster. Kleber is among Germany's most insightful and sophisticated observers of America and is both knowledgeable and unbiased in his assessment and journalistic coverage of the United States.

In the months following the Iraq War, Kleber was involved in an ambitious two-part documentary film project under the title "Omnipotent America," designed to gain insight into the international order that had arisen as a result of overwhelming U.S. military dominance. Kleber produced the first installment of the series, entitled "The World in Its Grasp," which sought to capture the essence of the U.S. military—and America's unique role in the world—and convey this to the German viewing public. In the late spring of 2003, Kleber approached me about this project, and my office provided logistical assistance to him and his staff in his contacts with U.S. military authorities and other U.S. officials in developing the film. The results were impressive: The documentary, first aired on August 27, 2003, portrayed an accurate and comprehensive picture of U.S. global security interests and commitments as well as the professionalism, dedication, and human side of those serving in the U.S. armed forces. The impact of the film was such that the Radio in the American Sector (RIAS) Berlin Commission, an NGO that promotes German-American dialogue and understanding through the broadcast and new media and that is the successor institution to the Cold War broadcaster RIAS in Berlin, gave the film its top award for the promotion of German-American understanding in 2003.[18]

While the film had a positive overall message and impact, one aspect of the film troubled me and in my view reflected a perception—and concern—that widely characterizes European views of the U.S. military: that it is largely staffed by America's poor and underprivileged. This comes through in one segment of the film that depicts in a poignant and emotional manner the story of a poor, white American mother whose son had joined the military. The message was that the socioeconomic circumstances of this family made it almost inevitable that—in light of the limited educational and employment prospects that the son faced in his family's impoverished, rural environment—joining the military represented his only viable option; he was, in essence, not a "volunteer" at all. The worry and sadness of the mother—whose physical appearance and surroundings conveyed poverty and want—at her son's "choice" to join the military reinforced what I believe are broadly accepted stereotypes concerning the U.S. military that many Europeans hold. The conclusion of many is that the Iraq War has been undertaken at the behest of America's elite but is being fought by America's disadvantaged.

One factor behind European attitudes toward the U.S. approach to its military is the fact that, unlike the United States, most European countries have compulsory national service, an obligation that usually involves a stint in the military (but in many countries can also be discharged through social service of one type or another). The universality of such national service—most commonly military service—is seen by many Europeans as more equitable than the U.S. approach, a viewpoint that also colors attitudes by many Europeans toward the United States and the U.S. military generally.

WHO IS FIGHTING THIS WAR?

The issue of "who is fighting this war" is one that has also been aired intermittently in U.S. media, academic, and think tank circles. Many Americans share the perception that, in the era of the all-volunteer force, the socially and economically disadvantaged—and especially racial minorities—are overrepresented in the U.S. armed forces and are bearing an unfair share of the sacrifice that the war has entailed. This is an important national discussion to have, since while in many ways the all-volunteer approach to the military has been a major success in the capability and professionalization of the armed forces and has had positive indirect consequences in such areas of providing opportunity and promoting tolerance, the elimination of the draft has changed fundamentally the relationship between the American people and those who defend our nation. One advocate of reinstituting the draft is Democratic Congressman Charles Rangel, whose sentiments on the issue reflect those of many who have opposed the war in Iraq; as he stated: "There's no question in my mind that this president and this administration would never have invaded Iraq, especially on the flimsy evidence that was presented to the Congress, if indeed we had a draft and members of Congress and the administration thought that their kids from their communities would be placed in harm's way."[19]

We are now in the midst of the first sustained combat in the era of the all-volunteer force, and while the members of the armed forces have acquitted themselves exceedingly well, and recruitment for the armed forces continues to be largely on target, the experience of the Iraq War will be an important one in assessing the concept of an all-volunteer military.

What research has been conducted into the demographics of the all-volunteer force has revealed some imbalances in ethnic, economic, and geographic representation in today's U.S. military of which Americans—and American policymakers—should be mindful. Most of these imbalances have turned out not to be large, and some go against common beliefs. For example, while it is true that—as many perhaps suspect—African-Americans are overrepresented in the military, this overrepresentation is attributable to high participation by African-American women: while African-Americans comprise some 13.4 percent of the U.S. population, 16.9 percent of deployed forces are African-American (including the 3.2 percent who are female).[20] Somewhat paradoxically, urban areas are underrepresented in the U.S. military, while rural areas are overrepresented, suggesting that competing employment prospects (generally more available in cities than in rural communities) do have an impact on enlistment rates. Perhaps somewhat surprisingly, both the "underclass" and the upper- and upper-middle classes are underrepresented in the military, while the middle class is overrepresented. The southern region of the United States is also overrepresented in the military.[21]

One change from previous U.S. experience in deploying military forces abroad is the fact that the all-volunteer military has resulted in a very different demographic for the personnel involved in the wars in Iraq and Afghanistan. More than one-third of deployed forces are thirty years of age or older, and for the first time in history more than half of U.S. deployed forces are married.[22] These kinds of outcomes to an all-volunteer approach to the staffing of our military warrant close tracking and regular public discussion. They require policies, regulations, and support structures geared to the new realities brought on by the all-volunteer force, and should significant sociodemographic imbalances arise, these need to be acknowledged and addressed in order to ensure that public policy related to the military, one of the nation's most important institutions—from placing its members in harm's way, to allocating national resources for its maintenance and support—reflect the interests and welfare of the full spectrum of the American people.

The issue of the experience of the nation's leaders vis-à-vis the military should also be part of the national discussion. Since the United States moved to an all-volunteer military with the end of the draft in 1973, studies have shown that—overall—the socioeconomic and educational levels of those in the armed forces are above the national average; anecdotal evidence, however, suggests (and it seems to be generally believed) that the direct involvement of the nation's elite in the U.S. military has steadily declined. One area in which this decline can be documented is in the record of military service by members of Congress. In the newly elected 110th Congress, 131 members have served in the military: 102 of the 440 members of the House of Representatives (including its five nonvoting delegates), and 29 of the 100 members of the Senate. The number of members of the 109th Congress who had served in the military was 141; the 108th Congress had 154 military veterans, and the 107th had 155.[23]

One factor in this decline in military participation by members of Congress is the increase in the number of women serving in Congress: There are ninety women in the 110th Congress, an all-time high, with seventy-four in the House (including three delegates) and sixteen in the Senate. Because women historically serve in far fewer numbers in the military than men,[24] this demographic change in the Congress has had the effect of reducing the percentage of members with previous military service. Nonetheless, as the Congressional Research Service noted in its most recent comprehensive statistical overview of the Congress—that for the 2004–06 109th Congress—the decline in military service on the part of members of Congress "may in part be attributed to the end of the Selective Service System draft in 1973."[25] In short, the apparent unintended consequence of the move to an all-volunteer force in reducing the level of personal experience in the military on the part of the nation's political leaders and other elites should also be monitored and discussed as we continue to assess the impact of the policies that determine who takes up arms to defend the country and the circumstances under which the military should be sent into battle.

SACRIFICE, HEROISM, AND "BAGHDAD ER"

The flurry of attention in media and other circles that arose in the spring of 2006 in connection with an HBO documentary entitled *Baghdad ER* provides an interesting case study of the message complexity and perception of bias that typically accompanies such a project. The documentary portrays the daily struggle and heroics of the 86th Combat Support Hospital (CSH) in Baghdad's International Zone in treating wounded soldiers. The media discussion surrounding its airing in April 2006 focused largely on the supposedly inevitable "antiwar" message and impact of such a film.

As most media reviews of the film noted, the Pentagon had initially given the documentary its full backing and support, as it was intended to show (and does accurately and sympathetically portray) the real-life efforts of the CSH's medical personnel in a battle zone and (as all of the reviews of the film noted) underscores that in Iraq fully 90 percent of those injured on the battlefield survive, a far higher rate than in any other war in history.

Having attended a special screening of the film at the Smithsonian Institution in the presence of the film's producers and directors, along with several of the military men and women who appear in the film, what struck me was not that it conveys a message either in support of or in opposition to U.S. policy in Iraq, but rather that it movingly depicts the level of sacrifice and heroism that war produces. My sense coming away from the showing was that this is a film that all Americans (at least of a certain age—it is extremely graphic and unsettling) should see. No Americans should be under any illusion that war is not the bloody, deadly horror that it is. Any national decision to go to war must presume that the people of the nation understand what war involves; *Baghdad ER* graphically conveys the violent and tragic personal impact of war.

Nonetheless, while the threshold for entering into something as horrible and destructive as war should be high—and the in-your-face gore of a film like *Baghdad ER* certainly helps ensure that this threshold remains high—the film should be somewhat unsettling to critics of the Iraq War as well. Several times in the film, injured soldiers are shown to be eager to get back to their units, to carry on work that they clearly understand to be important. Their commitment and dedication to their fellow soldiers are inspirational. Yes, all soldiers in all wars demonstrate a certain level of bonding and brotherhood such as that shown by the injured soldiers in *Baghdad ER*. Nonetheless, those here in the United States—who have not been asked to make any contribution to the effort that these soldiers are risking their lives for on behalf of their fellow Americans half a world away—must find it somewhat unsettling to witness the courage and dedication of the young men and women portrayed in the film. Any acknowledgment that these heroic military men and women are actually engaged in a mortal struggle to address the conditions that led to the events of 9/11—so as to prevent a recurrence of such a tragedy—would likely engender considerable cognitive dissonance on the part of an American TV viewer whose day-to-day experiences are entirely disengaged from the current struggle in Iraq.

One enlightening, if somewhat disconcerting, experience I had in connection to this aspect of the potential impact of a film such as

Baghdad ER on U.S. viewing audiences occurred in speaking with a colleague about the film and the issue of what our soldiers are actually involved in through their efforts in Iraq. The colleague did not seem to understand the point I was making—that Americans might be discomforted in witnessing the tragedy and sacrifice these soldiers were enduring to defend their freedom and security. Rather, in the colleague's mind, the heroism of *Baghdad ER* reflected simply the age-old camaraderie that binds soldiers on the battlefield and was not related to any sense of being involved in a larger purpose of confronting a threat to our nation and addressing the basic U.S. security challenges that emanate from the region. This experience was a wake-up call to me about just how much of a disconnect has developed across the spectrum of opinion in America concerning the U.S. effort in Iraq.

At the end of the screening of *Baghdad ER* at the Smithsonian, the mother of a young Marine whose death—after a valiant struggle to live—is portrayed at the end of the film spoke movingly about the solace she found in the footage that the documentarians had captured of her son's final moments. She conveyed her belief that the film provided an important contribution to the national discussion on Iraq, but her comments were those of a grieving mother and were neither partisan nor political. As a parent of three children who are now young adults, I could not imagine the pain of having to grieve the loss of a child, for any reason. Those parents who have suffered such a loss through the wars in Iraq and Afghanistan are—along with their children in uniform and the other members of the military serving in harm's way in these two war zones—the true heroes of our time. However, while these parents deserve our support and respect, we should be cautious in viewing them as having greater insight into or understanding of the struggle under way in both countries as a result of the personal tragedy that they are having to endure. Certainly theirs represents a sacrifice almost beyond comprehension and healing; my mother and father both lost brothers in World War II, and for both of their families the sense of loss continues to this day, more than sixty years later. Nonetheless, while decisions as weighty as those involved in war and peace must be informed by such voices as those of *Baghdad ER* and the families of those lost on the battlefield, we could see our vulnerability greatly increase—along with the ambition and daring of our enemies—if the voices and views of those directly affected by the trauma of the battlefield were to become determinative of national policies.

SAVAGERY AND ABSOLUTE SAVAGERY

The issue of graphically displaying the reality of war, which as noted above is an element in the public and media treatment of the documentary *Baghdad ER*, has been one that has arisen regularly during the course of the war in Iraq. The most common manifestation of this discussion has come in connection with the issue of prohibiting photos from being taken of the flag-draped coffins of service men and women killed in action. The Pentagon's policy of not allowing the release of such photos has been criticized as preventing the media from conveying to the American public the full story—and impact—of the war.

In my view, more significant than this aspect of reporting the horror of war is the fact of the insurgents' use in Iraq of the Internet and other media to disseminate images of unspeakable savagery as an element of its psychological warfare against Iraqis, the Iraqi government, and the coalition. The ready availability of such media to worldwide audiences, and the complete lack of morality or restraint by the insurgents in their gruesome treatment of human beings, ensures that demoralizing images of indescribable suffering, torture, and murder will be at hand to undermine the will of their enemies.

In a column on this unprecedented aspect of psychological warfare, entitled "Savagery's Stranglehold," *New York Times* columnist David Brooks examines the impact of such calculated cruelty and depravity and suggests that this phenomenon may have created an unprecedented challenge to the United States and the rest of the civilized world. He writes:

> [I]n our debates at home we are searching for ways to exercise enough power to defeat the insurgents while still behaving in accordance with our national conscience. We are seeking a sweet spot that satisfies both the demands of power and of principle. But it could be that given the circumstances we have allowed the insurgents to create, that sweet spot no longer exists."[26]

Brooks goes on to observe that "[T]he lesson is that if you are willing to defy all norms and codes of morality, you can undermine your enemy's willingness to fight."[27]

Multi-National Forces-Iraq Commanding General David H. Petraeus struck a similar theme in a message to U.S. service members upon his assumption of the MNF-I command:

> The enemies of Iraq will shrink at no act, however, barbaric. They will do all that they can to shake the confidence of the people and to convince the world that this effort is doomed. We must not underestimate them.[28]

My own take is that the level of resilience, sophistication, and understanding on the part of the American public concerning the struggle in Iraq and the violence and human suffering and tragedy that it entails is considerably underestimated by U.S. leaders and U.S. elites. It is, of course, repugnant and discouraging to witness images of calculated violence and cruelty by one's enemies against fellow citizens or one's partners and allies, but at the same time such images help define the parameters of the stakes in the struggle. Americans are aware that a central element of our current struggle in the Middle East is against exactly those in Middle Eastern societies whose moral values and world views justify such barbaric behavior. Americans are not naive about the nature of war; moreover, in principle there should be, as part of any involvement of our nation in war, a clear understanding—and image—of what such involvement entails. Such information and images are now—in the Information Age—an unavoidable element of modern warfare. However, while this state of affairs can be viewed as a disadvantage when we are in a struggle with a ruthless adversary, I believe that by and large the American public has the perspective—and stomach—to be able to deal with such images intelligently and to understand and accept the tragic consequences of warfare without surrendering to despair and abandoning the critical struggle that is today centered in Iraq.

6
The Coalition of the Unwilling

The story is told of a European tourist visiting a seaside resort in the United States. He is sitting at a dockside restaurant preparing to have a meal when he sees a large and obviously very expensive yacht sailing into the harbor. He then spies a youthful American waiter coming his way to take his food order.

Appalled by the ostentatious display of wealth represented by the yacht, he decides that he will engage this young American of apparently modest circumstances in a conversation on equality and fairness in society, and express his disgust at the opulence and decadence embodied in the yacht. As he's about to launch into his diatribe on this subject, the waiter notices the European visitor observing the yacht; before the tourist has a chance to begin to speak, however, the young American blurts out: "Yeh, someday I'm gonna get me one of those!"

This apocryphal tale, shared with me by an American friend in Germany, conveys in a light-hearted way one element of a disconnect in basic world views on the two sides of the Atlantic—differing views on the "morality" of wealth and on the proper balance between individual rights and personal wealth, on the one hand, and social equality and personal responsibility on the other.

After my return to Germany in June 2000 to head the U.S. embassy's Public Diplomacy Office in Berlin (I had left Germany in 1996 after serving for four years as the press attaché at the U.S. embassy in Bonn), I found that the issue of a "values-difference," such as is reflected in the tale above, had come to dominate the German-American dialogue. While then-President Bill Clinton was personally quite popular with Germans and Europeans, a growing list of "values" issues—global warming, the International Criminal Court, capital punishment, labor laws, etc.—had become of dominant interest in the German-American dialogue to our German interlocutors and the German public.

This aspect of German-American relations was placed in stark relief on the occasion of the U.S. presidential election in November of that year. As was tradition, the embassy's Public Diplomacy Office organized a reception at the embassy-operated *Amerika Haus* (the U.S. cultural center in Berlin) on the evening of the election, and some 1,400 German guests attended to partake of an "American election experience." As is also traditional, we conducted a straw poll of the attendees as a mock vote for the U.S. president. Given outgoing President Bill Clinton's popularity in Germany, and the generally more "liberal" political views of most Germans, we had fully expected that among the German "voters" we would find a preference for Clinton's vice president, Democratic candidate Al Gore, over Republican candidate George W. Bush. What turned out to be surprising, however, was the extent of this preference: The results of the poll gave Al Gore more than 70 percent of the vote; Ralph Nader came in second, with a percentage in the high teens; George W. Bush's percentage was in the low teens.

Once George W. Bush's term in office began, German attitudes toward the new president only deteriorated. Bush's assumption of the presidency with fewer votes than his Democratic rival Al Gore, and his doing so as a result of the most disputed presidential election in U.S. history, weakened the legitimacy of his victory in the eyes of many Europeans, just as it did for many Americans. The initial months of Bush's presidency then saw a string of policy decisions on such issues as the Kyoto Treaty on global warming, the Anti-Ballistic Missile Treaty, the International Landmine Treaty, the International Criminal Court, and the Biological Weapons Treaty, all of which took positions opposite to those that European leaders and publics supported. The announcement of these decisions was often done without coordination with or warning to our European allies and in some cases with insufficient coordination and public affairs planning even within the U.S. government itself. The impact was steadily rising antipathy on the part of the German public toward the new U.S. president and his administration.

This cloud over transatlantic relations was lifted by the attacks of September 11, 2001, less than eight months into President George W. Bush's term of office. These terrorist actions reminded both Americans and Europeans of the fundamental values that we shared and that we had defended together for more than half a century. The important, but more superficial, disputes that had recently come to the fore in the transatlantic relationship once again took a back seat to the existential foundation of this relationship, a foundation that was now seen to be under attack by the perpetrators of the 9/11 attacks. There was a recognition on both sides of the Atlantic that our shared fundamental values, and the way of life that they define, were being threatened by a ruthless enemy. As the *Le Monde* headline of 9/12 famously proclaimed: "Today we are all Americans."[1]

At the American embassy in Berlin, we received more than fifteen thousand messages of condolence (and the ambassador, Daniel R. Coats, answered them all); German mourners placed hundreds of bouquets of flowers around the embassy perimeter, and hundreds of thousands of Germans turned out four days later when Ambassador Coats joined German Chancellor Gerhard Schroeder, German President Johannes Rau, and other German leaders at Berlin's Brandenburg Gate for a memorial to the victims of the 9/11 attacks. The gate itself, a national German symbol, was draped with a banner that read: "Wir trauern—our deepest sympathy." The Public Affairs Office produced a special, German-language publication—"Gemeinsam gegen den Terror" ("Together against Terror")—which documented the heartfelt outpouring of sympathy and solidarity from Germans of all walks of life, including reproductions of several drawings depicting German-American friendship that German schoolchildren sent to the embassy. We printed and disseminated tens of thousands of copies (but still could not keep up with demand from school classes and others) and made it available on the embassy's Web site (the German version can be found at http://usa.usembassy.de/gemeinsam/index.htm; the English version at http://usa.usembassy.de/gemeinsam/indexe.htm). I consider this publication—combining as it does both message and feeling, both the personal and the political, incorporating both images and text, reaching across generations, and disseminated to both the broad public and the elite—to be among the most effective public diplomacy undertakings in which I have been involved during my Foreign Service career.

The depth of German solidarity with the United States following 9/11 was again reflected a few weeks later when the embassy sought to place notices in major German newspapers thanking the German people for their support. The papers gladly ran the notices, but all but one refused to accept payment for the tens of thousands of dollars worth of newspaper space they were providing us. The following month, German troops joined their American counterparts in

Operation Enduring Freedom in Afghanistan, and while there were some voices of protest within the pacifist segment of the German public, the effort to dislodge the Taliban from Afghanistan and root out al-Qaeda from that failed state was largely, if passively, supported by the German people.

The situation took a negative turn, however, when President Bush delivered his first State of the Union Address the following January. His use of the term "axis of evil" to describe the regimes in Iraq, Iran, and North Korea struck a nerve in the country. To many Germans, there was a sense of a U.S. religiosity rubbing up against a well-entrenched European secularism.

The German-American dynamic, however, was redirected onto a much more positive path when President Bush visited Berlin in May 2002 and addressed the German Bundestag. A ham-handed attempt at protest of the president's appearance before the Germany body as the president began to speak won him early sympathy and support. Sitting in the gallery, it was easy to sense the positive response of the Germans in attendance to encountering President Bush in person. In his remarks, the president proceeded in a soft-spoken manner to deliver a message of conciliation and cooperation, a message that was very well received by his German audience. The president's clear indication that no decision had been made on a military option for addressing the developing Iraq crisis, and his commitment to coordinate Iraq policy closely with America's allies—including Germany—had a markedly positive effect on German attitudes toward him and his policies. His personal charisma, and his bonding with Chancellor Schroeder over traditional German fare at a Berlin eatery the evening of his arrival in the city, also softened the negative attitudes toward him that had arisen in the wake of the "axis of evil" comments several months earlier. Importantly, Bush and Schroeder agreed not to "use" Iraq as a political issue in the German-American relationship.

Unfortunately, this U.S.-German detente on the Iraq issue was not to last. By late summer, Chancellor Schroeder was in the midst of a difficult reelection campaign and found himself behind in the polls. As the September election approached, he clearly needed a change of strategy to boost his electoral prospects. On August 26, Vice President Dick Cheney addressed the 103rd National Convention of the Veterans of Foreign Wars in Nashville, Tennessee. In the speech, the vice president treated the Iraq issue in some depth, laying out the argument for Saddam's possession of WMD and the threat that this posed to the international community. He also stated that "a return of inspectors would provide no assurance whatsoever of his [Saddam's] compliance with UN resolutions." He then proceeded to quote former Secretary of State Henry Kissinger: "The imminence of proliferation of weapons of mass destruction, the huge dangers it involves, the rejection of a viable inspection system, and the demonstrated hostility of Saddam Hussein combine to produce an imperative for preemptive action." At the same time, however, the vice president also stressed that, in dealing with Iraq, the president would "proceed with care, deliberation, and consultation with our allies" and would "consult widely with the Congress and with our friends and allies before deciding on a course of action."

As we later learned from a well-connected German security researcher, in view of Chancellor Schroeder's precarious electoral position at the time, he and his campaign team were looking for cover to renege on his agreement with President Bush not to use the Iraq issue for domestic political advantage. They seized on the vice president's remarks to the Veterans of Foreign Wars as that cover, and Schroeder proceeded to announce his opposition to a military solution to the Iraq crisis "under all circumstances." This caused a major political rift between President Bush and Chancellor Schroeder, a rift that soured German-American relations through the entire period of the Iraq crisis and until Chancellor Schroeder left office in October 2005. Here was yet another case, all too familiar to Americans conducting public diplomacy abroad, of a message crafted for domestic political effect—that of the vice president, aimed at his audience of U.S. military veterans—having an unintended impact overseas.

A BITTER MEDIA ENVIRONMENT

In the climate of strained German-American relations during the period leading up to the Iraq War in March 2003, several German media contacts confided to me that any attempt they made at "balanced" coverage of the Iraq issue provoked criticism and push-back from their editors, especially in light of the fact that such articles often elicited angry reactions from readers, including several cases of subscribers canceling their newspaper subscriptions in response.

Our media endeavors included at least one truly sublime moment, the time our public diplomacy efforts led to the headline

"With Iraq War, the U.S. Is Counting on Escalation in the Entire Middle East / Attack by Saddam Hussein on Israel Feared / Assistant Secretary: Nuclear Weapons Could Then Be Used" on the front page of *Der Tagesspiegel,* one of Berlin's leading dailies.[2] Our outreach to German opinion leaders on Iraq and other issues involved in our bilateral dialogue included an on-the-record breakfast meeting hosted by Ambassador Daniel Coats for visiting Assistant Secretary of State for European Affairs A. Elizabeth Jones. Gathered around Assistant Secretary Jones were half-a-dozen key Berlin-based German foreign policy correspondents, and the discussion focused almost exclusively on the Iraq issue. At the breakfast, one of the journalists was persistent in posing hypothetical questions about the possibility that Saddam had nuclear weapons and that, with his back to the wall in the event of a U.S. military attack, he might use them. After Jones several times dismissed this occurrence as extremely far-fetched, the journalist's relentless questioning on this issue ultimately succeeded in getting her to acknowledge that such a scenario, while being highly unlikely, was within the realm of possibility. It was this admission that sparked the front-page headline cited above, itself a telling reflection of the attitude and atmosphere of some in the German media in the period before the Iraq War.

The transatlantic dialogue degenerated at times into verbal sparring, with instances of then-Defense Secretary Donald Rumsfeld making a light-hearted but biting comment about "old Europe"[3] and citing "Libya, Cuba and Germany" as countries that would not help in U.S.-led efforts to deal with Iraq.[4] Both remarks were made shortly before the annual European security conference in Munich ("Wehrkunde"), February 7-9, 2003, which Rumsfeld attended and for which I and other Foreign Service colleagues were on hand to provide press and other public affairs support. Given the atmosphere that these comments had generated, Rumsfeld's appearance at Wehrkunde 2003 was among the most contentious public appearances by a senior U.S. official that I have witnessed in my diplomatic career.

In the ensuing weeks the transatlantic vitriol continued. A phrase that the *National Review's* Jonah Goldberg had used frequently since the late 1990s—from an old episode of "The Simpsons" TV show[5]—to describe the French—"cheese-eating surrender monkeys"—was picked up and entered into the daily lexicon of transatlantic discourse. The tabloid *New York Post* chimed in with its banner headline (and front page photo) of the "axis of weasels," referring to France, Germany, and Russia, and as the international intrigue over Iraq intensified the emergence of such a "coalition of the unwilling" involving these three nations became ever more evident.

In the end, during the lead-up to the Iraq War in 2003, we at the U.S. embassy in Berlin found ourselves unable to break through this atmosphere of recrimination, coupled with a broad German mindset against the U.S. approach and policy toward Iraq. Once hostilities were under way, and while the hot war was still very real, as the embassy's senior Public Affairs Officer—the person who was supposed to have insight into the communication environment and, in this case, our communication failure—I prepared a paper for embassy and Washington colleagues that sought to summarize and explain the factors that I viewed as having contributed to the deterioration in our bilateral relations over the Iraq issue. I titled my analysis "A Perfect Storm in German-American Relations"; herewith are some excerpts:

A Perfect Storm in German-American Relations: April 3, 2003:

The unusual and unexpected confluence of factors which have resulted in the current tattered state of the German-American relationship can usefully be conceptualized in the "perfect storm" scenario: a series of independent developments—political, social, economic, and historical; on both sides of the Atlantic—have coalesced to a common effect: to undermine long-held common perceptions and policy goals which have defined German-American relations for more than half a century. This paper seeks to identify these factors, along several dimensions—recent political / electoral developments; the aftermath of 9/11; cultural, social and societal characteristics; historical influences; and demographic trends—which need to be kept in mind as we undertake to rebuild German-American relations in a post-Saddam world.

The first "eastern German" chancellor

The most recent national election campaigns in both the U.S and Germany accentuated the fundamentally divergent political philosophies and programs of the U.S. and German governments. On the U.S. side, the fact that George W. Bush assumed the presidency as a result of the most disputed and drawn out presidential election outcome in U.S. history added a perception of "illegitimacy" towards the president to an already existing German mindset which largely rejects Bush's conservative political philosophy. . . . Germans' generally skeptical disposition towards the president . . . was followed in the Administration's first year by policy decisions on such issues as the Kyoto Protocol, the International Criminal Court, and the Anti-Ballistic Missile Treaty which ran counter to Germany's position on these issues. . . .

On the German side, with the election of Chancellor Gerhard Schroeder to head a "red-green" (i.e., SPD-Greens) coalition government in 1998, Germany had already chosen a chancellor with the least affinity for the U.S. of any German leader in the post-war era (Schroeder had cut his political teeth thirty years earlier as the head of the Young Socialists, the youth wing of the SPD, during the Vietnam era). . . . [W]hen Schroeder found himself facing near certain defeat in the September 2002 elections he decided to seek victory through a conscientious appeal to "anti-Americanism" (in the guise of opposition, under all conditions, to military action in Iraq).

This strategy worked, and Schroeder won a narrow election victory—with the margin of victory delivered in the new German states, making Schroeder effectively the first German Chancellor selected by eastern German voters. . . .These developments—on both the U.S. and German sides—have resulted in governments in the two countries whose political philosophies and perspectives are further out of sync than at any other time in the post-war period.

Why the anti-Americanism card worked

Several developments in the post-Cold War era have independently led to a weakening of the historical bonds that united Germans and Americans during the Cold War years. . . .These developments are examined below.

Pre-9/11 perceptions in a post-9/11 world

Perhaps the single most significant element defining diverging American and German perspectives—and policies deriving from these perspectives—is the distinction on the two sides of the Atlantic in reacting to the events of 9/11. While sympathetic to the tragedy which America suffered on that day, and concerned to address the factors that led to such atrocities, unlike in the U.S. there has in Germany been no fundamental reanalysis of the elemental threats now faced by civilization through the nexus of terrorism, failed / rogue states, and weapons of mass destruction. This . . . together with a prevailing perception that it is the U.S., not Germany, which faces the greatest threat, has led to a disconnect in perceptions—

and willingness to act—in this critical area.

American caricatures and the European moral high road

German perceptions gained through pervasive popular American culture have supported widely-held caricatures of U.S. society and the current U.S. administration. One telling indication of this is the wild success which the works of American gadfly Michael Moore are having in Germany. His scathingly critical documentary "Bowling for Columbine" has now been seen by more than 800,000 Germans, and continues to play to packed theaters around the country; many in the audience are school classes taken to see the film by their '68-generation teachers. Moore's equally hysterical screed, *Stupid White Men*, has been atop the non-fiction best-seller list in Germany for months. Without the American context in which to assess these works for what they are—extremist perspectives intended to provoke shock and outrage—they are taken largely at face value by their often naive, impressionistic German audiences. As *Wall Street Journal* Europe editor Fred Kempe recently noted: "It is telling that perhaps the most popular American in Germany is Michael Moore."

Moore's skewed analysis has fallen on particularly fertile ground here due to a variety of factors. Pervasive German perceptions of widespread economic and social inequity in the U.S.—based on issues ranging from access to health care and health insurance, to income disparities, to the social welfare system, to educational inequality—contribute to a sense of Europe being on a "moral high road" in comparison to the U.S. Selective interpretation of history—from the massacre of Native Americans, to slavery, to the use of the atomic bomb on Japan, to U.S. "creation of" / support for undemocratic regimes during the Cold War—feeds a tendency for Germans to interpret European views, policies and actions as being more highly-principled than those of the U.S., and thus as being intrinsically morally superior.

Pacifism and the halo factor

American columnist Robert Samuelson recently captured much of the essence of what he called "the anti-American fury" in Europe as follows:

"It makes people feel good. It gives them a sense of moral superiority. It doesn't cost them anything. It diverts attention from domestic discontents. It doesn't require hard decisions or hard thinking. It's a convenient moral exhibitionism that, on inspection, is full of delusion, shortsightedness and moral hypocrisy."

Or, as Munich historian Michael Wolfenson recently noted, "a visceral, moralizing pacifism pervades all elements of the German elite." Both observations capture essential elements of the atmosphere here. The public psyche is influenced by a sense of powerlessness (militarily), insecurity (economically), and fear of the future (demographically)....

"Weakness corrupts; absolute weakness corrupts absolutely"

This wry and provocative observation by Germany's most respected America-watcher, *Die Zeit* co-publisher Josef Joffe, captures an important element of the transatlantic debate, and one which particularly shapes German-American relations. While the perception of a benign and omnipotent U.S. may actually be welcome in many quarters (the European 8,[6] the Vilnius 10,[7] the Arab states of the Gulf), Germany is in the group of mid-sized powers whose world view is threatened by a sole superpower, and thus sees its interest in "balancing" out-sized American power through multilateral treaties and institutions....

Victimhood and gratitude fatigue

Even among Germany's older generation—those who experienced World War II and its immediate aftermath—that generation which has historically been most pro-American—a curious catharsis has been taking place lately. Largely as a result of the publication in late 2002 of a work entitled "The Fire," by Berlin historian Joerg Friedrich, the concept of Germans as victims of the war has come out into the open. Friedrich's provocative work treats the Allied fire bombing campaign during WWII, and—as the *New York Times* recently reported—has sparked "documentaries shown almost nightly on German television in recent months as part of a lengthy national re-examination of the Allied air war." Since, as the instigators of WWII, Germans were never really allowed to grieve their own losses after the war, the current departure of the war generation from the scene appears to have triggered a sort of catharsis that this generation never went through—with the at first looming, and now actual, military conflict in Iraq as the backdrop (and, perhaps, proximate cause).

The successor generations, for their part, appear to have decided that gratitude towards the U.S.—for its role in delivering Germany from the Nazi dictatorship, for planting the seeds for a successful democracy, for coming to the country's aid on numerous occasions in the immediate postwar period, for defending the country for four decades from the Soviet empire; and, in the more recent past, supporting (and pushing through) German unity in the face of strong opposition from . . . European neighbors—is governed by a statute of limitations. . . .

The children's crusade
One somewhat surprising development here since the start of hostilities in Iraq has been the widespread involvement of school children in anti-war marches and demonstrations. The phenomenon emerged on the first day of military action, when a "smart mob" of cell phone-empowered students—some 8,000 strong—gathered at Berlin's Brandenburg Gate, rather than reporting to school. In addition to sparking a widespread debate about "truancy for a higher cause," such activity has been repeated around the country in the two weeks since the war began. . . .While there appears to be a certain degree of cynicism associated with this excuse for skipping class, there is certainly also an element of political consciousness-raising (with inherent anti-American overtones) which will impact our public diplomacy efforts in the aftermath of the current Iraq crisis, and which underscores the urgency for reaching out to German youth.

Post-unification malaise
Thirteen years after the euphoria of the fall of the Berlin Wall and the subsequent reunification of the country, a . . . pessimism pervades the country, with relations between the former east and west German states characterized by a mutually-recriminating atmosphere. With the economies in the eastern states on a continuous downward course for half a decade now, and a steady out-migration of population (especially of the younger and more capable and ambitious residents), the resentment of the "easterners" towards their (still better off) western compatriots is a fundamental element of Germany's current socio-political climate; "Ost-algie"—a . . . reverie for the old German Democratic Republic—is pervasive. . . .

Fear Factors
Both economic and demographic trends feed a pessimism which increasingly colors the German national outlook. German economic growth has lagged the European Union for some ten years now, and unemployment levels are stuck above 10% (and much higher in the East). Germans are only now, and very painfully, coming to the conclusion that the "national holiday" (Germany as a national amusement park, as characterized by former Chancellor

Helmut Kohl in the mid-90s) must come to an end. The U.S., however, does not escape unscathed in this discussion: "cutthroat capitalism" as practiced in the U.S.—and as evidenced in "hire and fire" U.S. labor laws, weak social welfare arrangements, and large income disparities—is rejected by Germans, and to the extent that such economic arrangements in the U.S. are perceived here as undermining German competitiveness in the global marketplace, they breed a resentment towards the U.S.

The demographic outlook here is also a cause for German discouragement. With a less than replacement birthrate for some time now, Germans now recognize not only that their generous government-funded retirement system is unsustainable, but that they as a people are slowly dying out. Since there is effectively political gridlock on the issue of increasing immigration into the country, even this (controversial) route to an economically viable future is precluded, for the present at least. . . .

The relationship in a post-Saddam world
As outlined above, the public affairs climate in which we will be launching our post-Saddam-Iraq public affairs efforts here will need to take into account the endemic elements of envy / distrust, moral superiority, [and] insecurity . . . which color German attitudes towards the U.S. To succeed in such a climate, our efforts must be structured to communicate a message—universally accepted by Americans, but increasingly questioned by Germans—that the U.S. is basically a just and benign country whose power and dominance in economic, cultural and military affairs supports universal values of benefit to all mankind.

To successfully convey this message will require that we convince a skeptical German public of the intrinsic value of U.S. policies and structures in social, political, security, environmental and other spheres of common interest between our two societies. If handled well, this period of discomfort and distrust could provide an opportunity for a fundamental reassessment of assumptions, perceptions and values which underlie our relationship. The demons could be identified, so to speak, and then exorcised.

The prevalent attitude at the time toward U.S. filmmaker and gadfly Michael Moore, alluded to above, is particularly instructive to examine. I recall attending a showing of his film "Bowling for Columbine" one Sunday afternoon in Berlin and finding the theater packed with young Germans. In watching the film, I was particularly struck by—and concerned about—an animated sequence depicting

The Coalition of the Unwilling 127

U.S. actions over the previous decades, from the bombings of Hiroshima and Nagasaki to a string of Cold War events including the installing of the Shah of Iran in power, support for the bloody coup that placed General Pinochet in power in Chile, etc. These were the iconic images that young Germans were being fed of America, its values, and its role in the world.

As it happened, the period following the nadir in German-American relations in the spring of 2003 did feature a renewed German-American dialogue, one largely undertaken with the youth of the country, and most prominently with youth in eastern Germany. One of the highlights of this outreach effort was an appearance by Secretary of State Colin Powell in a German gymnasium (college-prep secondary school) in eastern Berlin in April 2004, a session in which he was challenged on issues from Iraq, to racial relations, to economic inequality. The secretary's easy banter with these skeptical but respectful young Germans—most of whom had been born in the late 1980s into a communist dictatorship in which such an open dialogue would have been unthinkable—was inspiring, both to those of us among the embassy staff on hand who had been through the very rough period in German-American relations just one year earlier and to the German students who were confronted with the reality of an African-American leader openly discussing many of the social and economic challenges which the United States continues to face, but doing so with affection and a commitment to contribute to improving an America that remains a work in progress. I was told that Secretary Powell himself viewed his exchange with these bright, engaging young Germans as one of the highlights of his entire four-year tenure as secretary of State. The fact that it was only with great reluctance that he eventually agreed to conclude the extended session in order to attend to some important diplomatic tasks with the German government reinforces this perception. And the positive media coverage that the event engendered—it was carried live on German national television—contributed greatly to improving our public dialogue in Germany.

My own experience in speaking with young people from Germany's eastern states was similarly enlightening, and encouraging. I would make it a point to bring with me a copy of Moore's book *Stupid White Men* whenever I would speak at a German school (I also made it required reading for my staff). This had the intended effect of surprise and proved to be an excellent ice-breaker.

Through my appearances at German schools it became clear

that young Germans—like young people everywhere—were actually most interested in practical issues that affected their personal lives and future prospects, such as education and employment. I recall one session in a fairly remote (and economically disadvantaged) area of the East in which one student raised the issue of the "outrageous" expense of higher education in the United States (in Germany, a university education is provided by the government, at no cost, to all who qualify). Seizing the opening, I described my own personal situation at the time, with two children in college at a cost of around $40,000 each per year. This fact elicited audible gasps from the students. I then proceeded to explain that not only is financial aid available to the needy, but that the quality of the education my children were getting was world class. Moreover, my children were both well aware (and quite appreciative) of the opportunity they were receiving, and the fact that their parents were sacrificing financially for them to receive such an opportunity contributed to the familial bond. Finally—and from a parent's point of view perhaps most importantly—in view of the high cost, my children were going to finish college in four years (unlike the more common six-to-eight years at university for German students).

We then did the math: once my children completed their university studies, they were likely to get good-paying jobs, and after working for a few years they would be gaining both real-world employment experience and earning an income. In fact, I pointed out, eight or so years following the start of their university studies, a financial comparison of their situation to that of a comparable young German would essentially be a wash (educational costs offset by income earned), but in contrast to most of their German counterparts, each would already be a productive, contributing member of society. I do not know how many converts I made that day among my attentive German audience, but I am confident that afterwards they at least saw the issue of the "outrageous cost" of higher education in the United States in a new light.

I tell this story in some detail because I believe it illustrates one of the persistent obstacles to transatlantic understanding—the all-too-frequent superficiality in the discussion and understanding of issues on which the United States and the European states have elected to take different societal approaches. These areas, in addition to education, include health care, labor laws, criminal justice, taxation, and others. In the case of each of these issues, it seems clear that both sides could make improvements over present practice, and, importantly, both sides could learn from each other's approach and experience.

Since the change in the German government in October 2005, the atmosphere in the German-American relationship has improved considerably. My sense is that, after the acrimony of the Iraq debate, there was a recognition that things were allowed to go "too far," and that—while the "perfect storm" may have been necessary to get long-festering issues out into the open and to clear the air—a new era is now at hand in which the transatlantic dialogue will be more focused on the synergy of shared values and goals and less on anger and distrust based on differing foreign and social policy choices being made by our two countries. One ironic footnote to the Michael Moore phenomenon in Germany was the circumstance that caused it to start unraveling—Moore's visit to the country on a book promotion tour at the height of his acclaim in Germany in November 2003. Moore drew audiences in the thousands as he spoke in various German cities, and one of his appearances was aired on national TV. The presence in person of this glib, disheveled, overweight American, and the sight of audience members walking out on his disjointed, largely incomprehensible rant during his nationally televised appearance, was a publicist's nightmare.

Now approaching the fourth anniversary of the fall of Saddam Hussein's regime, we are in a much better place with our European allies than we were in April 2003. Both sides have undertaken extensive and successful fence-mending since that time, and cooperation on a number of major international challenges—including Iran, North Korea, Lebanon, and Afghanistan—is extensive and effective.

This is not to say, however, that Europe and America do not still have some issues with respect to Iraq. In addition to the general challenge of convincing European countries to step up their contributions of personnel and resources to assist Iraq on its course of democratic and economic development—and getting these countries to be willing to deploy those personnel and resources on the ground in Iraq—two specific Iraq-related issues continue to impact relations: capital punishment and hostage policy.

CAPITAL PUNISHMENT

European opposition to capital punishment led to no European assistance in prosecuting Saddam Hussein. This attitude toward capital punishment continues to block European support for the Iraqi government's effort to bring leaders of the former regime to justice, because the Iraqi penal code includes the death penalty as a possible sanction for grievous crimes. The United States has pressed the Europeans since day one to lend support to this process, and they have consistently cited concerns with the death penalty in their refusal to do so.

Indeed, the European Convention on Human Rights can be interpreted as preventing support to a country whose criminal code allows the imposition of capital punishment. However, the United Kingdom's (UK) Attorney General Lord Peter Goldsmith has argued that European efforts can be channeled in a way that supports non-death-penalty-related aspects of the Iraq High Tribunal (IHT), which is responsible for bringing senior members of the former Iraqi regime to justice. Goldsmith has tried to sell the UK view to others in the European community, but they have declined to pursue it. The appearance is that some European countries do not want to be seen as supporting any post-war activities—such as the IHT—that might bolster the coalition intervention in Iraq. The fact is that in various instances around the world, Europeans support justice systems in countries that countenance capital punishment. Furthermore, the Europeans are providing support (including judicial training) to the regular justice system in Iraq, a system that also allows the death penalty. In fact, capital punishment is not a special feature of the IHT but derives from the regular justice system in Iraq; the IHT statute states simply that "the maximum penalty shall be the maximum penalty prescribed by Iraqi law." When the death sentence was imposed on Saddam Hussein on November 5, 2006, European leaders from UK Prime Minister Tony Blair, to German Chancellor Angela Merkel, to Italian Prime Minister Romano Prodi all expressed their disagreement with the sentence.

The distancing of themselves and their countries from the work of the IHT by European leaders negatively affects the legitimacy of the IHT, because it fosters a perception that the IHT is an Iraqi-American undertaking and does not have the support of the international community. That stigma undermines the efforts of the brave judges and prosecutors who are putting their lives on the line to bring members of the former regime to justice and thus help Iraq address the national trauma that the Saddam regime inflicted on the country. In addition, lack of European support for the IHT has resulted in the absence of European personnel, technical, and financial support for this effort. The fact that it is falling primarily to U.S. government employees and contractors to fill the gap harms the IHT's credibility.

Of course, the abhorrent manner in which the Iraqi government actually carried out the execution of Saddam Hussein on December 30, 2006, and the botched handling of the hanging of Saddam's half-brother Barzan Ibrahim al-Hassan on January 15, 2007, causing his decapitation, has only increased the international outcry against the imposition of capital punishment on former Iraqi officials. Although the video documentation that emerged of the execution of Saddam indicated that senior Iraqi judicial officials sought to maintain appropriate decorum as the sentence was carried out, the execution site was infiltrated by enough thugs and miscreants to disrupt and debase the entire proceeding. The smuggled cell phone video of the event that has been seen around the world represents a significant setback to the Iraqi government's interest in conveying that rule of law and impartial justice are attributes of the new Iraq.

HOSTAGE POLICY

The second Iraq-related area in which European and American approaches and principles continue to be at odds involves the endemic problem of hostage-taking in the country. While the United States has steadfastly refused to pay ransom for Americans taken hostage in Iraq (with tragic results for many individual U.S. hostages), a number of high-profile kidnappings of Europeans in Iraq have been resolved in a manner that has raised strong suspicions that ransoms were paid. European media accounts have cited figures in the millions of euros in connection with ransoms that have alleged to have been paid for the release of European hostages in Iraq. On November 26, 2006, the *New York Times* cited a U.S. government report that it had obtained that estimated that "unnamed foreign governments" paid $30 million in ransom to Iraqi kidnappers the previous year. The *Times* article went on to report:

> Another challenge for the United States, the report says, was to persuade foreign governments to "stop paying ransoms." It gives no details, but American officials have said previously that France paid a multimillion-dollar ransom for the release in December

2004 of two French reporters held hostage by an insurgent group. Italy, these officials have said, paid ransoms on at least two occasions, in September 2004 for the release of two women, both aid workers, and in March 2005, a reported $5 million for the release of Giuliana Sgrena, a journalist for the Rome newspaper *Il Manifesto*.[8]

From the U.S. perspective, it is troubling that European countries, especially those whose military forces are not at risk in Iraq, might have provided financial resources to insurgents in Iraq in order to gain the release of their citizens who have been taken hostage in the country, resources that are then available to the insurgents to support attacks on U.S. and other coalition forces in the country.

THE ABSENCE OF INTERNATIONAL INSTITUTIONS

In concluding this discussion of the "Coalition of the Unwilling," it would perhaps be useful to note the impact of the strategy by the al-Qaeda and Baathist insurgents in Iraq toward international institutions in post-Saddam Iraq. The determination of the terrorists to thwart the emergence of a free and democratic Iraq by attacking international institutions that could contribute to such an outcome, especially the United Nations (whose Baghdad headquarters was attacked on August 19, 2003, killing almost two dozen people) and the International Committee of the Red Cross (whose Baghdad headquarters was attacked on October 27, 2003, killing twelve), represents an unprecedented effort to neutralize these institutions as agents of postwar stability and recovery. With these institutions, and most other international NGOs now largely intimidated from operating within Iraq in support of the postwar rehabilitation of the country, the terrorists succeeded in limiting the outside contribution to this effort primarily to those countries that were involved in the military campaign to remove the Saddam regime. This, in turn, has undermined the legitimacy of this effort in the eyes of the Arab world and of the international community in general.

The fact that the presence of the Multi-National Forces in Iraq has the express consent of the Iraqi government under the authority of UN Security Council Resolution 1637, for the laudable goal of "support[ing] the Iraqi people in their pursuit of peace, stability, security, democracy and prosperity," is a generally overlooked point of reference in policy, media, or other discussions of the process currently unfolding in the country. The insurgents' success in largely keeping legitimizing international institutions from participating in Iraq's current transition represents a troubling precedent as a possible model for groups that aspire to impose their will and to seize power in a country through terrorism and armed insurrection.

7
Violence in Iraq: The Insurgency/Sectarian Conflict

One of the most complex, even contradictory, elements of the Iraq equation is the nature of the "insurgency" that has been active in the country since about six months after the fall of the Saddam regime. Indeed, to some extent the complexity of the insurgency reflects the competing and conflicting dynamics that affect many aspects of the Middle East region. Compounding the insecurity in the country, in the first half of 2006 the violence in Iraq mutated from being essentially insurgency based to containing significant—perhaps even dominant—elements of sectarian conflict. I examine both phenomena in this chapter.

THE NATURE OF THE INSURGENCY IN IRAQ

Although of greatly varying strengths and influences on the overall pattern of violence that is visible daily in Iraq, one can analyze the "insurgency" in that country as being comprised of essentially six elements:

1. Wahhabist Islamic fundamentalists (al-Qaeda in Iraq);

2. the Sunni armed resistance (all from Iraq's Sunni community, but ranging from former senior officials in the Saddam government, to those loyal to the Baathist ideology, to those who retain the hope that sufficient mayhem will lead the coalition to abandon the country and permit them to reestablish Sunni political hegemony, to those who are using violence in

order to strike the best bargain they can with the Shi'a-majority political order);

3. criminals (whose sole motivation is financial gain);

4. those seeking revenge for personal losses suffered at the hands of the coalition;

5. the economically desperate; and

6. "fence-sitters" (i.e., "passive" supporters of the insurgency).

Of these groups, only the first two present a serious, potentially long-term threat to the establishment of a secure and stable Iraq. And even among the various factions of the Sunni armed resistance, only the first two subgroups noted above will likely be able to be defeated only by being either killed or captured. The other elements of the insurgency listed above would be expected to decline (and essentially disappear) in an environment in which post-Saddam political, economic, and law enforcement processes take root. However, as is discussed below, the element of large-scale sectarian conflict that has emerged in Iraq since the bombing of the Shiiite Al-Askari Mosque in Samarra in February 2006 has inflicted a fundamental blow to such a scenario.

THE IRAQI "FENCE SITTERS"

There have been two parallel dynamics ongoing in Iraq since the Saddam regime was removed: a political process that seeks to guide Iraq to a "fair," "free," and secure landing in the aftermath of several decades of domestic disaster and destruction, and a violent effort on the part of Baathist fascists, on the one hand, and Islamic fundamentalists, on the other, to foil such an outcome and establish (or, in the case of the Baathists, reestablish) hegemony in the country. Most Iraqis—either through uncertainty or intimidation—are currently watching from the sidelines, unwilling publicly to tip their hands in favor of that dynamic that polls indicate they overwhelmingly support: a political process leading to freedom and representative government.

The uncertainty that most Iraqis feel about the prospects of success for the current political process in the country is a major factor in the passive attitude by many toward the insurgency (or sectarian violence). While most Iraqis support the creation of a free, largely secular, largely democratic political order, most remain on the fence while they continue to evaluate the prospects for such an outcome to the current struggle. Recent Iraq history is replete with cases of vicious retaliation against those who committed too early to what turned out to be failed efforts for political change. For this reason, Iraq today is largely a country of fence-sitters. Memories of the post-Gulf War carnage that the Saddam regime inflicted on the Iraqi Shi'a and Kurdish communities are still fresh; in light of this relatively recent experience, combined with the awareness within Iraq of the public debate in the United States about our willingness to continue to pay the price in blood and treasure that supporting Iraq's transformation from dictatorship to democracy is exacting, Iraqis see good reason to hedge their bets on the outcome of the country's current struggle. This dynamic, unfortunately, fosters a permissive operating environment for Iraq's insurgents.

ECONOMICALLY DRIVEN "INSURGENCY"

Those "insurgents" motivated not by political but solely by economic considerations may well be the largest contingent of "insurgents" of all in Iraq. Those who commit acts of violence or sabotage against coalition forces or the Iraqi government "for pay" are, of course, not actually "insurgents" at all, but are—in most cases, at least—simply resorting to acts of criminality to provide sustenance for themselves and their families. During the year I spent in Iraq, stories of children as young as ten years old being paid $50 to drop a hand grenade on a group of coalition soldiers, or a young man being paid $100 to blow up a fuel pipeline or plant an improvised explosive device, were commonplace. It is likely that, in terms of sheer numbers, the majority of acts of "insurgency" that have taken place in Iraq have been carried out by "economic insurgents," those with no political or ideological agenda or ax to grind; they are simply available as mercenaries to the real insurgent ringleaders, who use their extensive financial resources—either secreted around the country before the demise of the old regime, smuggled into Iraq through its porous borders, or acquired through criminal activity or corruption—to pursue their political goal of preventing the emergence of a free society and functioning state in Iraq.

AN EYE FOR AN EYE

The element of the postliberation violence in Iraq that can be ascribed to the next group—those seeking retribution for personal losses at the hands of the coalition—is difficult to quantify. Tom Ricks devotes most of his book, *Fiasco*, to the argument that the actions of coalition forces in the first year of the insurgency were a major contributing factor to the scope and strength of the insurgency. He documents at length that standard security procedures and military rules of engagement routinely violated the dignity of Iraqis, mostly Sunnis, and that in an honor-based society such as Iraq, in which personal dignity is as important as life itself, the coalition approach triggered many acts of revenge and score settling. While this is no doubt true, what is missing from Ricks' account is any analysis of the broader motivations among the Sunni community to launch and support an insurgency against the emerging order in Iraq. Coalition actions and policies in seeking to impose order and establish security during the first year of the insurgency can now be seen to have been in many respects counterproductive. But whether this approach was a marginal or a major contributing factor to the level of the insurgency remains very difficult to assess.

The possible role played by the Arab tradition of retribution in the current level of violence in Iraq was brought home to me personally in a discussion with a Sunni leader in the spring of 2005. This representative of the Sunni community had sought out a U.S. official in order to convey a list of grievances that that community wanted addressed as part of the process of their being brought into the political process. Of the issues that the Sunni leader raised, the one that carried by far the greatest emotional weight was the treatment of Sunni women by MNF-I forces. My Sunni interlocutor was quite animated in condemning actions in which Sunni women were either searched or detained by such forces; as he stressed, Iraqis would rather see their women killed than taken into custody by foreigners, and the policy of taking women family members into custody in order to lure male relatives into surrendering was simply unacceptable. While this Sunni leader's list of grievances was not accompanied by threats or other indications that a continuation of such acts against Sunni women would be met with violence, the level of feeling and forcefulness with which his message was conveyed convinced me that actions such as these were surely triggering acts of violence against coalition troops from Iraq's Sunni population.

Since that time, the MNF-I leadership has fundamentally and successfully changed MNF-I's approach to its mission to be one of active counterinsurgency—"winning hearts and minds"—an approach that includes exercising respect for the personal dignity of persons being detained; increased efforts at community engagement; considered treatment of suspects, their family members, and Iraqis at large; and paying compensation for destroying property and "blood money" to family members of those inadvertently killed or injured by their actions. These new counterinsurgency efforts notwithstanding, since the bombing of the Shiite mosque in Samarra on February 22, 2006, the dynamic in Iraq has changed fundamentally; revenge killing—not directed against the coalition, but rather in the form of Sunni-Shi'a tit-for-tat violence—has come to assume a dominant role in the violence rampant in the country today.

CRIMINALITY

It is difficult to estimate the contribution of purely criminal elements to the violence that is wracking Iraq today, but indications are that it is significant. The most common reflection of such a criminal element is the rampant kidnapping for ransom that is seen throughout the country, but most clearly in Baghdad. The emptying of Iraq's prisons in the final months of the Saddam regime has certainly contributed to the general deterioration in public order in the country. Today, the threat of kidnapping affects all aspects of how Iraqis live their lives and adds an element of fear and tension to the already difficult public environment in the country. The Iraqi government is, of course, committed to the full establishment of civic order and reduction of crime, but given all that this government faces at the moment, it can be expected that it will take some time for Iraq's institutions successfully to address this aspect of the violence currently afflicting the country.

RUTHLESSNESS AND RELIGIOUSLY INSPIRED FANATICISM

The two key groups that are at the core of the true insurgency in Iraq and that are conducting guerrilla warfare against the Iraqi political process are the Sunni armed resistance and the Wahhabist Islamists who call themselves "al-Qaeda in Iraq." The Sunni camp seems to be led (or at least organized and supported) by former regime elements who have nothing to lose in an all-out effort to prevent the establishment of a stable, peaceful Iraq; after all, they are the ones who, in large part, will have to answer to Iraq's new government and the Iraqi people for their crimes under the previous regime if an Iraq emerges with sufficient stability and security to bring them to justice.

In league with this group appear to be some elements of the mainstream Sunni community who are simply not (yet) willing to accept their new minority political status in the country. By waging (or simply supporting, actively or passively) resistance to the open and democratic political process currently under way in the country, this group appears to hope for, at best, a complete unraveling of the political process leading to an outcome in which—somehow—the Sunni minority would once again be able to reestablish its dominance of the country or, at least, ensure that their resistance to the current political process will win for them the best possible political deal as the process moves forward.

The other group at the core of the Iraqi insurgency—the (largely) foreign Wahhabist jihadis, i.e., al-Qaeda in Iraq—finds itself in a situation much like that of the Iraqi former regime elements: They also have nothing to lose in opposing—to the death—the emergence of a free, democratic, and constitutionally secular Iraq. They recognize, as do most observers of the region, that should Iraq emerge as a model of tolerance, accountable government, and freedom for those in other countries in the region to emulate, this would almost certainly amount to a death knell for the efforts of al-Qaeda to establish fundamentalist Wahhabi Islam as the governing paradigm for the region. In that sense, Iraq (potentially) represents al-Qaeda's last stand.

The sole path toward gaining anything more than marginal popular support for the oppressive style of governance that the Islamic fundamentalists advocate has been to offer such a state as the only alternative to the autocratic regimes that currently dominate the region. As noted in chapter 3, as citizens' distaste for such regimes has grown in the current context of increased access to information about the shortcomings of their societies, accompanied by the region's continued economic decline under such regimes, significant elements of Arab publics have given at least passive support to the efforts of radical Islamists to force a change in the region's status quo. Stirrings of democratic reform in the Middle East would work quickly and powerfully to the detriment of the interests of the Islamic fundamentalists. They are well aware of this fact, which is why they are fighting so hard to oppose it.

Paradoxically, the two groups at the core of the Iraqi insurgency—the Sunni armed resistance and al-Qaeda in Iraq—envision diametrically opposite outcomes to the current struggle: The former seeks to reestablish (secular) Sunni political hegemony in Iraq, while the latter is attempting to found in Iraq a Taliban-like Wahhabist Islamic state. The only element they have in common is the short-term goal of keeping the aspirations of the majority of Iraqis—as well as the international community in general—for the establishment of a modern, democratic state in Iraq from being achieved.

The ruthless tactics of these two core elements of the Iraqi insurgency have taken the West, and even many Iraqis, by surprise. Iraqis, of course, had experienced a culture of depravity under the Saddam regime. The psychopathic behavior of Saddam's son Uday was legendary. Around the time of my arrival in Baghdad in June 2004, one apocryphal story making the rounds concerned the "pet" lions kept by Uday Hussein at his private zoo in the Green Zone. When this area was liberated, it was said that those in the U.S. military who took over the care of Uday's "pets" found that the lions rejected the normal food (the meat of dead animals) that they were being fed. As the story goes, the caretakers came to learn that Uday had regularly fed the lions humans, in some cases reportedly often young women whom he had just finished raping. It apparently took some time and effort to get the lions to accept normal food again.[1]

Fast forward to present-day Iraq and the nature of the current insurgency. In my observation, the level of depravity of those opposed to current political developments in the country appears to shock even many Iraqis. I recall with considerable discomfort the time I came across a member of my staff at the U.S. embassy in Baghdad mesmerized by something he was viewing on his computer screen.

Violence in Iraq: The Insurgency/Sectarian Conflict

When I walked by and glanced over, I saw that he was watching the slow beheading, with a dull knife, of an Iraqi translator whom the terrorists had captured. The translator was being executed for working with the coalition. My staff member had worked with this translator in a previous job, and while the two were not close personal friends, the barbarism of the terrorists' actions on this individual, whom he knew personally, was clearly having its intended effect of intimidating and terrorizing anyone who dared contribute toward the creation of a successful democratic Iraq.

In the period since the start of the Iraq War, it has become routine to hear accounts from the country that bespeak a barbarism that should shock anyone with normal human sensitivity. Within the Iraqi context, however, such occurrences have become almost numbingly commonplace:

- On Iraqi election day, January 30, 2005, the terrorists used a nineteen-year old Iraqi youth with Down's Syndrome as a suicide bomber. The young man, named Amar, had the mind of a four-year-old, and was, of course, incapable of knowing what the terrorists were using him for. He was apparently lured or kidnapped by terrorists, who strapped explosives to his chest and guided him to an Iraqi voting center.

- In mid-July of 2005 twenty-seven people, most of them children, were killed by a suicide truck bomb as they gathered around an army vehicle where U.S. troops were handing out candy.

- On November 10, 2005, Iraqi suicide bombers—apparently at the behest of the late Jordanian-born terrorist Abu Musab Al-Zarqawi—struck three hotels in Amman, Jordan, hitting, among other targets, a wedding party, and killing more than fifty people.

- On March 30, 2006, the regional Arabic daily *Al Hayat* carried an item stating that "the 'unknown insurgents' no longer possess any moral qualms, given the discovery of mass quantities of booby-trapped candy and the distribution of poisoned medicines."

Other outrages have already entered the common database of collective experience with Iraq:

- the bombings of the UN's headquarters and the Jordanian embassy in Baghdad in August 2003;
- the bombing of the Imam Ali Mosque in Najaf, also in August 2003, killing 125, including revered Shi'a religious leader Ayatollah Mohammad Baqir al-Hakim;
- the March 2004 burning and mutilating of the bodies of four murdered U.S. security contractors, before they were strung up on a bridge in Fallujah;
- the May 2004 kidnapping and beheading of U.S. contractor Nicholas Berg and, subsequently, several other U.S. workers kidnapped in the country; and,
- the July 2004 kidnapping and murder of Iraqi-British CARE official Margaret Hassan; and so on.

It is arguable that U.S. and other western military and occupation planners would have been hard pressed to anticipate such a level of depravity on the part of the two groups that underpin the current insurgency in Iraq. Just like the failure of imagination that caused the intelligence failure before 9/11, the level of barbarism and inhumanity that has been on display in Iraq over the past several years reveals another failure of imagination, in this case to anticipate the fanaticism and ruthlessness with which ousted leaders of the Saddam regime, and Islamic fundamentalists in the region, would react to the prospect of the emergence of a free and democratic Iraq.

SECTARIAN CONFLICT

With the Samarra bombing of February 2006, the insurgents finally succeeded in their long-standing goal of introducing two specific destabilizing elements into the dynamic of post-Saddam Iraqi society: sectarian victimhood, and sectarian displacement. It had been clear since the early days of the insurgency that the primary goal of the hard-core insurgents—especially al-Qaeda in Iraq, and its now deceased former leader Abu Musab Al-Zarqawi—was to thwart the success of the country's political process by igniting sectarian strife, a civil war between Iraq's Shi'a and Sunni communities. The effort seems to have been aimed at drawing into the Iraq dynamic the involvement of the Sunni-majority Arab states that border Iraq on the side of the Sunni minority community within Iraq. The wisdom and patience of Iraq's most influential Shi'a cleric—Grand Ayatollah Ali al-Sistani—however, successfully countered that strategy during the initial years of the insurgency. He directed his followers not to seek retribution for the violence being visited upon their communities by the (Sunni) insurgents but rather to seek the power and influence that was their due through the political process and the ballot box. In view of the wholesale slaughter that the insurgents were inflicting on Shi'a communities within Iraq, the willingness of Iraqi Shi'a by and large to heed al-Sistani's directive is both remarkable and commendable.

Unfortunately, as the insurgents escalated the ruthlessness of their attacks—the Samarra mosque bombing has been the most spectacular and effective to date—they have been able to provoke enough sectarian-based revenge killing by Shi'a to trigger a significant element of victimhood and internal displacement so that now these two factors have been added to the list of challenges that Iraq's leaders face as they seek to quell the insurgency and reestablish security and normalcy in the country. The fact that the single most violent day to date in post-Saddam Iraq occurred on Thanksgiving Day 2006, when a series of car bombs in Baghdad's Sadr City killed some two hundred Shiites, is a testament to the determination and viciousness of al-Qaeda and its supporters within Iraq's Sunni community in its efforts to ignite full-scale civil war in the country. Compounding the true sectarian impetus behind the displacement of Iraqi's from their homes and communities, an Iraqi Sunni women from Baghdad—in a discussion in Washington in late 2006—described reports she has received from friends and family of Baghdadis being driven from their homes by sectarian rivals not because of sectarian hatred but simply to acquire valuable or desirable property owned by those being driven out.

Iraqi leaders, senior U.S. officials and diplomats, and senior MNF-I military commanders on the ground in Iraq have all affirmed their recognition of this new element in the violence that continues to wrack the country and their determination to confront it. One positive factor is that Iraq's senior Shi'a cleric, Grand Ayatollah Ali al-Sistani, continues to urge Iraq's Shi'a to refrain from violence and retribution for the provocations of Sunni extremists, and Iraq's Shi'a-led governing coalition has been consistent in denouncing this sectarian violence, including by Shi'a militias and death squads.

Moreover, opinion polling continues to support the long-held view that Iraqis on the whole reject sectarian segregation or ethnic cleansing. An International Republican Institute poll in July 2006 found that 78 percent of Iraqis countrywide held this view, and even in heavily religiously mixed Baghdad, 76 percent of the population opposed such separation.[2] However, such goodwill and determination by Iraqi leaders and Iraqi citizens is being sorely tested by the provocations of minorities on both the Shi'a and Sunni sides who continue to wage fierce sectarian violence.

8
Iraq and the Media

A great deal has been written and debated concerning the coverage of Iraq in the U.S. and international media. Many among those who continue to support U.S. policy in Iraq have charged journalists covering the country with communicating only a partial picture—and an inaccurately negative one at that—of the true situation in the country today. Others have criticized the media for "hotel journalism," for claiming to cover Iraq without being able or willing to leave their fortified offices and residences. Still others have aggressively come to the defense of these journalists, noting the large number of journalists who have been killed in the conflict (already far more journalists have died in the three-plus years of the Iraq conflict than died in all the years of U.S. military involvement in Vietnam) and their heroism in trying to cover this difficult and dangerous story.

There is, of course, an element of truth in all three claims. In my experience, however, the dominant perception is of a courageous and determined U.S., international, and Iraqi press corps seeking to get and report the Iraq story as fully and accurately as possible. As my colleague, State Department spokesman Sean McCormack, noted in early 2006:

> I think it is important for everyone to understand that there are those two realities in Iraq at the moment. You see a lot of the very difficult, difficult stuff. You see the results of terrorist acts, the IEDs [improvised explosive devices], the bombings, the killing of innocent civilians. But there is also another story to tell as well, and we see many reporters on the ground telling that story.[1]

This is not to dismiss the frustrations of those who perceive one-sided and incomplete reporting in the media coverage that Americans see coming out of Iraq. However, to the extent that they exist, these shortcomings result from the situation on the ground and the nature of "news" and not—in my view at least—from bias, timidity, or a lack of professionalism on the media's part.

The two stories unfolding simultaneously in Iraq, as those who have been involved in the basic societal and political transformation that has been taking place in Iraq since April 2003 are well aware, present themselves very differently for media coverage. One, more visible and visual (and thus more amenable to media coverage) is the raging insurgency and sectarian violence, i.e., the violent opposition on the part of various groups to the establishment of a stable and secure social order under the control of a representative government, along with—since early 2006—the mounting tit-for-tat sectarian revenge killing and sectarian cleansing. The daily events wrought by the insurgents, with the death and destruction they entail, are designed for maximal media (and, thus, propaganda) effect, and they represent the kinds of occurrences that, since they are exceptional and tragic, are a natural focus of media attention, and, while not as visual, the high body counts resulting from the sectarian reprisal killings are also an essential aspect of the "news" from Iraq. No one can, or should, fault the media for covering this "news."

The other "story" that is unfolding in Iraq is the country's slow but steady path of political, civic, social, and economic transformation from a corrupt, violent dictatorship to a society that is striving to incorporate into its mores rule of law, personal freedom, individual rights, and tolerance for ethnic and sectarian differences. Progress on this path of "liberalization" (for want of a better word) has been sporadic and uneven, but each day that goes by in which average Iraqis experience the freedom of the new Iraqi order—even in the midst of considerable violence—represents another setback for those who seek to return the country to its fascist past or hijack Iraq's future in the name of Islamic extremism.

The latter story is difficult to cover in the context of daily media reporting; it is more conducive to being explicated, for example, in a lengthy academic or think tank monograph than in a daily newspaper. Nonetheless, a great deal of creative and energetic media coverage of this subtle but important storyline does appear and is a great credit to the many journalists on the ground in Iraq who seek to report beyond the daily carnage.

While the journalists who have been filing such analytical reporting are legion, let me illustrate my take on this phenomenon with the case of the young and enterprising *Washington Post* reporter Jonathan Finer, who reported from Iraq in 2005 and 2006. I first met Finer a few weeks before I completed my tour in Iraq in June 2005.

He was relatively new in the country, and the occasion of our meeting was an interview he had requested on the topic of the media in Iraq. He was doing an in-depth piece for the *Post* on the role of the emerging Iraqi media in the transformation of the country, focusing largely on the courage of Iraqi journalists in the face of the danger that comes from playing a watchdog role in society (which is a great way to make enemies, and in a violent environment such as exists in Iraq, one is wise to avoid antagonizing dangerous or powerful people).

In our discussion, I stressed the great importance that the U.S. government placed on helping the Iraqi media develop the capabilities and skills needed to perform their crucial role in the type of society toward which Iraq was evolving. I also outlined for Finer the many programs that my office in the Embassy was supporting to assist in this development, for example:

- training programs for journalists in a variety of thematic and professional skill areas, including election coverage, economic reporting, and using Internet resources;

- exchange programs for journalists and editors to expose them to media practices and professionals in the United States and elsewhere;

- weekly press briefings for Iraqi journalists to help them hone their "on-their-feet" questioning and reporting skills;

- grants to Iraqi civil society organizations to foster professional development activities for women journalists; etc.

Finer proceeded to publish an excellent and comprehensive piece on the Iraqi media in the *Post* on June 6, 2005.[2]

After returning to the United States in late June 2005, I continued to follow Finer's reporting from Baghdad and remained impressed with the regular, in-depth, thoughtful pieces that he filed during his time there. He and his *Washington Post* colleagues in Baghdad have covered the steady stream of insurgent (and, lately, militia) violence in detail, as they should. However, they have also run excellent analytical pieces on social issues (such as on reform in the Iraqi educational system, and on the country's divorce rate), on reconstruction activities (including successes), on anticorruption efforts, on political evolution in the country, on cooperation between Sunnis and Shi'a in opposing al-Qaeda in Iraq, on Iraq's engagement with its neighbors in addressing border security issues, and even on Iraqis' obsession with the World Cup soccer tournament. These features usually appeared with multiple bylines but often with Finer among the contributors.

In the second half of 2006, Finer's mantle was taken up by another *Washington Post* journalist, Josh White. Over a several-month period, White filed an impressive array of insightful local-color, human-interest, and contextual pieces that collectively embodied a great deal of information and insight into important aspects of the country's current course. White's in-depth features on efforts at economic revitalization and unemployment, on difficult and complex border issues, and on Iraqi communities in various parts of the country and their varied conditions and circumstances (sometimes surprisingly upbeat, other times not so), provided interested readers with a window on the complexity of the Iraq issue and complemented the "hard news" coverage of almost daily violence and bloodshed that largely defines the U.S. public's perceptions of the country.

My own sense while I was in the country was that, like those observers who have been frustrated with the media coverage coming out of Iraq, many of the correspondents on the ground were also less-than-satisfied with the picture that emerged from their reporting. On several occasions during my time in Iraq, for example, when I expressed concern or displeasure to a journalist over a dramatic headline on a piece of reporting from Baghdad, I was told that the "sensationalist" headline writing is the product of their stateside editors, not the journalists filing the story. As someone with years of experience in working with the press, I am familiar with that common disclaimer; nonetheless, my sense in Iraq was that it reflected a considerable element of truth. The journalists were aware that the circumstances that applied in Iraq already challenged their ability to produce comprehensive and balanced reporting; attempts by editors at home to try to highlight a story by using a provocative headline further compounded the challenge of their already very difficult journalistic efforts.

The severe limitation on the number of staff that news organizations maintained in Iraq—a result of the great expense and danger involved in having reporters in the country—led to pressure on the limited number who were there to provide a steady stream of reporting on the "breaking" news of the latest violence, to some extent at the expense of more substantive, analytical reporting that might have conveyed a more nuanced—and complete—picture of the course of events unfolding in the country.

As it happened, we on the U.S. government side also played a (reluctant) role in circumscribing coverage of the full scope of the Iraq story, this due to the success (and ruthlessness) of the insurgents in targeting our reconstruction projects. Aware that the generously funded U.S. efforts to help rebuild Iraq's badly deteriorated essential services sector—electrical generation and distribution, water and sewage treatment, etc.—would undermine their agenda in post-Saddam Iraq, the insurgents consistently targeted such infrastructure projects in their terror campaign. Perhaps the most vicious of these attacks was a September 30, 2004, car bombing that killed thirty-four Iraqi children at a ribbon-cutting ceremony in Baghdad for a sewage treatment plant. Following that incident, we in the embassy, and our military counterparts, severely limited the publication and dissemination of information about U.S.-funded reconstruction projects. We could not risk a repeat of the carnage wrought by that incident and were also very mindful of the need to keep the existence of such projects quiet in order to avoid having newly built infrastructure facilities destroyed by the insurgents. This approach—while clearly appropriate under the circumstances—was disappointing and frustrating to many members of the press corps, who were eager to cover this important aspect of the Iraq story. In this case, the terrorists had achieved their objective—assuring that an important part of the Iraq narrative would remain untold.

Finally, even when media organizations allotted space or time for in-depth coverage of current developments in Iraq, the scenario would often involve considerable coverage of (typically negative) current, headline-grabbing developments up front, with context buried more deeply inside the article. An illustrative example is an excellent piece by Jonathan Finer and John Ward Anderson in the *Washington Post* on the April 9, 2006, third anniversary of the fall of Baghdad to coalition forces. Under the fully accurate and fair headline "The Battle for Baghdad's Future," and subhead "Three Years after the Fall, Capital is Pivotal to U.S. Success in Iraq, Officers Say," Finer and Anderson wrote a 1,600-word article that provided great insight into the situation in Baghdad and the role the city is playing in the agendas of the various parties vying for Iraq's future. Before moving to the issue of these varying perspectives, the article's fifth paragraph described the current conditions in the city:

> Three years after U.S. forces swept Saddam Hussein's government from power, car bombing and political assassinations are near daily occurrences. Neighborhoods, now torn along sectarian lines, are plagued by increasingly violent militias and dysfunctional public services, and occupied by tens of thousands of foreign troops.

This information is accurate and essential for an understanding of the issue treated in the article; it needs to be included. However, one has to read through to paragraph twenty-five in the article, very near the end, to come across the following "contextual" information:

> Many independent analysts here say that they do not believe that Baghdad or Iraq has descended into the kind of full-blown civil war in which sectarian militias engage in gun battles and artillery duels and residents pack up and move in massive numbers.

Two paragraphs later, the article concludes:

> "Despite the bad security situation, I am optimistic," said Ali Hussein, 46, who lives in the Amiriyah neighborhood in western Baghdad. Salaries have gone up since the U.S. invasion, he said, and the Iraqi army is improving. "Everything comes gradually. People should know that what is happening is not easy. It takes time."

The piece, overall, provides an excellent account of the situation—and stakes—in Baghdad three years after the city fell. Nonetheless, only the patient reader—the one who is willing to read through to the end of a 1,600-word story—will get the full picture. The reader who reaches paragraph five and decides he or she has read enough about the ceaseless violence in Iraq will come away with the view reinforced that the situation in the country is hopeless and that Iraqis have retreated into sectarian and ethnic enclaves, despairing of the future and resigned to a permanent state of ethnic and sectarian conflict, or worse.

I do not wish to overstate the extent to which one article can be taken as reflecting inherent limitations on the ability of journalists to convey the complexity and nuances of the Iraq issue through daily reporting. In fact, in any given week one can find excellent and comprehensive behind-the-headlines coverage of key aspects of the Iraq issue throughout the U.S. media. The point is simply to suggest that the story of a political transformation slowly taking root in a country wracked by daily, headline-grabbing violence is a difficult one to tell through daily journalism. It is perhaps even more difficult to get the U.S. public to focus on and delve into the story to a depth that leads to sufficient understanding in order to evaluate properly the current Iraqi, U.S., and coalition efforts in the country. The reasons involve the nature of "news," the attention spans (and interest levels) of consumers of the media (an element of "Iraq fatigue" has long since affected most Americans), the danger and difficulty inherent in reporting from Iraq, and the subtlety of the "second"—the "political evolution"—storyline of the Iraq issue. In my view, we in the embassy and the journalists with whom we interacted were all making a good-faith effort to provide candid, accurate, and useful information to help foster as complete an understanding of the Iraq issue as possible under the circumstances.

COVERING IRAQ

In the early days following the reopening of the U.S. embassy after the June 28, 2004, return of governing authority to a sovereign Iraqi government, we quickly learned that a perception existed among many in the U.S. and international media of a "credibility deficit" on the part of the U.S. government. Those of us newly arrived in the country in connection with the opening of the U.S. embassy, however, were given the benefit by the press corps of starting with a clean slate, and we had the advantage of representing not a governing authority—as did our Coalition Provisional Authority predecessors—but rather a foreign government (the United States) in a sovereign foreign country (Iraq).

Our approach was to endeavor to provide as much information as we could to help the U.S. and international press corps understand and knowledgeably report on developments in the country. We supplemented this Baghdad-based strategy by occasionally offering to provide logistical support for media excursions around the country, thereby attempting to facilitate coverage that was otherwise largely precluded by the security situation in the country.

The most high-profile element of our media efforts was the holding of regular, on-the-record briefings for the U.S., the international, and the Iraqi media with Ambassador John Negroponte. Similarly, the frequent visiting U.S. government officials always included on-the-record media events (interviews and press conferences) on their schedules. These typical on-the-record media activities notwithstanding, however, what came to be a central pillar in our media engagement was the somewhat unusual (for a U.S. Embassy) but very effective tactic of holding frequent background briefings for the U.S. and international press with senior embassy officers involved in political, economic, and other on-going developments in the country. For this approach to succeed, however, two conditions were required: Our briefers had to be candid and fully credible with the journalists, and the journalists had to be fully trustworthy to abide by the ground rules of the briefings.

Over time, the sincerity and insight of the embassy officers involved in these background briefings won the confidence of the originally somewhat skeptical press corps; these officers came to be in high demand, to the point where the frequency of their work with the press took considerable time away from their "day jobs" of handling the embassy's political and other portfolios. Without fail, however, these officers placed a very high priority on helping with the critical public affairs work of trying to ensure that reporting on Iraq was based on understanding and insight and not on ignorance and speculation. For myself, and I suspect for other embassy Public Diplomacy Office colleagues as well, this was an inspiring case of selfless teamwork in pursuit of the most urgent current foreign policy priority of the U.S. government.

For their part, the journalists never once violated the trust we placed in them to handle the candid and at times potentially controversial information that our briefers shared with them in accordance with the ground rules that had been agreed upon. I saw this as a case in which the crucible that was Iraq forged an alliance between potential antagonists—the press and the U.S. government—that honorably served the best interests of both. My perception of this bond was reinforced when I learned that a U.S. soldier who was assisting seriously wounded CBS correspondent Kimberly Dozier—who at the time of her almost fatal injury was embedded with U.S. troops and whom I and my fellow Public Diplomacy Office staff had come to know and respect for her excellent and courageous reporting from Iraq—gave her a Purple Heart that he had earned for being wounded on the battlefield.

Our interaction with the U.S. media also entailed other unusual elements, sparked by the unique and challenging circumstances involved in reporting from a country experiencing considerable violence and one whose newly formed sovereign government was still busy getting its feet on the ground. Security was a top priority for all of the journalists in Iraq, and we at embassy Baghdad (and our MNF-I colleagues) placed a high priority on working with the U.S. press corps to help ensure their safety. This involved regular meetings with the journalists and the private security contractors that their media organizations had engaged to discuss and coordinate security issues and information. The media were given considerable access to reports on violence and security threats and incidents—for use in their security planning, not reporting—and never once misused this information. A certain camaraderie developed, fostered by the circumstance of living and working in a war zone.

An additional (and likewise unusual) element of cooperation between the embassy's Public Diplomacy Office and the U.S. press corps involved assistance in dealing with Iraq's still-evolving entrance rules and procedures. Because only a small number of Iraqi embassies had stood up the ability to issue visas, it was difficult for most journalists to get a visa to enter the country before arriving at Baghdad International Airport (BIAP). And immigration procedures at BIAP were anything but smooth and predictable. As a result, at the request of the journalists, we worked with the Iraqi government to create a system by which we would "vouch" for U.S. journalists by providing them with a letter that I signed confirming their bona fides and expediting their entry into the country. The system worked (and works) well: I continue to receive occasional reports from journalist friends of such letters bearing my signature still being used by U.S. journalists to enter Baghdad.

For its part, the cohesion of the embassy team in its work with the press was rarely marred by unauthorized leaks to the media, and while this did happen on infrequent occasions, these were typically petty and bothersome rather than substantive and serious. I recall that shortly after my office disseminated a list of standard guidelines for embassy staff to follow in dealing with the media, elements of this message appeared in a British newspaper. The circulation of such guidelines is basically standard procedure for any U.S. embassy of any size, and their purpose is to alert embassy staff to the fact that the work of the embassy is of interest to the media and thus embassy staffers should keep this in mind should they find themselves in contact with members of the press. The coverage of our guidelines essentially amounted to quoting the prescription to be "circumspect" in dealing with the press; it was insignificant.

The only other instances that involved unauthorized sharing of embassy information with the Baghdad-based press corps tended to occur when mortars or rockets struck or landed near the embassy compound. In such cases, it was clear that some journalists had made arrangements with some person or persons on the embassy staff to alert them to any such occurrences (any embassy staff member who made such an arrangement with the media was, of course, violating embassy policy), and in most cases the impact of having such information provided almost in real-time to journalists who then reported it to the world was mostly limited to the surprise of seeing the report on the wire before our office even received media inquiries about the incident.

One such incident, however, was more troublesome than that: the night of January 29, 2005—the evening before Iraq's first national election, an election that it seemed the insurgents would try at all costs to disrupt. That evening, a rocket hit the Republican Palace where the embassy had most of its offices, killing two staff members. Before we were able to fully assess the damage and confirm the extent of deaths and injuries to the staff, we saw press reports on the attack, including mention of two fatalities. In light of this, we became concerned for the anxiety that this report would cause for the families back home of the hundreds of embassy Baghdad employees who, upon seeing these press reports, would not know if it was their loved one who had been killed. This incident reminded many of us of what was perhaps the most difficult aspect of serving in Iraq: knowing the anxiety that our being in Iraq was causing family members and friends concerning our safety and welfare.

THE POST-AL-JAZEERA ERA

The evolving Iraqi media environment came to encompass some unexpected and, ultimately, somewhat revolutionary developments. Since the time of its establishment in 1996, Qatar-based Al-Jazeera satellite television had been the dominant international broadcaster in the region. During the period from its inception up to and through the overthrow of the Saddam regime, Al-Jazeera was an untiring champion of a downtrodden Iraqi people suffering under the (in Al-

Jazeera's view, U.S.-inspired) UN sanctions against Iraq. With hostilities under way, however, the message morphed into one of wanton U.S. military destruction and the killing of innocents (an agenda captured well in the 2004 documentary film "Control Room"). Al-Jazeera's unrelenting message of U.S. (war) criminality and Arab humiliation continued through the period of the CPA and into the new era of restored Iraqi governing authority. Then, the regional Iraqi media story turned a corner.

One major element in this development was the launching of the Saudi Arabia-financed, Dubai-based Al-Arabiya satellite TV broadcaster in 2003, which displayed a more neutral, less agenda-driven approach to the Iraq issue. Then, in August 2004, the new Iraqi prime minister, Ayad Allawi, suspended Al-Jazeera from operating from its premises in Baghdad, citing the station's Iraq coverage as "incitement to violence" against the new regime; a ban on the station's Iraq-wide operations then went into effect the following month. Through the autumn of 2004, however, despite the official ban on its operations in Iraq, Al-Jazeera continued to play its role of providing moral support to the displaced Sunni minority, in particular in its coverage of the retaking of Fallujah from insurgents in November 2004 by Iraqi and coalition forces. Using biased sources—mostly former Baathist officials who claimed to have witnessed everything from the deaths of thousands of civilians to the use of chemical and nuclear weapons by multi-national forces—Al-Jazeera kept its regional viewers (overwhelmingly Sunni Arabs) pleased with its storyline of heroic Sunni resistance to the evil Americans and their Iraqi (Shi'a) lackeys. But then reality began to impinge on Al-Jazeera's narrative. First, there were the successful national elections on January 30, 2005, in which Iraq's Shi'a and Kurdish communities voted in large numbers, while their Sunni compatriots mostly sat out the polling. The scenes of jubilant Iraqi voters could not be ignored or suppressed, nor could a message which was poignantly expressed by one disillusioned Iraqi partisan of the station, who after witnessing the huge electoral turnout and peaceful balloting, was caught on camera exclaiming "Al-Jazeera lied to us."

At around the same time, Iraq's national TV station, Al-Iraqiya, which had recently been turned over to full Iraqi control, began airing a must-see nightly program called "Terrorists in the Hands of Justice"—a sort of (involuntary) reality TV for insurgents. This program, based in the northern city of Mosul and produced with the support of Iraq's Interior ministry, featured captured members of the insurgency, who spoke of their crimes and the motivation for their actions. The disheveled, uneducated, and weak individuals who were paraded on the program night after night conveyed a message that the insurgents—rather than the supermen they had come to be viewed as by most Iraqis—were in fact losers of the first order. The program moved Al-Iraqiya to the top of the ratings in Iraq, while greatly bolstering the morale of the Iraqi people and strengthening their determination to root out and defeat those who stood in the way of a secure and prosperous future for their country.

The proliferating satellite media environment in the region continued to challenge Al-Jazeera in its effort to dominate the news environment, and the station continued to lose its place with the Iraqi viewing public within the media pecking order. Al-Arabiya became the most-viewed regional broadcaster in Iraq, replaying Al-Jazeera (which remained dominant only among Iraq's Sunni population). Al-Arabiya's success in attracting Iraqi viewers with balanced and fair coverage of Iraqi, regional, and international news was effectively validated when insurgents attacked the station's Baghdad bureau with a car bomb on October 30, 2004, killing five members of Al-Arabiya's staff. On February 23, 2006, Al-Arabiya's well-known female correspondent Atwar Bahjat was killed by unknown gunmen in a targeted assassination while she was interviewing Iraqis outside Samarra. Just as the insurgents had done previously by attacking the UN headquarters and the International Red Cross in Baghdad in 2003, they once again showed their recognition that their agenda was threatened by anyone or any institution that operated in an unbiased, nonideological manner in post-Saddam Iraq, and by so doing supported, by example, the effort to create a successful and equitable Iraq out of the dysfunctional state that had resulted from Saddam's misrule.

MEDIA EVOLUTION WITHIN IRAQ

One of the true success stories in post-Saddam Iraq has been the remarkable proliferation of media of all kinds in the country. Dozens of TV stations, almost two hundred newspapers, and robust Internet and blogosphere cultures now provide Iraqis with the freest information environment in the Arab world.

One of the most inspirational anecdotes concerning the Iraqi media that came to my attention during my time in the country concerned the Iraqi talk-radio broadcaster "Radio Dijla." Founded by Iraqi journalist Ahmad al-Rikaby, Radio Dijla,[3] with its call-in format and open and unbiased approach, has performed a "social networking" function for Baghdad residents since it went on the air in April 2004.

The anecdote, which encapsulates the kind of epiphany that came slowly to most Iraqis—including Iraqi journalists—following the country's liberation, is described in an item from London's *The Independent* newspaper of August 4, 2004; it concerns al-Rikaby's effort to get a capable, but still cowed-by-authority member of his staff to edit a simple public service announcement:

> Rikaby . . . is still proud of weaning some of those journalists off their previous subservience, recounting how he asked one scriptwriter to rewrite an Arabic public service announcement he himself had drafted. The scriptwriter came back some time later trembling with fear and begged him not to be angry. "The guy had changed the word 'trash' to 'garbage.' I told him if I hadn't trusted him I wouldn't have asked him to rewrite it, that he was free now." He started crying.[4]

Sadly, Radio Dijla, like the satellite TV network Al-Arabiya, has incurred the wrath of the insurgents in Iraq, most likely because it embodies a voice of moderation and conciliation, two attributes that the terrorists and insurgents are determined to eradicate from the country. Four of Radio Dijla's staff members have been assassinated in the two-plus years that it has been on the air.

THE IRAQI MEDIA NETWORK AND THE MINISTRY OF INFORMATION MENTALITY

As the above tale reflects, one challenge to Iraq's transformation after its citizens have suffered under decades of violence and intimidation is to adjust their thinking concerning the functioning of the country's institutions, in the case of the Radio Dijla anecdote, the Iraqi media. Similarly, Iraq continues to face major challenges in rethinking and redefining its fundamental social and civic institutions, including those involved with the government's approach to the media and to its information activities. In the Arab world, it is the norm for governments to operate a Ministry of Information, whose purpose is essentially to propagandize the country's own citizenry. Before the fall of the Saddam regime, when Iraq's Ministry of Information ceased to exist, only one Arab country had disband its Information ministry, the government of Qatar, which did so when it created the regional broadcaster Al-Jazeera in 1996.

In Iraq, coalition authorities sought to use the infrastructure and personnel that remained from Iraq's defunct Ministry of Information to launch a new media entity, one that would be unique in the region—a "public broadcaster" on the model of Britain's BBC [British Broadcasting Company] and America's PBS [Public Broadcasting System]; that is, a broadcast entity that is publicly financed but that is independent of government control or influence. This new entity, called the Iraq Media Network (IMN), was begun shortly after the change of regime in Iraq, and it continues to this day. It comprises three elements—the daily newspaper *Al-Sabah*, Al-Iraqiya TV, and Al-Iraqiya radio. IMN has had a turbulent history in the years since its launch, especially Al-Iraqiya TV. While Al-Iraqiya TV's programming and technical sophistication still leave much to be desired, its feel for the cares and concerns of average Iraqis has enabled it to generate considerable interest in its "public affairs" and other programming. It has been a very positive force for informing and educating Iraqis on developments in the country and the issues of the day. This impact has been particularly effective in connection with the country's elections and its constitutional processes, as well as in public affairs programming involving economic reform, the judicial proceedings concerning former regime officials, and the insurgency.

In the early days of the Iraqi Interim Government (IIG), in the months after the transfer of governing authority from the CPA to the IIG, we at the U.S. embassy had a lively, ongoing dialogue with the press and public affairs elements of the IIG concerning the IMN and its role in the new Iraq. Some within the IIG were convinced that the government needed a "media organ"—such as the IMN—to communicate effectively with the Iraqi people, an institution along the lines of a Ministry of Information. In their view, the IMN—which had been created out of the defunct Ministry of Information—should, now that Iraqis once again exercised governing authority in their own country, return to its former mission as the official voice of the Iraqi government.

Fortunately, this view was opposed by others involved in the new government's public information and outreach efforts, who understood the new dynamics taking hold in the country and who sought to emulate the more typical western approach to government information activities: a professional office of public affairs to handle media inquiries, arrange media events for officials, monitor media coverage of the government, and undertake proactive media messaging and information dissemination—but not government ownership and control of media organs themselves. Our office, and our counterparts at the British embassy, provided considerable support to these elements of the IIG's information efforts, and the quality and success of the IIG's media activities improved over time. The outcome was a functioning and credible system, and one unique among Arab governments, in which the public is served and informed by an independent media entity (IMN) while the government undertakes its outreach efforts to its citizens not through media outlets that it operates itself but through engagement with the free and independent media that dominate the media scene in Iraq.

CENSORSHIP

One vestige of "old-think" that our efforts in Iraq were not able to eliminate entirely, however, was an inclination by Iraqi authorities to revert to the use of media censorship to address biased and harmful reporting. In the early months of the IIG, the impact of the agenda-driven, anti-Iraqi reporting by Al-Jazeera was a cause of ever-increasing concern and anger to the IIG leadership. Prime Minister Ayad Allawi repeatedly warned Al-Jazeera that its reporting on Iraq was inciting violence and strife in the country and that if this did not change he would have no choice but to ban the broadcaster's operations from the country. Through the summer of 2004, as the IIG—which had assumed power on June 28—continued to get its footing, the provocative coverage of Iraq by Al-Jazeera continued. As noted earlier, by August the prime minister was losing patience with Al-Jazeera and temporarily closed its Baghdad office while demanding that the broadcaster provide the IIG with "written explanations" about why it was being "hostile to the Iraqi people" in its coverage of the country. By September, in the absence of any reply from Al-Jazeera to his ultimatum, Allawi extended the closure of Al-Jazeera to its operations throughout the country and made the closure indefinite; the closure of Al-Jazeera's operations in Iraq officially remains in effect to the present day. The ban, however, has not prevented Al-Jazeera from reporting from Iraq, and—somewhat ironically—Al-Jazeera's coverage of the country has even included appearances on the broadcaster by senior Iraqi officials when they were traveling outside of Iraq.

For our part, we in the embassy Baghdad Public Diplomacy Office urged our contacts at the IIG not to support the banning of Al-Jazeera, even though we acknowledged that its coverage of Iraq was provocative and potentially a source for inciting violence. In this case, however, our arguments in the end did not hold sway, and the IIG banned the regional broadcaster.

9
Inside Iraq

In the early days following Iraq's liberation, the U.S. approach to Iraq's three major communities—the Kurds, the Shi'a, and the Sunnis—was largely been perceived within Iraq as one in which the United States favored the Kurds, tolerated the Shi'a, and saw the Sunni as adversaries. In pursuit of U.S. policy goals, we at embassy Baghdad sought to correct this perception and to convey a balanced approach to these communities:

- We sought to convince the Kurds that we expected them to make reasonable compromises with the other communities and that we would not support them in maintaining maximalist political demands.

- We sought to convince the Shi'a that we trusted them and accepted their political majority status in the country, while indicating that we expected moderation and inclusiveness—not high-handedness—on their part.

- We sought to convince the Sunnis that we did not hold them collectively responsible for the crimes of the previous regime and that they could trust that Iraq's political process would not be vindictive toward them, would give them a voice, and would protect their community and their minority rights and thus that they should join the political process.

These aspects of developments in post-Saddam Iraq have received considerable attention in the media and in statements by U.S. officials in speeches, hearings, and other public fora in the wake of rising insurgent and sectarian violence in Iraq over the past three years. In my travels around the country and meetings with government officials, media representatives, academics, and other opinion leaders, I found Iraqis who uniformly professed support for a moderate, inclusive, representative and "nonsectarian" government but who also felt the need to express—and in particular to convey to U.S.

officials—the grievances and "claims" of their community and the "needs" of that community in the new Iraq. There was a sincerity in the desire to convey such messages to "the Americans," since most did accept U.S. intentions toward their country as benign and, indeed, saw U.S. involvement in and commitment to their country as the only path toward a united, free, and stable future for Iraq.

THE KURDISH COMMUNITY

In listening to the various stories of my Iraqi interlocutors, the Byzantine complexity of the issues facing Iraq took on an added clarity. For example, in March 2005 in discussions with senior officials in Dohuk—a very peaceful, scenic, and prosperous Kurdish town located not far from the Turkish border—I was told that one nonnegotiable condition for the territory of the Kurdistan regional government remaining part of a unified, federal Iraq is that the Kurdish regional government must have the authority to decide whether U.S. forces could remain stationed in that part of the country. The message was clear—that the Kurds would require an indefinite U.S. military presence on their territory—i.e., "permanent U.S. bases" on the territory of the Kurdistan regional government—as a necessary guarantee against a repeat of the historic violence perpetrated against the Kurdish community by Baghdad governments since the founding of the Iraqi state. This demand, of course, flies in the face of the oft-leveled criticism that the United States invaded Iraq for the purpose of establishing permanent military bases in the country and must depart Iraq as soon as is practical in order to demonstrate the falseness of this claim.

    Other comments I heard during my talks—that Kurds would never accept any role for Islamic law (*Shari'a*) in Iraqi governance; that Iraqi Kurdistan would never fly the Iraqi flag ("the three stars represent Iraq, Syria, and Egypt, from the defunct United Arab Republic, a fascist political union reviled by Kurds"); that the safety and stability of Iraqi Kurdistan argued for more U.S. aid for this region ("you know, not a single U.S. soldier has been killed in Kurdistan since the war began"); etc.—convinced me that Iraq remained a country of red lines among its many and diverse ethnic and sectarian groups and that there was still a great deal of "venting" that had to take place—and Americans were as good a target for such venting as anyone—before the country could move on to a new chapter of hoped-for internal peace and reconciliation.

KIRKUK

I encountered a similar experience—and message—when I accompanied two prominent U.S. foreign policy experts—Leslie Gelb, president emeritus of the Council on Foreign Relations, and Fouad Ajami, a Middle East scholar at The Johns Hopkins University—on a visit to the contentious mixed-ethnicity city of Kirkuk, and the Kurdish cities of Sulaimaniyah and Erbil, in April 2005. The discussions in Kirkuk centered on the multiethnic nature of the city, its history under the Saddam regime of ethnic cleansing and displacement, and the fact of the region's considerable oil wealth. In discussions with representatives from the Kirkuk leadership and community, the various ethnic groups invariably used "the floor" to outline their history, their grievances, and their claims on Kirkuk's resources and future. Kurds insisted on speaking in Kurdish, and Turkmen in the Turkmen language. The Kurds stated their right to the city and to having it be part of the territory of the Kurdistan regional government; Arabs claimed that they will abide by an open and honest vote on the matter by all residents—they clearly felt that their numbers would give them a stronger position than most others think in such a vote; and Turkmen simply wanted their rights—as a minority, no matter how you slice it—guaranteed.

Among the Kurds, Turkmen, and Christians there was considerable concern at the prospect of some type of *Shari'a* being imposed on Iraq by its Shi'a majority. There was anger by all communities that Kirkuk's oil wealth had not benefited the city at all; 100 percent had heretofore been taken by the central government for use elsewhere in the country. Several said that at least 15 percent of the revenues from Kirkuk's oil production income should be set aside for Kirkuk.

There was also frustration expressed by the fact that the slowness to form a government in Baghdad had delayed the ability of the Kirkuk government to get down to business. One woman spoke up for the need to educate the people on democratic concepts. When the issue of internally displaced persons came up, pandemonium almost broke out, and we had to intervene to move away from that subject.

The final status of Kirkuk in the new Iraq—whether it will be incorporated into the Kurdistan regional government or not—is one of the most contentious issues facing the country today. The constitution calls for the issue to be decided by a plebescite among the people of Kirkuk before the end of 2007. The disposition of the immense oil wealth of Kirkuk hangs in the balance.

IRAQI KURDISTAN

The following day, in the prosperous Kurdish city of Sulaimaniyah, the discussions with officials and academics centered on Kurdish needs (i.e., "demands") in the new federal Iraq. Our interlocutors expressed a clear desire for maximum regional autonomy—a loose confederation more than a unified federal state—with at least one person openly expressing what clearly many really want—full independence for Kurdistan. There is, however, enough realism—at least among the Kurdish leadership and elite—to realize that an independent Kurdistan would likely bring more harm than good to Kurds: "a country of a few million with Turkey, Iran, Iraq, and Syria on its borders would be very vulnerable," as one participant put it. Thus, the Kurds seem to have accepted the reality of remaining within a loosely confederated but unified Iraq. This situation, however, still leaves several issues to resolve:

- *Shari'a:* There are great misgivings that—despite saying all the right things—the Shi'a leadership will pursue a policy of "creeping Islamism." The parallel is drawn to Khomeini's Iran: when he first came to power, Khomeini said the country needed to retain its multiparty political system, but in fact he moved the country over time to a single-party Shi'a theocracy. There was considerable Kurdish skepticism that Grand Ayatollah Ali al-Sistani is "really" pro-Iraqi and moderate on the role of religion in public life; there is fear that he will do Iran's bidding and support—if not clerical rule, per se, as in Iran—a dominant role of *Shari'a* in Iraqi life.

- *Security:* The long-suffering history of the Kurds at the hands of various Iraqi governments has left an indelible skepticism, even paranoia, regarding Iraqi national security forces. They will never allow themselves to be put in a position where they do not have the means to protect themselves. If a way can be worked out to use the Kurdish security forces (Pesh Merga) to do this as part of a national security force, fine; if not, then the Pesh will remain to defend Iraqi Kurdistan.

- *U.S. guarantees:* Likewise, as noted above, the Kurds are in no hurry to see U.S. forces depart Iraq or Iraqi Kurdistan. In an ideal world, from the Kurdish viewpoint, the United States would establish a permanent military presence in Iraq's Kurdish region.

These problems notwithstanding, there is great pride among Kurds that a Kurd—Jalal Talibani—has become the Iraqi president and a basic sense of realism—at least among the intellectual leadership—about what the problems are and what the limits are that the Kurds cannot overstep in trying to solve these problems.

THE SUNNI COMMUNITY

A discussion I had in April 2005 with a prominent Sunni from the Mosul area reinforced to me both the political and very practical challenges that bedevil efforts to address the root causes for the support of the Iraqi insurgency among many Iraqi Sunnis. The meeting took place at the Sunni leader's request, in order for him to have an opportunity to convey to a "U.S. official" his concerns about issues (and U.S. government policies) that he felt adversely affected the Sunni community in Mosul. Among these were the following:

- The result of the January 2005 election left the Mosul Provincial Council with a 95 percent Kurdish makeup, this in an area that has traditionally had a large Sunni Arab population. The Sunnis, who boycotted the elections, felt disenfranchised and unrepresented.
- One result has been what the Sunnis perceive as "Kurdish arrogance," similar to what Sunnis view as Shi'a arrogance in the South;
- The Sunni community in Iraq suffered under the previous regime, just as the Shi'a and Kurdish communities did; however, they perceive that they are being treated by the coalition

and the other Iraqi communities like the "opposition," as if the Sunnis writ large are Iraq's oppressors.

- The Sunni community is being shortchanged on welfare payments and public works projects.

- The Sunnis want the occupation to end; the United States needs to better explain why the military is here and when it will leave.

- U.S. actions often offend Sunnis' religion and dignity: Americans confiscate Sunni weapons, subject Sunnis to random arrest, etc.

- There is a connection between unemployment and terrorism: The terrorists pay ordinary Iraqis to commit terrorist acts.

- High inflation has put people in financial jeopardy.

- There is resentment of the "haves": only the corrupt and criminals get ahead in present-day Iraq; honest, religious people are the losers. There are now two classes of Iraqis: kleptocrats and honorable people.

He then proceeded to outline a list of actions that needed to be taken:

- more support for agriculture, help for unemployed farmers;

- ensuring that people get their full monthly food rations;

- more public works projects need to be undertaken in Baghdad and in Sunni regions;

- there must be limits on Shi'a political control in areas of Sunni majorities;

- Sunni youth should be encouraged to join the Iraqi security forces;

- Shi'a National Guard troops should not be used in Sunni areas;

- former Baathists who did not commit crimes should not be penalized; and

- Sunni detainees should not be taken to non-Sunni areas of the country.

This litany is very familiar to anyone who has been involved in Iraq or in U.S. efforts to develop policies that would foster stability, intercommunal harmony, and support among Iraqis for a free and democratic Iraq. All of the critical issues are there: corruption; economic development; political "balance"; nonsectarian security forces; limits on de-Baathification; etc. One of the underappreciated psychological obstacles to gaining buy-in from the Sunni community into the new Iraq is the absence in Iraq's history of the protection of minority rights. With no experience or relevant model to encourage that community to trust that it will be treated equitably in the new Iraq, many have withheld their support for the establishment of the new order in the country.

As late as December 2006, in a visit to Washington, DC, the highest-ranking Sunni in Iraq's government—Vice President Tariq al-Hashimi—continued to express concern that the United States supports "collective punishment" of Iraq's Sunni community in response to the violence taking place in the country. In remarks at the U.S. Institute of Peace, al-Hashimi suggested that it is still widely believed within Iraq's Sunni community that the United States supports compensation for Iraq's Shi'a community at the expense of Iraqi Sunnis for past atrocities committed against the Shi'a by Saddam's regime. To underscore his point that the government of Saddam Hussein was by no means a monolithic Sunni entity, al-Hashimi noted that of the fifty-five officials depicted on the playing cards that were distributed in spring 2003 of the most-wanted Iraqi officials from the deposed Baathist regime, thirty-five are Shi'a.

THE SHI'A COMMUNITY

The post-Saddam behavior of Iraq's largest community—the Arab Shi'a, which is estimated to account for 60 percent of the country's population—has reflected the many facets of this large group. Most important to know about Iraq's Shi'a community—and the Shi'a sect of Islam generally—is that, unlike Sunnis, Shi'a are acolytes of specific religious figures and in Iraq the most influential such Shi'a leader is Grand Ayatollah Ali al-Sistani. Al-Sistani is one of the small number of senior Shi'a clergy (*marjaiyah*) in the country, all based in the Shi'a holy and pilgrimage city of Najaf. Al-Sistani is himself a follower of the "quietist" school of Shi'a Islam, which holds that clergy should have an advisory role in governance but should not themselves occupy political offices. This is in contrast to neighboring Iran—where al-Sistani was born—and has been an essential factor in the political development of Iraq since Saddam was removed. This position by al-Sistani, together with his almost preternatural forbearance in the face of the atrocities that the Iraqi Shi'a community has suffered since Saddam's removal from power at the hands of its enemies, has been key in keeping the bulk of Iraq's Shi'a community behind the effort to create a representative and accountable government in the country, a goal that al-Sistani supports (and is the course that the country has, in fact, taken, which has given the majority Shi'a community effective political hegemony).

At the margins of the Shi'a community there are those who would like to take the country in a more overtly Islamic direction. Most well known within this group is the young cleric Moqtada al-Sadr, whose familial connections provide him with a certain amount of influence and recognition but whose personal religious credentials (and thus authority) are viewed by most Iraqis as ranging from suspect to nonexistent. Nonetheless, in the chaos of post-Saddam Iraq, al-Sadr has attracted the support of large numbers of poor and dispossessed Shi'a, and he has used this support to create the large and powerful Al-Mahdi militia.

The accepted wisdom about Iraq, one which is still oft-repeated today, is that Iraqis are largely secular in their personal orientation and that the diverse Iraqi population—some 60 percent Arab Shi'a, 15–20 percent Arab Sunni, 15–20 percent Kurd (all Muslim, largely Sunni) and about 5 percent "other" (Christian, Turkmen, Yazidi, etc.)—ensures that affairs of religion and affairs of state must and will remain separate. This viewpoint was key in the projections concerning post-Saddam Iraq on the part of U.S. policymakers. Given this circumstance, as well as what was known concerning the state of Iraq's infrastructure, the quality of the civil service and of civilian security forces, the extent of Iraq's oil resources (and thus a projected considerable steady national income), and the availability to a post-Saddam Iraq of a group of experienced (and tough) Iraqi expatriates—such as secular Shi'a Ahmed Chalabi and Ayad Allawi—a scenario was assumed in which these various elements working together would successfully segue Iraq from the dictatorship of Saddam Hussein to a stable and secure social order and an effective representative and constitutional government.

As Iraq's recent history has shown, this is not what occurred. However, postulating such a scenario was not unreasonable. Iraqis had been through two straight decades of war and hardship; it made sense to assume that they would welcome the opportunity to live under a stable, responsive, and accountable government. The world had progressed during that time from an ideological confrontation between capitalist democracy and socialist totalitarianism to the "end of history"—a broad acceptance that a free market economy and representative government embody the optimal paradigms for organizing societies for the greatest common good. The view was that the secular, smart, and long-suffering Iraqi people would certainly support the establishment of such a society. All opinion polling that has been done in Iraq in the post-Saddam period has supported such a view. As Rutgers University Political Science Professor Eric Davis put it in an October 2005 report he authored for the United States Institute of Peace: "The idea of a democratic Iraq is not one imposed by foreign powers, but rather one that Iraqis themselves vigorously support."[1]

What was not anticipated was the determination to defeat the democratic agenda in Iraq on the part of those whose perquisites, interests, or agendas would suffer under such an outcome: Iraqi (Sunni) Baathists (and the Sunni community more broadly); international Islamic terrorists (al-Qaeda, et al.); Iraqi Shi'a Islamists (such as Moqtada al-Sadr); the tens of thousands of criminals whom Saddam freed from Iraqi prisons before his downfall; and autocrats and entrenched elites in the region. Iraqis, and coalition forces, have paid dearly for this miscalculation.

THE IRAQ WAR: PHASE IV

In light of the sustained and very violent insurgency that has taken hold in Iraq since the removal of the Saddam regime, a cottage industry of commentary has emerged on whether or not this development was foreseen (or foreseeable) or not, and who should shoulder the blame for the failure to anticipate and prepare for it. This is likely to be another issue related to the Iraq War that historians will research and debate for years to come.

Various published commentaries by retired senior U.S. military officers that appeared in the spring of 2006 largely attributed blame in this area to former Secretary of Defense Donald Rumsfeld, mostly for an alleged failure to provide sufficient forces to ensure security in the country following Saddam's removal. One commentary on this issue that emerged in response to the published criticisms of former senior military officers was that of retired Marine Lieutenant General Michael DeLong, the second in command at CENTCOM from the period of 9/11 through the Iraq War, who published an op-ed in the *New York Times* on April 16, 2006. General DeLong noted that "such criticisms [of insufficient troop strength] ignore that the agreed-upon plan was for a lightning operation into Baghdad. In addition, it would have been well-nigh impossible to bring many more soldiers through the bottleneck in Kuwait. And doing so would have carried its own risk: you cannot sustain a fighting force of 300,000 or 500,000 men for long."

In his *New York Times* op-ed, General DeLong also commented on aspects of the war's aftermath:

> The outcome and ramifications of a war, however, are impossible to predict. Saddam Hussein had twice opened his jails, flooding the streets with criminals. The Iraqi police walked out of their uniforms in the face of the invasion, compounding domestic chaos. We did not expect these developments."

In his piece, General DeLong does cite two areas in which decisions "could have been better": "We banned the entire Baath Party"; and "We dissolved the entire Iraqi Army." He also notes that "[W]e relied too much on the supposed expertise of Iraqi exiles like Ahmad Chalabi who assured us that once Saddam was gone Sunni Arabs, Shiites and Kurds would unite in harmony."

Finally, in concluding his op-ed, General DeLong addressed the issue of post-War Iraq—"Phase IV":

> "But that doesn't mean that a 'What's next?' plan didn't exist. It did; it was known as Phase IV of the overall operation. General Franks drafted it and the Joint Chiefs of Staff, the State Department, the Pentagon, the Treasury Department and all members of the Cabinet had input. It was thoroughly 'war-gamed' by the Joint Chiefs."

More recently, several writers and op-ed columnists have published general claims indicating that elements of the career bureaucracy—in particular, the CIA and the State Department—had anticipated the emergence of violent sectarian (Baathist) and jihadist opposition to coalition goals for the new Iraq. Ron Suskind, in his book *The One Percent Doctrine*, for example, writes: "The State Department's Office of Intelligence Analysis had produced a variety of reports before the Iraq war predicting, for the most part, the explosive mix of insurgency and inertia that had defined the first year of the U.S. occupation. The CIA had also done its share—with bleak assessments of how a U.S. invasion would stoke *jihadist* anger worldwide and nourish a widening base of violence-prone recruits."[2] *Washington Post* columnist Richard Cohen added: "Even before the invasion of Iraq, the term 'civil war' was being bruited about."[3]

The CIA's assessment of the impact of military action in deposing Saddam is laid out in considerable detail by former CIA analyst Paul Pillar in a *Foreign Policy* article in the journal's March/April 2006 issue entitled "Intelligence, Policy and the War in Iraq." Pillar's account, in its entirety, is as follows:

> Before the war, on its own initiative, the intelligence community considered the principle challenges that any post-invasion authority in Iraq would be likely to face. It presented a picture of a political culture that would not provide fertile ground for democracy and foretold a long, difficult, and turbulent transition. It projected that a Marshall Plan-type effort would be required to restore the Iraqi economy, despite Iraq's abundant oil resources. It forecast that in a deeply divided society, with Sunnis resentful over the loss of their dominant position and Shiites seeking power commensurate with their majority status, there was a significant chance that the groups would engage in violent conflict unless an occupying power prevented it. And it anticipated that a foreign occupying force would itself be the target of resentment and attacks—including by guerrilla warfare—unless it established security and put Iraq on the road to prosperity in the first few weeks or months after the fall of Saddam.
>
> In addition, the intelligence community offered its assessment of the likely regional repercussions of ousting Saddam. It argues that any value Iraq might have as a democratic exemplar would be minimal and would depend on the stability of a new Iraqi government and the extent to which democracy in Iraq was seen as developing

from within rather than being imposed by an outside power. More likely, war and occupation would boost political Islam and increase sympathy for terrorists' objectives—and Iraq would become a magnet for extremists from elsewhere in the Middle East.

While much of what has occurred in post-Saddam Iraq is reflected in Pillar's account above, many of the problems that have arisen in Iraq would have been avoided had there not developed a fundamental dynamic of a one-sided, broadly supported (both within Iraq and in the neighboring Sunni-majority Arab countries) and well-resourced Sunni insurgency against efforts of the Iraqi majority and the international community to establish accountable governance and rule of law in the country. This development was unforeseen, however, in large part because the conventional wisdom was that the neighboring (Sunni) Arab states supported the deposing of Saddam Hussein.

The operative view concerning Iraq's Arab neighbors was that expressed by Bob Woodward in *Plan of Attack*. Woodward lists eight Arab countries whose support—either tacit or overt—would be solicited for undertaking military action to remove Saddam: Egypt, Oman, the United Arab Emirates, Saudi Arabia, Yemen, Bahrain, Qatar, and Jordan. As Woodward stated: "All these Arab or Muslim countries would be publicly against a war, but nearly all privately wanted Saddam out."[4] The fact that elements of coalition military activity against Saddam's Iraq were conducted on or from many of these countries does indicate that their leaderships were supportive of the removal of Saddam from power. However, in the wake of his demise, the policies and actions of these countries have, in several cases, evidenced an ambivalence (or worse) against the emerging political direction in post-Saddam Iraq of representative government under Shi'a political dominance.

Aside from Pillar's insider's account of the intelligence community's thinking and predicting vis-à-vis post-Saddam Iraq, other accounts of prewar analysis of post-Saddam Iraq have appeared in several publications. The most thorough efforts that I have come across to document the analysis and public discussion of prewar expectations concerning potential postwar, worst-case scenarios in Iraq appeared in three published accounts: Tom Ricks' *Fiasco*; Michael Gordon and Bernard Trainor's *Cobra II*; and *Washington*

Post journalist Karen DeYoung's biography of Colin Powell, *Soldier: The Life of Colin Powell*.

In *Fiasco*, Ricks methodically documents every instance he can find of a politician, pundit, academic, or other public voice warning about post-Saddam sectarian conflict, economic turmoil, or al-Qaeda infiltration. To me, the striking impression left by Ricks' treatment is that it betrays essentially an absence among experts, commentators, and pundits of any comprehensive, thoughtful analysis of the real probable challenges that would follow Saddam's removal. The picture Ricks paints, rather than demonstrating that there were clear, loud voices in the prewar public discussion making legitimate, ultimately correct predictions of postwar violence and chaos, actually conveys the impression that, surprisingly, no one ever seems to have systematically analyzed the issue of who those persons and groups would be whose interests would be undermined by the emergence of a post-Saddam Iraq along the lines envisioned by the United States and the coalition when they undertook to remove Saddam.[5]

In *Cobra II*, Gordon and Trainor cite a January 2003 National Intelligence Council (NIC) report entitled "Principal Challenges in Post-Saddam Iraq." Among many potential political, economic, security, and other problems the report treats in its "key judgments," it states the following concerning potential friction among the country's three major communities:

> Iraq would be unlikely to split apart, but a post-Saddam authority would face a deeply divided society with a significant chance that domestic groups would engage in violent conflict with each other unless an occupying force prevented them from doing so. Sunni Arabs would face possible loss of their longstanding privileged position, while Shi'a would seek power commensurate with their majority status. Kurds could try to take advantage of Saddam's departure by seizing some of the large northern oil fields, a move that would elicit forceful responses from Sunni Arabs and from Turkey. Score-settling would occur throughout Iraq.[6]

As Gordon and Trainor themselves characterize the NIC report, it "chronicled a long list of potential problems. It noted, but did not emphasize the issues."[7]

In *Soldier*, DeYoung cites an analysis prepared for Secretary of State Colin Powell by two senior diplomats with considerable Middle

Eastern expertise. As she recounts it:

> In mid-December, months before the war began, Powell tasked NEA [Near East Asia] Assistant Secretary William Burns with preparing "a memo on everything that could go wrong" after a military victory. Burns and his deputy, Ryan Crocker, worked into the night to produce a dozen single-spaced pages they called "The Perfect Storm."
>
> The memo explained Iraq's complicated ethnic and religious divisions and the tight lid Saddam Hussein's dictatorship and his Sunni-dominated Ba'ath Party had kept on them for decades. Released from his brutal control, Iraqi factions—especially the majority Shiites and Kurds—might try to settle accounts and would vie, perhaps violently, for dominance over the minority Sunnis or even for territorial separation. The Sunnis themselves would not give up power easily. Powerful exile figures from all factions would flood Baghdad to compete with and perhaps overwhelm emerging local leaders, while other countries in the region, including Iran, Saudi Arabia and Syria, would try to exert influence on their newly-liberated neighbor. A whole new political framework would have to be established, along with a private economy to replace Saddam's centralized system that supplied at least 60 percent of the Iraqi population with everything from jobs to rationed food and fuel. After years of sanctions and corruption, Iraq's infrastructure was in tatters.
>
> The earlier conclusion of the State Department's Future of Iraq project—compiled into 13 volumes that were handed over to Rumsfeld at the end of 2002—included the possibility of widespread looting and lawlessness and emphasized the need to quickly repair Iraq's infrastructure.[8]

Like the NIC report discussed above, the Burns / Crocker memo certainly covered the waterfront on possible difficulties that could result from removing Saddam from power, but from DeYoung's account at least it, like the NIC product, provided no sense of priority or probability. That the Shiites and Kurds might inflict violent revenge on Sunnis after Saddam's removal (which did not happen) is presented alongside "the Sunnis themselves would not give up power easily" (which became essentially the entire story of post-Saddam Iraq). While comprehensive in its identification of possible post-Saddam challenges, it—like the other reports and analyses that have emerged since the war and that in some quarters have been cited as showing that everything that has taken place in post-Saddam was in fact predicted—contains no evidence that it was a systematic analysis of exactly whose perquisites and agendas were threatened by Saddam's removal and thus who posed the greatest challenge to coalition success in post-Saddam Iraq.

Had such an analysis taken place, it would not have been hard to anticipate that the outcome would have been a list of exactly those who have conducted or incited violence in Iraq following the removal of Saddam's regime:

- former senior figures in that regime who remain at large (with the acquiescence of significant elements of the Sunni community from which they came), who do not want to face personal accountability for their actions under the old regime and who—together with many in their community—still cling to a hope that Sunni political dominance can be reestablished;

- al-Qaeda, a Sunni Islamic fundamentalist organization that disdains Shi'a Islam and for which a successful, secular, democratic Iraq would represent a counterweight to its ambitions in the region;

- Iranian provocateurs, who oppose secular, democratic governance of the type supported by Iraq's Shi'a leadership;

- the Sunni elites in the neighboring autocratic Arab countries, who fear the impact of a democratic Arab country in their midst and also oppose, in general, the idea of Shi'a political hegemony in an Arab country; and

- the thousands of criminals whom Saddam freed from Iraqi prisons in the months leading up to the war.

In my own efforts to determine if military planners, intelligence officials, and diplomats might have anticipated the kind of multifaceted insurgency that emerged in Iraq after the removal of the Saddam regime, I sought out an official who was aware of CIA prewar intelligence efforts on Iraq, who—when asked about pervasive anti-Shi'a sentiment on the part of Sunni Arabs in the face of Shi'a political ascendancy in Iraq—commented that "more attention should have been paid to the Sunni-Shi'a aspect of post-Saddam Iraq." He acknowledged that this element of the Iraq equation—and specifically the unhelpful, postwar reactions of the Sunni-majority Arab states on Iraq's borders—was not properly analyzed and anticipated in the run-up to the war. In addition, according to this official and a second person informed on CIA prewar intelligence with whom I spoke, it was universally accepted within the intelligence community that Iraq's Shi'a—and the Shi'a religious leadership in Iraq—were committed secularists and opposed to clerical rule in the country. This view was again validated in early February 2007. A *Washington Post* article on the national intelligence estimate on Iraq issued on February 2, 2007 cites a senior intelligence official referring to earlier intelligence assessments on Iraq as stating that "analysts failed to predict the 'rapid degree of intensification of sectarian mobilization and consciousness, and the speed in which that happened. I don't think we were that insightful'."[9] Thus, at least two key elements—the broader Sunni-Shi'a conflict that the Iraq War sparked, and efforts by some within Iraq's Shi'a community to impose Islamic strictures in the emerging Iraqi political and social infrastructure—were essentially unforeseen (or at least underappreciated) in the lead-up to the Iraq War.

INTERNAL DYNAMICS INSIDE IRAQ

In looking at the present dynamics within Iraq that are playing an important role in the prospects for the success of current U.S. policy and the current political process in Iraq, there are three issues that will determine the ultimate success or failure of the ongoing enterprise in the country: (1) the need for the various Iraqi communities to achieve *reconciliation*—and not just coexistence; (2) the urgent need for *economic reform* to lay the conditions for the economic progress that will be needed to anchor a democratic political order; and (3) the need to address the prevalence of *corruption and criminality* in the public sector.

RECONCILIATION AMONG IRAQ'S COMMUNITIES

The dynamic now playing itself out inside Iraq is complex and unpredictable. Centuries of complicated history; decades of violent, corrupt despotism; a wounded and abused national psyche; and infrastructure and economic devastation have all taken their toll, and all are affecting the unfolding drama in Iraq today. The most helpful contribution that the United States and like-minded countries can make toward influencing Iraq's internal developments in the current period is to ensure that we are committed to help Iraq achieve a future of freedom, justice, tolerance, and good governance. Iraqis will decide exactly what path their country will take, but in doing so they need to know that certain choices will result in support and assistance from the world's democracies, and other decisions could undermine such support. As departing U.S. Ambassador Zalmay Khalilzad has stated: "They will make their choices. We will make our choices, based on their choices."[10]

During my year in Iraq, we at embassy Baghdad gave a high priority to fostering the reconciliation that needs to be achieved among Iraq's various communities. One role that we played was, as noted previously, to serve as a sounding board to enable Iraqis to vent their grievances and make the case for their views and desires concerning the emerging new Iraqi political and social order. Beyond this, we used various programs at our disposal to directly promote intercommunal dialogue and reconciliation. Most prominent among these was the International Visitor Leadership Program, one of the State Department's flagship programs and a vehicle that for more than fifty years has advanced U.S. foreign policy interests by bringing up-and-coming foreign leaders to the United States for an intensive professional and cultural experience. As noted earlier, during my time in Iraq, my office sent more than eighty Iraqis on this program, in a variety of projects covering issues ranging from the media, to women's issues, to minority rights. Perhaps the most significant of the projects undertaken during my Iraq tour was that involving a group of fourteen religious leaders representing the full spectrum of the Iraqi religious landscape. The three weeks that these religious leaders spent in the United States—meeting with government officials, community leaders, representatives of U.S. religious organizations, and others, as well as living and traveling with one another—showcased the pragmatism, tolerance, and compromise that characterizes the workings of America's diverse society. It was this insight that these leaders brought back with them to Iraq from their U.S. experience.

The issue of reconciliation among Iraq's sectarian and ethnic communities has taken on increased prominence since the bombing of the Golden Mosque in Samarra in February 2006 and the sectarian violence that that incident sparked. Prime Minister Nouri al-Maliki acknowledged the urgency of this challenge in announcing, on June 25, 2006, the creation of a National Reconciliation and Dialog Project and a twenty-four-point reconciliation plan.[11] The project, which includes a proposal for a limited amnesty and other inducements to encourage current supporters of the insurgency to renounce violence and join the political process, is claimed to have the backing of the leadership of Iraq's Shi'a, Sunni, and Kurdish communities.

In a discussion with an Iraqi acquaintance who was visiting Washington in late summer of 2006, I asked how this effort at reconciliation was faring. Unfortunately, the answer I received was that, to that point, there had been no observable effort or impact stemming from the prime minister's reconciliation initiative. This Iraqi interlocutor, a secular Sunni whose family has lived for generations in Baghdad, commented that Iraqis have been waiting and hoping for a positive contribution by the reconciliation commission toward ending the current sectarian strife but have been disappointed by the inaction that has been observed to date. The operative mentality, this Iraqi added, among political leaders from Iraq's three largest communities—Shi'a, Sunni, and Kurd—has been and remains one of "favoritism toward one's own." This is reflected in the fact that it is commonplace to find that each ministry's staff is coming to reflect the communal affiliation of its minister: Shi'a-led ministries purge non-Shi'a from their ranks; Sunni-led ministries favor Sunnis; and Kurdish-led ministries do the same for Kurds. Thus, while success in gaining Sunni participation in the political process has been a significant step toward creating a stable and inclusive civic environment in the country, the record to date reflects that moving the country from coexistence to reconciliation among its sectarian and ethnic communities has remained elusive. It is this state of affairs that led to President Bush's initiative in early 2007 to "surge" additional troops into Baghdad and Al-Anbar Province in order to create the security climate needed for Iraq's leaders and the Iraq people to take the steps—and risks—required for reconciliation.

Such a policy of communal reconciliation within Iraq, coupled with a convincingly conveyed commitment by the West to stay engaged over time in the task of encouraging and facilitating Iraq's recovery and renaissance, is the course that offers the best chance both for Iraq's interests and for achieving the West's key security goal in the current decade: fostering political reform and, with it, economic development that will address the genuine grievances of the angry populations of the Arab world and help restore their lost sense of dignity. This course thus offers the current best chance of addressing the root cause of the greatest threat to the world in the twenty-first century—the possible nexus of Middle East-based international terrorism with weapons of mass destruction.

ECONOMIC REFORM

The challenge of economic reform in present-day Iraqi presents a Catch-22 to the Iraqi government and the international community working with that government to help the country out of the economic crisis it inherited from the Saddam regime. Under the Baathists, Iraq's was a centrally planned, command economy, on the Soviet model. Industry was dominated by large, inefficient, state-owned enterprises (SOEs). The SOEs, together with the government itself, provided the bulk of employment in the country. Under the UN sanctions of the 1990s and early years of the current decade, these enterprises became less and less productive, and their operation more and more corrupt. At the time of the removal of the Saddam regime, they had lost any capacity to function as a competitive industrial base for the country. However, as with government employment, any effort to terminate the employment (and paychecks) of the large workforces of the SOEs (estimated at more than half a million) would contribute significantly to anger and possible violence against the new Iraqi government and coalition forces. Thus, the significant drain on Iraq's resources represented by "ghost employment" in the SOEs continues to this day. The issue of addressing the high unemployment in Iraq as a major contributing factor to insurgent violence took on a new urgency in late 2006, and the U.S. military began a crash effort to bring some of the SOEs back into production and identify customers—including the U.S. military itself—for their products.

The period of UN sanctions also strengthened the harmful economic practice in Iraq of providing massive subsidies for food and other essential goods and services. Iraqis grew used to receiving a monthly food basket of staples such as rice, flour, and sugar, and efforts to modify or monetize these subsidized foodstuffs have met with considerable popular resistance. The inefficiency and corruption associated with this program (it is estimated that some 25 percent of the funds expended are siphoned off) amounts to a major waste of the limited government resources available to address the country's many economic, infrastructure, and other needs.

The situation is similar in the energy sector. Stories about long gasoline lines at Iraqi service stations—in a country with the second highest proven oil reserves in the world—are commonplace. The part of the story that is generally not told, however, is that the "shortages" that such lines represent are not actual shortages of gasoline but rather are a response to the enterprise of Iraqis in "buying low and selling high." Gasoline at the pump is subsidized by the government, and until December 2005 was priced at about 5 cents per gallon. At that time, the price was increased eightfold, to around 40 cents per gallon. Under the old pricing system, an estimated 25 percent of the gasoline sold in Iraq was resold on the black market, mostly in neighboring countries. The large price increase of December 2005 has cut into the black marketeering of Iraqi gasoline but has not eliminated it. The situation with the availability of gasoline in Iraq is compounded by the manyfold increase in automobiles in the country since the fall of the former regime. The absence of restrictions—and customs duties—on importing automobiles into the country for a lengthy period following the April 2003 regime change caused the number of automobiles in the country—and the associated demand for gasoline—to surge. Iraq's infrastructure and pricing system has yet to adjust to this new reality, and the precarious security and economic climate in the country largely prevents the Iraqi government from directly addressing these problems.

The situation with electricity in Iraq is similarly complex. Since the ouster of the Saddam regime, demand for electricity has spiked; Iraqis now have the refrigerators, air conditioners, televisions, and other electrical appliances that were unavailable to them before. This has caused a major increase in demand for electricity in the country. At the same time, the government's ability to price and collect payment for electricity has largely broken down. The result is that much of what electricity is available is wasted, stolen, or otherwise not used wisely or to the benefit of most Iraqis.

The electrical power situation is further complicated by the fact that in the new Iraq, unlike in Iraq under Saddam Hussein, electricity is not used by the regime to "reward" or "punish" certain communities or areas of the country. This fairer sharing of the country's electricity resources has meant considerable reductions in the availability of electricity in certain formerly favored locations (such as Baghdad), while other regions (such as the largely Shi'a south) have seen their access to electricity improve.

Of course, the overall level of electricity in the country has also been negatively affected by the determination of insurgents to target the country's electrical grid as part of its campaign to destabilize Iraq. Furthermore, reconstruction efforts in the electricity sector by the United States and others have, in many cases, suffered from poor planning and implementation.[12] Taken together, a complicated mixture of increased demand, supply disruptions, infrastructure deterioration, and zero cost for usage has led to the well-documented shortage situation in the electricity sector in Iraq today.

Iraqis, however, are an ingenious and entrepreneurial people and in many cases have developed effective systems for supplementing the limited electricity that they get from the national grid. It is a startling sight to drive through Baghdad and see cartons of portable generators piled high along blocks and blocks of the city's sidewalks. Many Iraqi families now use such generators to supply the electricity they need during the many hours each day when the central grid is off-line. Alternatively, it is now quite common for a group of neighbors, or an enterprising individual on a city block, to set up a small, neighborhood electrical distribution system supplied by a local generator, and supply electricity to area residents for a fee. In this way, many Iraqis combine their free access to the national electrical grid—when it is operational—with fee-based access to a neighborhood electrical supplier—when it is not.

During my tenure in Iraq, we undertook public diplomacy programming to address the need for Iraqis to understand the broken state of their economic system and accept the need for significant economic restructuring in the country, including in the area of state subsidies. Our centerpiece effort was a grant to an energetic Iraqi economic research institute and think tank to spearhead this public education campaign. Our Iraqi counterparts parlayed this grant into an hour-long national weekly economic discussion program on Al-Iraqiya television. There, the moderator—who ran the economic institute to which we had provided the grant funding—would host guests from all sectors of Iraq's economy (and government) to discuss frankly the state of the country's economy and the steps needed to improve it. By all accounts, this program was quite popular among its Iraqi viewership. As a pragmatic, energetic people, Iraqis are under no illusions concerning the challenge they face in the economic sphere, and I strongly sensed that they were eager to understand what economic course likely lay before them and what their role would be in contributing to Iraq's economic recovery and revitalization.

CORRUPTION

Iraqis broadly lament the endemic corruption and criminality that became pervasive in the Iraqi public sector during the reign of Saddam Hussein and especially during the period under UN sanctions following the Gulf War. While recognizing the sad state of the public sector in their country today, Iraqis are quick to point out that not too long ago—in the late '70s, when the country reached its modern apex of economic, educational, and social achievement—Iraqi public servants were a model of efficiency and honesty, far ahead of their counterparts elsewhere in the Arab world. However, yet another disastrous legacy of the Saddam regime was the degrading of this system into one in which no aspect of life could be conducted without bribery, graft, kickbacks, theft, or other types of criminal and corrupt behavior.

Based on my experiences and observations during the year I spent in the country, I would count corruption—both actual and potential—as the most serious factor undermining efforts to defeat the insurgency and create the type of new Iraq that most Iraqis seek. Numerous incidents that have been reported underscore the fact that this factor works against every element involved in the current struggle in the country. For example,

- military equipment issued to Iraqi security forces is sold on the black market to insurgents, providing insurgents with weapons, ammunition, and protective gear for their use against coalition and Iraqi security forces;[13]

- names and phone numbers of citizens who report crime or insurgent activity are sold to criminals and insurgents, who then take retribution, virtually ensuring that average Iraqis will not alert authorities to crime or insurgent activity that they witness;

- petroleum products are stolen and smuggled out of the country, as is oil revenue itself, much of it winding up in the coffers of insurgents, financing their terrorist activities and depleting the Iraqi government of the funds it needs to meet the needs of its citizens and to combat the insurgency; and

- government procurement costs are inflated and the surplus funds stolen, also often by those supporting the insurgency, with the same effect of funding insurgent activities while denying Iraqis essential resources and services.

While I was working at embassy Baghdad, we were concerned daily with the possibility that one of the Iraqi employees of the embassy would betray the identities of other Iraqis working there, thus exposing them to targeting by insurgents. One day we did learn of a report that an employee of one of the Iraqi ministries had been caught selling the names of all of the ministry's employees to insurgents, who clearly were interested in targeting these Iraqis who, by working for the Iraqi government, were in their view collaborating with the "occupiers."

Such corruption, when paired with the impact of the uncertainty among Iraqis concerning the strength of the U.S. commitment to stand with them until their struggle is won, largely accounts for the tremendous difficulty that the coalition and Iraqi security forces are experiencing in trying to quell the insurgency. As Judge Radhi Radhi, the head of Iraq's Commission on Public Integrity (an independent Iraqi body initially established under the Coalition Provisional Authority to fight corruption) has commented: "Without corruption we would have been able to defeat the terrorists by now."[14]

In fact, corruption and criminality now appear to have become the primary sources for the funding of the insurgency in Iraq. A *New York Times* article published on November 26, 2006, cited a U.S. government report that "estimates that groups responsible for many insurgent and terrorist attacks are raising $70 million to $200 million a year from illegal activities." The article spells out quite succinctly the devastating connection between the insurgency, the lack of essential services and supplies, and corruption, when it states: "The oil ministry in Baghdad, for example, estimated earlier this year that 10 percent to 30 percent of the $4 billion to $5 billion in fuel imported for public consumption in 2005 was smuggled back out of the country for resale. At that time, the finance minister estimated that close to half of all smuggling profits was going to insurgents."[15]

An Iraqi acquaintance who has studied the issue of corruption cites insurgent financing as one of the primary reasons for the concerted effort to destroy Iraq's crude oil pipelines. By blowing up the pipelines, the insurgents force the government to transport its oil exports (and refined petroleum product imports) by tanker truck. While oil products transported by pipeline are relatively difficult to steal, those shipped by tanker truck are ripe for insurgents to intercept, with the collusion of corrupt Iraqi government officials.

One aspect of the atmosphere of corruption that permeates the Iraqi public sector is not just corruption itself but the impact of the potential for corruption on the functioning of the Iraqi government. The very possibility (likelihood) that anyone given authority to expend government funds might abuse that authority can make Iraqi government institutions dysfunctional. Two mundane but telling examples come to mind from my own experience in the country:

- On a visit to the Iraqi Media Network, I heard complaints by a talk show host on IMN's Al-Iraqiya television network that he had no funds even to provide refreshments for guests on the show. When I later asked the IMN director about this, he explained that if he did not retain sole authority to commit IMN funds and instead delegated that authority to others in the organization, he feared there would be a wave of fraudulent expenditures that would quickly deplete the IMN's resources;

- When discussing with an official in the prime minister's office the setting up of the infrastructure (computers, televisions, etc.) needed for a media reaction and monitoring unit, he conveyed to me an incident that had occurred a few days earlier: He had given a member of his staff a sum of money (cash; everything in Iraq is done in cash, another major element contributing to corruption in the country) to purchase such equipment in the city, but he had insisted that this staff member be accompanied by another member of the staff, who was waiting for him by the front door of the office. The staff member with the cash exited the building by a back door and went and purchased the equipment on his own. While he did get the equipment he was supposed to, he used all the funds he was given and, in the official's mind, without question extorted kickbacks in doing so.

As these incidents suggest, actual or potential dishonesty in the Iraqi public sector not only contributes directly to the insurgency that is wracking the country but also seriously undermines the functioning of the Iraqi government in its effort to defeat the insurgency, restore "normalcy" in civic life, and deliver basic services to the Iraqi people.

DISMEMBERING IRAQ

A major element of the discussion of internal factors affecting Iraq's prospects for success involves proposals that have been made that—since Iraq is actually an artificially created entity—the only real solution to its current predicament is to break it up along communal lines into its constituent parts: a Shi'a south; a Kurdish north; and a Sunni center. However, as critics of a break-up-the-country-to-save-Iraq strategy have correctly noted, Iraq is really composed of *four* entities:

- a Shi'a-dominated area in the south and south-central parts of the country, in which Islam plays an important role in civic, social, and political life;

- a Kurdish enclave in the north, with a determinedly secular population whose boundaries are currently defined by the borders of the Kurdistan Regional Government but whose peoples represent major—often majority—population elements in neighboring areas beyond these borders;

- a Sunni "triangle" centered on Al-Anbar Province just north of Baghdad that is not only Sunni dominated but—just as importantly—whose civic, social, and political structures are tribally defined; and,

- Baghdad, with a quarter of Iraq's people and characterized by a population in which many, perhaps even most families have members from more than one of Iraq's three major communities—Shi'a, Sunni, and Kurd—and that also has a significant (although now rapidly declining, sadly, through emigration) Christian minority.

A telling anecdote appeared in a *Washington Post* story about the impact of the current violence on the center of Baghdad's once thriving bookshop district, Mutanabi Street. The article quoted one bookseller lamenting the sectarian violence that now affects the area and portrays the well-known Baghdad phenomenon of a "sushi family" (i.e. Sunni-Shiite): "I am a Shiite. . . . All my daughters are married to Sunnis. And my son is married to a Sunni woman. No one used to mention Sunni and Shiite. This is all new to us."[16] This situation was reinforced to me in a December 2006 conversation that I had at Georgetown University with a Sunni member of the Iraqi Council of Representatives who commented, in the context of a discussion of whether or not Iraq had by that time entered into a civil war: "I am a Sunni; my wife is a Shi'a. There will not be civil war in Iraq until there is civil war within Iraqi families, and that will never happen."

The existence of this melting pot containing 25 percent of Iraq's population most directly precludes dismantling the country into separate Shi'a, Kurdish, and Sunni enclaves as a solution to Iraq's current strife. The most comprehensive (and sympathetic) treatment of the proposal to divide Iraq into separate entities appears in the book *The End of Iraq* by foreign policy expert (and former U.S. ambassador to Croatia) Peter W. Galbraith. But even Galbraith, a close friend of Iraq's Kurds and a strong supporter of their cause, falters when confronted with the dilemma of dealing with Baghdad in the process of the dismembering of the country: "Accepting partition," he writes, "is a way to get most coalition forces out of Iraq quickly. It does not solve the problem of Baghdad. That is because there is no good solution. . . . In Baghdad and other mixed Sunni-Shiite areas, the United States can not contribute to the solution because there is no solution, at least in the foreseeable future. It is a tragedy, and it is unsatisfying to admit that there is little that can be done about it."[17]

Moreover, the communal mixing that characterizes much of Iraq today is not the only obstacle to partitioning the country. Despite the frequently heard claim that there is no "Iraqi identity," in my experience I found this not to be the case. When a non-Iraqi asks an Iraqi if he or she is a Shi'a, Sunni, or Kurd, the typical response—given with some indignation—is that "I am an Iraqi." Data from the World Values Survey provide some quantification of Iraqi identity among Iraq's various communities, with 86 percent of Iraqi Arabs stating that they are "very proud" to be Iraqi, while 34 percent of Iraqi Kurds express the same viewpoint. For Iraqi Arabs, the percentage with such views of their national identity was higher than for eighty-one of the eighty-six countries included in the survey. And even for the Kurds, considering their circumstances of de facto independence from the rest of the country for the last twelve years of Saddam's rule and the treatment that they received at the hands of the Baathist regime, the 34 percent figure does not make the case that it is hopeless for the Kurds to remain Iraqis. After all, even in as stable, wealthy, and progressive a country as Switzerland, the percentage of those who are "very proud" to be Swiss is only 36 percent.

In February 2007 the *Wall Street Journal* cited data from the University of Michigan's Institute for Social Research which likewise provide encouragement for the view that Iraqi attitudes remain conducive to creating a unified, secular, and tolerant nation:

> Between 2004 and 2006 the number of Iraqis who supported the ideal of an Islamic state fell to 22% from 30%, while those agreeing that religion and politics ought to be separated rose to 41% from 27%, according to surveys conducted by the University of Michigan's Institute for Social Research. Even in Baghdad, site of so much of the sectarian killing, the number of respondents who put their Iraqi identity ahead of their Muslim one doubled to 60%. (By contrast, only 11% of Cairenes saw themselves as Egyptian first, Muslim second.) And 65% of Iraqis agreed that it was "very important" for Iraq to be a democracy, up from 59% two years before.[18]

In short, there is nothing about the current state of attitudes among Iraq's major communities that dooms the effort to assist Iraqis in working out a national compact that will keep the country intact under a system of shared or devolved powers within a federal or confederated system that meets the needs of Iraq's unique circumstances.

Of course, among Iraqis there is an awareness of ethnic and sectarian identity, but this is true of all multiethnic and multisectarian societies and does not automatically portend discord among the different communities. Opinion polling has consistently supported the view that Iraqis do not wish to see their country dismembered. An Oxford Research Institute poll conducted in March 2004 with a representative sample of Iraq's population found that "nearly 80% favored a unified state with a central government in Baghdad." As the poll company's director, Dr. Christoph Sahm, summarized the result: "the key finding is that Iraqis don't want to break up the country."[19]

While the sense of being "Iraqi" has certainly declined in the northern Kurdish community since the United States made that area a protected zone in the early 1990s and it began to economically, culturally, and linguistically evolve away from the rest of Iraq (most of the Kurdish area's younger generation has not learned to speak Arabic), the general impression I took away from my experience in dealing with Iraqis in all parts of the country was that there exists a foundation of Iraqi nationality that is broadly present among Iraqis. There are, to be sure, communal and sectarian tensions and grievances, but there is also a proud shared identity with Iraq's past glory as the cradle of civilization and the golden age of Islamic influence and culture. And even Iraqi Kurds, arguably the group in Iraq most alienated from the concept of an Iraqi identity, look back on a history in which one of their own—the famous Muslim warrior Salahaddin, who drove the Crusaders out of Jerusalem and ruled great swaths of the Middle East during the twelfth century—is among the most revered leaders in the history of the Middle East.

There are significant, probably insurmountable, regional considerations to a partitioning of Iraq as well. Turkish objection to an independent Kurdistan; Arab objection to an Iranian-allied Shi'a entity controlling the country's major oil wealth and being geopolitically threatening to the Arab Gulf countries; and the nonviability of an impoverished, resource-poor Sunni "Bantustan" are all realities standing in the way of a partitioning of Iraq that most Iraqis and other countries in the region recognize.

IRAQ AS SWITZERLAND

It is telling to note how often in the post-Saddam era literature on Iraq one encounters the caveat concerning efforts to remake Iraq conveyed in the phrase "no one expects Iraq to become a Switzerland." But this is not quite true. There is one group of people who actually did (and mostly still do) expect Iraq to become another Switzerland: the majority of Iraqis. In this connection, Francis Fukuyama had it right in his "end of history" treatise: The historical path of sociopolitical evolution had, by the final decade of the twentieth century, reached a point at which it became overwhelmingly accepted by publics worldwide that a free, secular, democratic, and free-market system represented the most advantageous and desirable political and economic model for the organizing of societies. Such a system became, as Fukuyama suggested, a universal aspiration, thus, in his term, bringing an end to "history" in the sense of ending any further argument about the most advantageous form of human social, political, and economic organization.[20]

The Iraqi people are no different from peoples elsewhere, and—when liberated from the tyranny under which they had long suffered—aspired to such a society for themselves. Oxford Research International, for example, has regularly conducted polling in Iraq since mid-2003; it reported in its December 2003 poll that "90.3% of interviewees said that they somewhat agreed or strongly agreed that the country needed an Iraqi democracy." Data from the World Values Survey cited earlier show that "In . . . Iraq . . . fully 85 percent of the public said that democracy was the best form of government, and there was no significant difference between Iraqi Kurds and Arabs on this point."[21] However, several factors have conspired so far to thwart the attainment of this goal. These include

- the total disintegration of any civic cohesion or allegiance among Iraqis, as a result of several decades of abuse under the Baathist regime and in particular during the desperate every-man-for-himself conditions that prevailed during the twelve years of UN sanctions on the country;

- the "petrocracy factor"—the fact that Iraq's oil wealth served as a magnet to some to lure the unscrupulous, rather than the patriotic, to seek (and then exploit for personal gain) leadership positions in the new Iraq;

- the tragic occurrences in the aftermath of the Gulf War, when Kurds and Shiites rose up against the Saddam regime with the expectation of U.S. military support and protection, leading to massacres of those communities when such support was not forthcoming;

- the insecurity and uncertainty that Iraqis experienced in the looting and lawlessness in the immediate aftermath of Saddam's removal, largely causing Iraqis to withhold overt commitment to and support for the efforts of their liberators to establish a benign and humane order in the country;

- the message of a possible U.S. loss of resolve and commitment in seeing its policy goals in Iraq through to success that has been conveyed in our domestic public and political dialogue on Iraq policy; and

- the clear strength and determination on the part of reactionary forces from both within Iraq and in the region violently to reimpose a tyranny of one sort or another on the country.

The psychological devastation that Iraqis have suffered in recent decades has only begun to be recognized and its effects appreciated in understanding the course the country has taken since Saddam's removal. Iraqi's I have spoken with routinely describe a descent of their society into an almost Hobbesian state as the paranoia of the Saddam regime grew (accompanied by growing distrust even of friends and neighbors as possible informants for the regime), corruption and black marketeering became endemic, and families took desperate measures—from selling precious heirlooms to engaging in prostitution—just to meet the basic necessities of life.

Research has shown that Iraqis evince a number of troubling psychosociological effects that corollate with the high level of insecurity that has characterized their lives for the past several decades. "Insecurity in Iraq seems to reflect both long-term factors linked with the reign of Saddam, and short-term factors linked with the disorder and terrorism that have prevailed since his fall," notes a study (first completed using 2004 data and then updated in 2006) based on the World Values Survey project of eighty countries, concluding that "the high levels of xenophobia and rejection of out-groups [Note: The study documented that Iraqis displayed such traits in the highest percentages of any people in the eighty countries studied] that currently exist in Iraq may hinder the emergence of stable democracy, for there is strong evidence that tolerance, trust and an egalitarian outlook are conducive to democracy."[22]

The petrocracy factor—the circumstance by which countries with great oil wealth use the exploitation of that wealth to circumvent the imperative, embodied in the end-of-history thesis, to take the measures needed to create a successful, wealth-generating economy in order to meet the needs and aspirations of their people—has also affected the post-Saddam era in Iraq. Rather than putting their efforts into supporting the types of policies (rule of law, social cohesion, accountable government) that would foster such economic success, and seeking the regional, communal, sectarian, and other cooperation needed to create a climate of stability and common purpose that are required as a foundation for economic success through the traditional means of investment and productivity, many of the players in post-Saddam Iraq have focused on gaining access to the spoils of the country's oil wealth. Evidence has emerged, for example, that several Iraqi officials who have served in post-Saddam governments have used their government positions to pursue illegitimate personal gain. The head of the Iraq Public Integrity Commission has estimated that Iraqi government officials have stolen up to $2.3 billion in the post-Saddam years, and several former cabinet-level officials are under investigation or indictment. The perception of such corruption and theft from public coffers by government officials is widespread among Iraqis, resulting in a pervasive "take-what-you-can-get" mindset in the country, a dynamic that is contributing to the difficulty in achieving a new order in Iraq.

10
Iraq's Neighborhood

One fact that has not been lost on those who have sought to understand and address the situation that Iraq has faced in the postwar phase of its efforts to establish stability and order in the country while confronting a multifaceted insurgency is the impact of Iraq's neighbors on this process. Transitioning from a political order that has been dominated for centuries by the country's Sunni minority to one in which the country's majority Shi'a population is establishing political hegemony has produced some difficult (and largely unanticipated) consequences and challenges vis-à-vis the neighboring Sunni-majority Arab countries to Iraq's west and south. To the east, Iraq's neighbor Iran—a Shi'a dominated, mullah-governed Persian Islamic state—has also influenced Iraq's internal developments since the country's liberation. And, to the north, the large and powerful Sunni Muslim nation of Turkey—like Iran, also non-Arab—has, in its own manner, influenced developments in Iraq (albeit in a more passive mode than have Iraq's Sunni Arab neighbors and Iran).

FEAR, OR LOATHING?

One impact of the Sunni-Shi'a divide on the situation in Iraq has been the apparent hesitancy of (Sunni) Arab regimes to say or do much in support of an Iraqi political process that is leading to Shi'a political dominance in the country. As the *New York Times* reported in May 2005, "For Sunni Arabs . . . the triumph of the Iraqi Shiites is a calamity. . . . one easily foreseen consequence of the Shiites' triumph could be a redoubling of the Sunni insurgents' efforts to disrupt and, ultimately, defeat the democratic government of Iraq."[1] In June 2006, Iraqi expatriate Kanan Makiya, author of the 1989 book *Republic of Fear*, which documented the pervasive, almost mundane nature of the Iraqi police state under Saddam Hussein, commented on this aspect of the current struggle in Iraq in a paper published by the Philadelphia-based Foreign Policy Research Institute entitled "Iraq's Democratic Prospects." In his words:

> If the war against the insurgency is not going as well as was hoped, in large part this is because the regimes on Iraq's borders—the very ones that would be most undermined by a success story in Iraq—are sustaining it by doing little or nothing to stop the infiltration of determined jihadis from slipping in and wreaking havoc. If anything, the neighboring regimes are aiding them.

Of the twenty-two Arab countries,[2] none had ever had a Shi'a-led government before the fall of Saddam Hussein.[3] Under the Iraqi Interim Government, which served from June 28, 2004, until May 2005, Prime Minister Ayad Allawi was the first Shi'a to lead the government of an Arab nation. The Iraqi Transitional Government, which came to power through the January 2005 election, was led by Shi'a Prime Minister Ibrahim Ja'fari and had a Shi'a majority in the Transitional National Assembly; it was thus the first Shi'a-dominated government in the Arab world. The current Iraqi government, as well, is led by a Shi'a prime minister, Nouri al-Maliki.

In the Arab Muslim community as a whole, members of the Sunni sect account for some 90 percent and those of the Shi'a sect about 10 percent. There are only two Arab countries with Shi'a majority populations—Iraq, and the small Persian Gulf island nation of Bahrain; and only one other Arab country—Lebanon—in which the Shi'a population outnumbers the Sunni population. Until the fall of Saddam Hussein, Iraqi governments have always been led by Sunnis. The other Shi'a majority Arab country—Bahrain—has a Sunni emir ruling a nation that has an estimated 75 percent Shi'a majority. The only other parts of the Arab world with significant Shi'a populations are Oman, Yemen, and the Eastern Province of Saudi Arabia. In the case of Saudi Arabia, its Shi'a population is located in the area of the country where all of its oil is located. In recent years, this population has begun to receive more equitable social and educational treatment and economic opportunity under an initiative of dialogue and reconciliation launched by King Abdullah. The process of bringing the Shi'a into the kingdom's societal mainstream, however, is still in its early stages.

The broad concern among Sunni Arabs about Shi'a political dominance in Iraq was perhaps best reflected in an ill-conceived remark by Jordan's King Abdullah II shortly after the removal of the Saddam regime. The king, who in fact is an enlightened and progressive influence in the region, commented in December 2004 that a "Shi'a crescent" was developing from Iran through Iraq and into the oil-rich Gulf states and that this was a disaster for the region. King Abdullah II soon distanced himself from this statement, but the fact that it was made by such a well-intentioned Sunni leader is indicative of the depth to which the ancient fears and prejudices on the part of Sunni Arabs affect their attitudes toward and willingness to coexist with their fellow Shi'a Arabs.

An interesting conclusion in this connection can be drawn from opinion polling done in the region by the U.S. polling organization Zogby Associates in 2004. The poll asked respondents in several Arab countries a number of questions related to U.S. policies, actions, and motives in the region. One question was the following: "Do you agree with the following statement? Force was not at all justified in Iraq." The percentage agreeing with this statement was 81 percent in Jordan, 80 percent in Syria, 80 percent in the Palestinian territories, and 70 percent in Egypt. In Lebanon, the figure was 48 percent. That is, in Lebanon, an Arab country with a Shi'a plurality and a significant Christian minority, a majority of those polled actually saw the military intervention in Iraq to depose Saddam as having been justified, a fact that certainly gives Lebanon a unique status among the Arab states. In every other Arab population polled—all with Sunni majorities—support ranged from less than one-third to less than one-fifth.

The attitudes of Sunni Arab populations toward the emergence of Shi'a political hegemony in Iraq may be based as much on fear as it is on prejudice. This seems to be the impetus behind King Abdullah II's remark cited above, as well as a comment by Saudi Foreign Minister Saud Al-Faisal in September 2005. The foreign minister's remark, that he had heard of "the entry of people, money, and weapons as well as meddling in political life" from Iran, provoked a heated response from Iraq's then Interior Minister, Bayan Jabr, who, while speaking to journalists in Amman on October 2, commented that Iraq would not be lectured by "some Bedouin riding a camel." As with the statement made by King Abdullah II, the Saudi foreign minister was warning against possible Iranian hegemony in Iraq and the possibly disastrous impact of this development on the Gulf region, with its massive oil reserves.

This sentiment continues to color the thinking of Sunni Arab leaders, as reflected in an April 9, 2006, remark by Egyptian President Hosni Mubarak to Al-Arabiya TV: "Shiites are 65% of the Iraqis . . . Most of the Shiites are loyal to Iran, and not to the countries they are living in." Mubarak came under intense criticism from Iraqi leaders and subsequently "clarified" his comments by explaining that they "did not carry any insult or doubt of the loyalty of Iraqi Shiites to their country, Iraq." And a remark cited by *New York Times* columnist Tom Friedman in a September 8, 2006, op-ed column entitled "The Central Truth" that "[E]arly in the Iraq war a prominent Sunni Arab leader said to me privately, 'Thomas, these Shiites, they are not real Muslims'" also reflects an historical animus of Sunni Muslims toward the Shi'a sect.[4]

Such attitudes toward the removal of the despotic Saddam regime and the ascendancy of Iraq's Shi'a may parallel a phenomenon I observed in West Germany in the 1980s. The German case involved the deployment of intermediate-range ballistic missiles in Europe (mostly in West Germany) to counter similar missiles that the Soviet Union had installed on the soil of several of its Eastern European allies. To U.S. policymakers and defense planners, the logic of responding to the Soviet provocation by countering with the deployment of similar missiles in the West was unimpeachable, but many Germans opposed the deployment. Logic aside, they saw such action as simply too dangerous, since any miscalculation would play out as a possible nuclear exchange on German soil. If one applies this thinking to the current situation with Iraq vis-à-vis the rest of the (Sunni) Arab world, an adverse Sunni reaction to the emergence of Shi'a political hegemony in Iraq can justifiably be seen to embody an element of fear at the possible adverse and unintended consequences for the region of the Persian Gulf, the Arabian Peninsula, and possibly beyond should this lead to regional Iranian hegemony or instability in areas with significant Shi'a populations in the region.

Developments vis-à-vis Saudi Arabia's Shi'a minority provide perhaps the best insight into the process that the Shi'a-Sunni divide may still need to undertake in Iraq. As recently as the 1950s, the Shi'a sect of Islam was not even recognized as "Islamic" in Saudi Arabia. Discrimination against the Shi'a community was pervasive. In my own personal experience, I observed some aspects of this phenomenon when I spent two years in the late 1970s teaching at King Faisal University in the Eastern Province capital of Dammam, the area of the kingdom in which almost all of Saudi Arabia's Shi'a population lives. Through conversations with students and graduate assistants at the university, as well as interaction with friends at the Arabian-American Oil Company (ARAMCO),[5] I learned of the circumstances affecting Saudi Arabia's Shi'a community. This experience and insight would be repeated when I returned to Saudi Arabia's Eastern Province to serve for three years at the American Consulate General in Dhahran from 1985 through 1988. Such close and prolonged interaction with Arab Shi'a is an unusual experience for a U.S. diplomat; most diplomats who serve in Arab countries spend most or all of their careers in communities with overwhelmingly Sunni populations and almost exclusively Sunni elites. In *The Assassin's Gate*, George Packer cites Iraqi exile Kanan Makiya as imputing a bias among State Department Arabists in favor of Sunni Arabs at the expense of the Shi'a:

> In his view," Packer writes, "the department's officials, and especially the Arabists at the Bureau of Near Eastern Affairs, were bulwarks of the Middle Eastern status quo—the kind of bureaucrats who had always favored leaving Saddam in charge of Iraq for the sake of "stability." They were compromised by their accommodation with the Sunni Arab dictators of the Middle East, Makiya thought, and disbelievers in the possibility of Arab democracy.[6]

This claim certainly does not reflect my experience and outlook in dealing with the Arab world.

During my tour of duty in Saudi Arabia in the mid-1980s, I had the opportunity to serve under a career Foreign Service Officer who is considered to have been among the most accomplished Arabists ever to serve in the U.S. Foreign Service, the late Ambassador Hume Horan,[7] who held ambassadorships in five countries during his career—in Cameroon, Equatorial Guinea, Sudan, Saudi Arabia, and the Ivory Coast. Among my experiences during my time of service in Dhahran was an occasion to accompany Ambassador Horan and a group of Saudi military officers on a visit to the aircraft carrier *USS Enterprise* in the Arabian Sea, where we received the full "Top Gun" treatment; this was certainly one of the more memorable experiences in my Foreign Service career. After retiring from the Foreign Service in 1998, Ambassador Horan answered his country's call to duty one last time to join the CPA and contribute his unique skills and experience to our post-Saddam efforts in Iraq. In *State of Denial*, Bob Woodward cites an intriguing exchange between Ambassador Horan and CPA Spokesman Dan Senor while both were in Iraq serving with the CPA:

> Horan told Senor they were doing full-blown nation building now, and estimated that their chance of building a democracy in Iraq was only about 30 percent. "Those are the highest odds we have ever had or will ever have in trying to pull this off," Horan said, referring to the whole Middle East. But even at 30%, they were right to give it a try. "It's worth doing," he said.[8]

Such a perspective on the part of one of America's most experienced and knowledgeable State Department Arabists speaks volumes about the importance, and difficulty, of the political reform agenda in the Arab world.

Over time, and in conjunction with rising educational levels and economic prosperity, attitudes on the part of Saudi Arabia's Sunni majority toward its Shi'a minority have softened considerably, and today the kingdom's Sunni leadership and Shi'a community are engaged in a process of dialogue and conciliation. However, in many locations in the Arab world, the starting point for such reconciliation can perhaps be likened to racial relations in the United States in the first half of the last century, when prejudice and discrimination were widespread and deep. In parts of the Arab world, among significant elements of the Sunni community, attitudes among Sunnis toward Shi'a have not progressed much beyond this stage. Thus, the success of the current western political enterprise in Iraq will hinge to a great extent on whether the process of overcoming deep-seated prejudice by Sunnis toward Shi'a can be telescoped from what would normally be expected to take decades into a period of just a few years (or even less).

REGIONAL DEMOCRATIC REFORM

The implications of the prospect of the taking hold of a democratic and representative political order in Iraq have not been lost on the leaders of the other Arab countries, almost all of which are ruled by a monarch or an autocrat. A series of UN Development Programme reports has documented the economic and educational underachievement of the Middle East region in recent decades and has cautiously called for reform in these areas, with the clear implication that such reform will also require the opening of greater political space for change in the countries of the region. Against this backdrop, the writing on the wall in which an Iraq that successfully transitions to a country with a politically representative and accountable government, the transparent and equitable rule of law, and a free-market economic system comes to dominate the region politically and economically is clear for all to see. Iraq's potential is unlimited; recognition of that fact is certainly one element driving the efforts of Iraq's external enemies to attempt to derail its transition.

There is an old adage in the region that says that books are written in Cairo, published in Beirut, and read in Baghdad. The value that Iraqis place on books was, to me, one of the most evident characteristics of the Iraqi people while I was in the country. During that year, we distributed tens of thousands of Arabic-language books to universities, schools, libraries, and other institutions around the country. This book distribution program was particularly highly valued by our colleagues in the regional embassy offices, as well as by the civil affairs officers among our military colleagues. We also opened more than a dozen "American Corners"—U.S.-themed reading rooms set up in already existing institutions that contain hundreds of books as well as video materials and computer equipment—all around the country, from Basra in the south to Dohuk in the north. In visiting several of these American Corners, I found the hosts—usually a university president or municipal library director—to be effusive in both their enthusiasm for the fact that this educational resource was now available at their institution and gratitude for our generosity in providing it.

The reputation of Iraqis as valuing education and having a pragmatic and productive work ethic underlies a subtle dynamic that appears to permeate attitudes and expectations toward Iraq in the region. The leaders, elites, and peoples in Iraq's neighborhood are well aware that an Iraq unleashed would very likely take off and come to dominate the region economically and serve as a lodestar politically. Iraq has the ingredients: an educated and historically industrious and entrepreneurial population, abundant water resources and arable land, and the second largest proven oil reserves in the world. If this combination of factors were to be combined with a stable, free, and accountable political order and a just society based on the rule of law, Iraq's rush to modernism would likely leave the rest of the Arab world in its wake.

To the leadership and entrenched elite of Iraq's neighboring autocracies, this sparks fear, as what would then be the "Iraq model" would represent a threat to their hold on power and their continuing influence. To the neighboring populations, the recognition of Iraq's potential breeds envy. In both cases, it triggers opposition to the transition of Iraq to a stable and successful country. In June 2005, shortly after the first freely elected government in the history of Iraq was installed in office, we worked with colleagues in the region to encourage officials in neighboring countries to make public statements in support of the new Iraqi government. Unfortunately, our efforts—and those of the new Iraqi government itself to elicit such overt support in the region—had little success.

One telling indication of this attitude on the part of Iraq's neighbors is their unwillingness to cancel any of the massive debt that Iraq accumulated under Saddam Hussein, debt that was largely incurred during Iraq's war with Iran when there was a not-too-subtle understanding in the region that Iraq's war against its Persian, largely Shi'a foe was also being fought on behalf of the Sunni Arab states. Despite windfall oil revenues in recent years, Iraq's Gulf Arab neighbors, which hold upwards of $65 billion in Iraqi debt, have to date refused to forgive any of that debt. In contrast, the Paris Club group of industrialized creditor nations, which hold some $40 billion in Iraqi debt, have agreed to forgive up to 80 percent of that debt. On November 22, 2004, in connection with the Paris Club's announcement of its debt forgiveness plan, the office of then-Prime Minister Ayad Allawi released a telling statement saying: "The prime minister looks forward to Iraq's Arab brothers forgiving their debts from Iraq in the very near future, to contribute both to Iraq's and their own security and development." No such debt cancellation from Iraq's Arab neighbors has yet been forthcoming.

One ironic and unforeseen outcome of the coalition-led effort to remove Saddam Hussein from power in Iraq and foster the emergence of Iraq as a model democratic Arab state and as such a possible spark for broader political reform in the region is the fact that this action caused world oil prices to jump from around $20 per barrel at the time of the Iraq War to upwards of $75 per barrel in summer 2006. The massive windfall that this revenue spike provided to the oil-rich Arab states has undermined the urgency for them to undertake the political and economic reforms for which many of their citizens had been agitating. One key impetus behind such calls for reform was the steadily declining per capita income in the Arab oil-exporting countries in recent decades. In Saudi Arabia, for example, stagnant world oil prices over the two decades before the Iraq War, coupled with an extremely high rate of population growth, cut the country's per capita income from around $25,000 at its high point in 1980 to around $7,000 in 1999. The decline in inflation-adjusted per capita income in the kingdom may well have been the steepest in any country in history. According to the U.S. Department of Energy, in 2004 Saudi Arabia's per capita export revenues, in inflation-adjusted terms, were only 13 percent of their 1980 figure.[9]

By the end of the 1990s, the revenue crunch that Arab oil exporters faced induced them to seek other economic paths to satisfy the employment and economic aspirations of their growing populations. This led to the prospect of increased accountability and political participation in these countries. Under recent world oil market conditions, however, this impetus to reform has declined drastically. In the case of Saudi Arabia, for example, oil export revenues increased 49 percent in 2005 over 2004, exceeding $150 billion. The oil-exporting regimes in the region now have the means to provide government services (such as education and health care), employment opportunities, and income streams to their citizens using their oil profits sufficient to counter popular sentiment toward economic (and political) reform. As *The Economist*, in an article in its July 1, 2006, edition under the headline "Democracy in the Arab world" put it: "Several factors explain the waning reform momentum. One is the high price of oil. Exporters, from Algeria and Libya to the monarchies of the Persian Gulf, find themselves so flush with cash that they can again buy off dissent." This development has thus undercut one of the key strategic goals of U.S. policy in deposing Saddam Hussein in Iraq.

IRAN

Much has been written about Iranian actions, and motives, concerning Iraq since the removal of the Saddam regime. Shi'a-dominated Iran—while Persian, not Arab—has close ties to the Shi'a community in southern Iraq, many of whose leaders spent years in exile during the Saddam era in Iran. Available evidence indicates that, since the change of regime in Iraq in 2003, Iranian agents have been active in the south and southwestern parts of the country seeking to influence developments there and to support elements of the Shi'a Islamist community. The U.S. government's perception concerning Iranian involvement in Iraq is reflected in comments made during an appearance in Washington in July 2006 by U.S. Ambassador to Iraq Zalmay Khalilzad: "Iran has played a role in providing extremist groups with arms, training and money." He went on to suggest that "Iran must decide if it is opposed to a stable, strong and democratic Iraq."[10]

Iran and Iraq have been regional rivals for many years, a rivalry most recently manifested in the bitter and destructive Iran-Iraq War from 1980 through 1988. While the period of open hostility between the two countries ended with the removal of the Saddam regime, there remain elements of tension between them. One important area of dispute between Iranian Shi'a leaders and the Shi'a leadership in Iraq is a fundamental difference in the political philosophy of the two groups: The dominant Shi'a leaders in Iraq—in particular the country's most influential cleric, Grand Ayatollah Ali al-Sistani—are of the "quietist" school of Shi'a clergy, which rejects clerical political rule; in Iran, by contrast, the Shi'a leadership advocates, and practices, having political rule in the hands of clerics. Thus, the emergence of a democratic Iraq under secular political leadership poses a threat to Iran's clerics in two respects: the freedom that such an Iraq would display right next door to a repressive Iran would be a potential source of destabilization for Iran, and a Shi'a-majority Iraq under successful secular democratic rule would provide an alternative political model that could undermine the Iranian theocracy. The Iranian leadership's apparent recognition of these potential challenges to its legitimacy and power seems to underlie its actions toward current developments in Iraq.

An additional complicating factor in Iran's relationship with Iraq involves the ongoing dispute between Iran and the international community regarding the possibility of Iran obtaining nuclear weapons technology. The U.S.-led effort to deny such technology to Iran has put the two countries on a collision course. In light of this fact, Iran's actions in Iraq have been interpreted by many as an effort to keep the U.S. military bogged down in that country's violence as a way to ensure that the United States does not attempt to use military means to resolve its dispute with Iran.

In his Washington appearance cited above, Ambassador Khalilzad shared a light-hearted anecdote that underscored just how complex—and unpredictable—U.S.-Iranian bilateral relations are. As Khalilzad said: "I used to meet with the Iranian ambassador . . . and I used to joke with him that 'you guys should be much more helpful to us, because look, you couldn't deal with the Taliban problem, you couldn't deal with the Saddam problem, and we've dealt with both.'" Alas, gratitude is not an operative factor in international relations.

TURKEY

Although non-Arab, as a Muslim-majority, democratic country, Turkey embodies a secular political order that could be a model for Iraq's evolving democracy. However, ethnic tensions involving two of Iraq's communities—the Kurds, and the Turkmen—color Turkey's relationship with the country and foster a certain wariness between the two.

The major source of tension is with Iraq's large Kurdish community, which is mostly located adjacent to Turkey's southern border and which, since the early 1990s, has maintained a largely autonomous governing enclave—the Kurdistan Regional Government. Ethnic Kurds inhabit large areas of four contiguous countries in the region—Iraq, Turkey, Iran, and Syria—but they have no state of their own. For several decades now a terrorist organization—the Kurdistan Workers Party, known by its Kurdish acronym PKK—has operated in the area, mostly in Turkey, seeking to force the creation of an independent Kurdish homeland. The governments in the four countries in which Kurdish communities are located are, of course, opposed to the creation of such a state, as it would necessarily be carved from their territory.

Of greatest concern to the Turkish government is the possibility that Iraqi Kurds might cross an understood "red line" and attempt to establish just such an independent homeland in northern Iraq. Turkey's concerns were not helped when, in conjunction with the January 2005 national election, almost 99 percent of Kurds living in the area governed by the Kurdistan Regional Government voted in a nonbinding referendum for such an independent Kurdistan. While this vote appears accurately to reflect the desires of Iraq's Kurdish population, Kurdish leaders—and, fundamentally, Iraqi Kurds themselves—accept that such a Kurdish state would not be politically viable, and its establishment is, in reality, not an option. Such a Kurdistan would be a landlocked enclave of a few million people surrounded on all sides by hostile neighbors. While an independent Kurdistan in northern Iraq could in principle be economically sustainable, based on the oil resources in the Kirkuk region (assuming that Kirkuk would be part of an independent Kurdistan; it is not currently part of the Kurdistan Regional Government), the hostility toward such a state on the part of all of its neighbors would almost certainly ensure that this oil could never be brought to market.

The other group in Iraq in which Turkey has a stake is the Turkmen community. This small group—estimated at under 2 percent of Iraq's population—is ethnically Turk and has historically comprised a major segment of the population in many towns and villages in the far northern part of the country. Turkmen make the claim, on the basis of Iraq's 1958 census, that their community at one time comprised a plurality of the population of the oil-rich city of Kirkuk. Given its ethnic and linguistic kinship with the Iraqi Turkmen, Turkey is concerned about the treatment and representation that Iraq's new political structure will afford to the several very small ethnic and religious minorities in the country. These include not only the Turkmen but such groups as the Chaldeans, Yazidis, Assyrians, and others, all of whom together comprise less than 5 percent of Iraq's population.

11
American Competence and Commitment

The U.S. experience in Iraq has raised concerns about U.S. institutional *competence* to undertake such an ambitious effort as we have in Iraq and about the factors involved in the U.S. *commitment* to sustain such a difficult undertaking long enough for it to have a chance to succeed. I examine these two issues in this final chapter.

COMPETENCE

America's experience in Iraq has broken new ground in the capabilities and institutional competencies needed to translate what was a fairly quick and efficient military victory into the geopolitical outcome that the war was meant to achieve. The removal of Saddam Hussein's regime from power in Iraq was intended to lead to a unified, cohesive country with a government chosen by and representative of the Iraqi people. Before the return of governing authority to Iraqi leaders by the Coalition Provisional Authority, UN Security Council Resolution #1546, passed on June 8, 2004, codified the international community's concept for the newly liberated country as "a federal, democratic, pluralist, and unified Iraq." As discussed above, a broad array of those opposed to such an Iraq has been endeavoring since the early days of the post-Saddam era to foil just such an outcome.

Moreover, as mentioned in the previous chapter, since Saddam's removal from power it has become clear that decades of oppressive dictatorial rule have left a legacy of devastation not only on Iraq's economy and infrastructure, but—more significantly—on the psychological state of the Iraqi people as well. In early 2005, retired General Gary E. Luck came to Iraq to conduct a wholesale review of coalition efforts in the country. In his report to Joint Chiefs of Staff Chairman Richard Myers, Luck stated: "[w]e have underestimated the effect Saddam Hussein and his regime had on the spirit of his people."[1] Luck continued: "Nobody got any credit for showing any initiative under Saddam Hussein. Now we're asking them to show all this initiative and they don't know how to do it."[2]

A telling anecdote is recounted by U.S. Air Force Colonel (ret.) Kim Olson, who served as executive officer to General. (ret.) Jay Garner, the U.S. first civilian administrator in post-Saddam Iraq. In an October 2006 talk at Georgetown University, Olson described touring a Baghdad hospital with General Garner shortly after their arrival in the country in May 2003:

> Conditions in the facility were abysmal, and the area outside the hospital was strewn with trash and the debris from an artillery shell which had hit the building during the recent fighting. Seeing this scene of destruction and neglect, Gen. Garner asked the hospital administrator why no one from the hospital had made any attempt to at least minimally clean up the hospital grounds. The administrator leaned close so as not to be overheard, and said softly: 'Because no one has told us to.'"

As these reports indicate, recovery by the Iraq people from the psychological devastation of the Saddam regime is an important aspect of the current struggle in Iraq.

The U.S.-led coalition has been faced with the task of addressing this situation, and, as several observers have documented, the capabilities and resources to master this challenge were often not up to the task. Several factors have contributed:

- The confusion and unrest immediately following the fall of the Saddam regime led most of Iraq's civil servants to abandon their positions. The essential disappearance of a visible police force further undermined an already tenuous public order, resulting in a status quo in Iraq a few weeks after the war that was much worse than anyone had anticipated, a situation from which the country is still trying to recover.

- As noted earlier, neither of the two U.S. governmental institutions—the Department of Defense nor the Department of State—had a standing bureaucratic structure with the experience and expertise to deal with the postwar situation in Iraq.

Thus, this capability had to be established in the midst of addressing the problem itself.

- As also discussed previously, factors of institutional culture (and perhaps rivalry) in these two institutions contributed to friction between them, or even worse.

- The "politicization" of the Iraq War contributed to an atmosphere in which many saw participation in the postwar effort as condoning the war itself. Thus, in the days of the Coalition Provisional Authority, many who volunteered to go to Iraq and serve had previous political associations with conservative institutions. Some claim that CPA staff members were selected for having political views supportive of the administration's Iraq policy; others counter that those brought on board were the only ones who stepped forward. Regardless of how it came about, to the degree that the staffing of the CPA was done from a restricted pool of the potential talent available this negatively affected the critical starting phase of the U.S. effort to help with the transition of post-Saddam Iraq.

Within governmental institutions I sensed another bias that affected the postwar effort in Iraq. In my own experience, after I had been asked to lead the Public Diplomacy Office upon the reopening of the U.S. embassy in Baghdad in June 2004, I had a surprising conversation with a Foreign Service colleague who commented that neither "the money" nor the (assumed) "career enhancement" associated with such an assignment could entice this Foreign Service officer to volunteer for service in Iraq. This Iraq-assignments-for-the-values-challenged attitude was disappointing in that it dismissed the possibility that if one has the needed skills and experience that might make a difference, one might volunteer for service in Iraq out of a sense of patriotism or professional commitment, rather than for self-serving reasons.

THE ARMY YOU'VE GOT

From a perspective gained largely through my first-hand, daily interaction with members of all branches of the U.S. armed forces all around Iraq during the year I spent there, I view today's U.S. military as a unique and highly admirable institution, one of the most selfless and altruistic organizations that exists anywhere. This hugely diverse institution molds the men and women in uniform into a disciplined, well-trained, dedicated force committed to self-sacrifice—even to the point of sacrificing one's life—for the greater good of the American people and the world community.

While our military capabilities proved themselves more than equal to the task of quickly and efficiently defeating the Iraqi military and liberating the country from Saddam's grip, where we were not adequately prepared was in dealing with the aftermath of Iraq's liberation. As various sections of this work have outlined, the conditions and challenges that the coalition faced in postliberation Iraq would have been daunting even for an experienced and talented corps of professionals operating within an institutional framework with a proven track record. However, neither such an institutional framework nor such a professional corps existed at the time of Iraq's liberation, and this clearly made our efforts in Iraq immensely more difficult.

My own arrival in Iraq, in June 2004, came during the final days of the Coalition Provisional Authority. From the perspective of that time frame, my perception is that those who answered the call of duty in the postliberation period—while well intentioned—did not represent the breadth of talent and experience that one would like to have had in dealing with these challenges. To be clear at the outset: I have nothing but the greatest admiration for those who accepted the considerable personal risk and physical hardship and answered the call to service on behalf of their country in the immediate postliberation period. Nonetheless, the fact is that this corps consisted of all volunteers who had to be enticed to accept this dangerous and difficult duty; accordingly, the eclectic group that was assembled consisted of individuals with diverse backgrounds, motivations, and capabilities. In many cases, moreover, what skills they had had never previously been applied abroad; many, possibly most, CPA staff members got their first passport in order to travel to Iraq and serve in the CPA.[3]

This state of affairs clearly did not serve the interests of the United States, or the Iraqi people, well. As a "lessons learned" report by the Special Inspector General for Iraq Reconstruction (SIGIR) issued in January 2006 noted, "[t]here were personnel in CPA without appropriate skills for the position to which they were assigned," and these personnel "could not, in some cases, overcome shortfalls in skills or experience."[4]

A U.S. Institute of Peace report that SIGIR cited has noted: "[t]here is simply no capacity in U.S. civilian government agencies to mobilize large numbers of the right people quickly. . . . [T]he CPA was the ultimate authority in the land and charged with rebuilding the country, but it was composed of a pickup team, and it underwent enormous turnover."[5] In *The Assassin's Gate*, George Packer cites a senior administration official as saying: "We sent an inexperienced, youthful, full-of-zest, full-of-courage team to do what seasoned professionals would have found extremely challenging, if not impossible."[6]

The contract volunteers who signed up to work with CPA were supplemented by career professionals from various governmental agencies, most prominently the State Department. However, as the above-mentioned SIGIR report also noted: "Relatively few agencies responded effectively to the call for volunteer detailees for CPA."[7]

The approach within the State Department to staffing Iraq provides a microcosm of the jury-rigged approach that was the U.S. government's effort to supply the skills and staffing for the needs of the postwar effort in that country. As the cohort of volunteers that I was among heard in predeparture briefings, Iraq represented a completely new approach for the department: heretofore, it had been State Department policy to draw down staff and, ultimately, to close overseas facilities in the face of rising threat environments. With Iraq, this approach was turned upside down. As the security climate in Iraq deteriorated, State staffing in the country increased.

Dealing with this new reality, however, has proven to be a major challenge for the State personnel system. The department has maintained a policy of staffing its Iraq positions only through volunteers; to date there have been no directed assignments. However, as circumstances on the ground have developed in unpredictable and unexpected ways, State's approach to filling its Iraq positions has gone through several iterations, raising issues of consistency and equity and sparking considerable discussion, and some discord, within the ranks of the Foreign Service.

The ups-and-downs of the incentive package for Iraq service, for example, have raised concerns. Even from the time of the CPA cohort of State staff in Iraq, there was an implied—and, more recently, a more overt—promise that Iraq service would be positively rewarded within both the assignment and promotion processes. This has not been well received by many in the Foreign Service, who view this as undermining the integrity of these systems, especially in the area of promotions. Indeed, the potential exists for a breakdown within the career Foreign Service between a "we"—who have served in the war zone of Iraq (or Afghanistan)—and a "they"—who have not—especially if efforts to fill Foreign Service positions in these two countries continue to become more difficult. Much of this discussion is summarized in the March 2006 issue of the *Foreign Service Journal*, which is largely devoted to the issue of service in Iraq. More broadly, the State Department—and the U.S. Foreign Service—are struggling mightily with the new reality that, worldwide, there are currently more than seven hundred one-year, unaccompanied (that is, no family members allowed) danger and hardship Foreign Service positions to be filled every year.

The institutional shortcoming within the U.S. government that our postconflict experience in Iraq exposed has been a difficult and costly lesson learned, both for Americans and Iraqis. One positive outcome, however, has been a recognition of this deficiency, accompanied by an effort to address it. As noted by the Special Inspector General for Iraq Reconstruction: "The CPA experience demonstrated the U.S. government's critical need for a reserve civilian corps of talented professionals, with the proper expertise, willing to work in a hostile environment during post-conflict stabilization and reconstruction periods." Noting deficiencies with the "pickup" team approach to postconflict Iraq, the SIGIR also stated: "The Iraq experience has shown the critical need for in-depth understanding among relief and reconstruction specialists of the cultural, political, and socioeconomic underpinnings of the post-conflict country or region," while noting that this need has been addressed by new National Security Presidential Directive 44, which assigns to the State Department responsibility "to coordinate all overseas reconstruction and stabilization activities."[8]

TRANSFORMATIONAL DIPLOMACY

On January 18, 2006, Secretary of State Condoleezza Rice unveiled a new approach to U.S. diplomatic efforts abroad in a speech at Georgetown University, an approach designed to reflect the new world in which we are living. The secretary designated this new approach "Transformational Diplomacy," whose objective she summarized as "to work with our many partners around the world, to build and sustain democratic, well-governed states that will respond to the needs of their people and conduct themselves responsibly in the international system." In line with this new approach, the secretary announced that the United States would change its diplomatic posture, reducing U.S. diplomatic positions in countries such as Germany and increasing such positions in key emerging nations such as China and India.

Secretary Rice went on to say that "to advance in their careers, our Foreign Service Officers must now serve in what we call hardship posts." She and her senior advisors have since worked with the career Foreign Service and its professional organization—the American Foreign Service Association (AFSA), which also serves as the collective bargaining unit for the Foreign Service—to implement the changes needed in personnel policies, administration, training, and other areas in order to implement her transformational diplomacy agenda. As the challenge of filling diplomatic positions in Iraq and Afghanistan has done, transformational diplomacy will change the Foreign Service. In a July 2006 meeting with AFSA representatives to chart progress on the transformational diplomacy initiative, Secretary Rice further outlined her vision of the Foreign Service as a professional corps that she sees as becoming more "expeditionary." As AFSA summarized her views for its members, transformational diplomacy will

> requir[e] employees to deploy more frequently in areas of crisis and conflict, sometimes on short notice. This, she said, will require sacrifice and a broad acceptance that the Foreign Service career may involve a greater proportion of difficult, dangerous, and unaccompanied postings in the future. We must start recruiting differently, she said, and new entrants into the Foreign Service will need to have different expectations.[9]

Although the concept of transformational diplomacy is just beginning to be developed and implemented, it is already clear that it will mean considerable change for America's career diplomats and will also spark varied responses abroad. One telling commentary appeared in Egypt's major national newspaper *Al-Ahram*, shortly after the secretary delivered her transformational diplomacy speech.

Egypt is, of course, a country in which the United States is encouraging political reform and steps toward more accountable governance, that is, a country that is likely to experience the impact and effects of U.S. transformational diplomacy. In *Al-Ahram's* view, however—a view that is likely dominant among Egypt's elite—transformational diplomacy is not considered a welcome development but instead represents what the *Al-Ahram* commentator dubbed "invasive" diplomacy.[10]

As this Egyptian comment suggests, the concept of transformational diplomacy raises the issue of U.S.—and, generally, "outside"— support for internal reform in other countries. Middle East scholar Michael Rubin, in answering the question "How should the U.S. aid dissidents?," provides an interesting take on this issue:

> The involvement of embassies—as is the case both with the Middle East Partnership Initiative and the Foundation for the Future funds[11]—often leads to conflicts of interest, as the diplomats' desire for stability trumps their willingness to support effective reform."[12]

The challenge to policymakers is in finding the proper balance between these two interests. As argued earlier in this work, the primacy in U.S. policy of stability over reform in the Arab world from the end of the Cold War until September 11, 2001, contributed to the root causes behind the terrorist attacks of that day. The removal of Saddam Hussein from power in Iraq in spring 2003 presented an opening for a new approach to the region, one which offered the possibility of a positive political change. Whether Saddam's removal will prove to have been a wise course of action will largely hinge on its impact on future political developments in the region, something that only history will be able to judge.

IN IRAQ, THE ENLIGHTENMENT MEETS RAMBO

To sit in the DFAC (dining facility) in the Republican Palace in Baghdad and to observe and engage the eclectic band of internationalists and adventurers who would be gathered there at any one time gave one a sense of glimpsing the future of the international order, an international scene in which the "end of history" scenario plays out through the application of transformational diplomacy by the United States and like-minded democratic nations. Perhaps this perception betrays an unrealistic optimism, but one could not avoid the feeling in Baghdad that the mixture of career military and military reservists, diplomats, contractors, security personnel, international civil servants, and sundry soldiers of fortune had found their way to that place and, together, created a critical mass of self-reinforcing—and self-reassuring—professionals committed to the challenging task that is the transformation of Iraq.

The quest is ambitious, meaningful, and controversial, and its outcome is as yet uncertain. But it did bring out the best in those who were participating. In a circumstance in which an in-coming mortar or rocket could land at any moment, petty annoyances, discomforts, and inconveniences received little airing. Beyond that, there was an aura of commitment, bravado, pride, confidence, selflessness, and simple humanity that—when perceived—conveyed an uplifting and motivating sense that, for all its foibles and shortcomings, at its core the effort by the international community to help Iraq transition to a brighter future was in the hands of a group of individuals who were pleased and excited to be part of something much larger than themselves.

(DIS-)CONNECTION

Another drawback in the Iraq effort has resulted from the circumstances of undertaking an enterprise such as the current coalition effort in Iraq from the platform of a wealthy, dominant country such as the United States. The fact is, there is no real need for the U.S. public on the whole to play the part of the "home front" in this effort and make tangible, daily sacrifices in support of Iraq policy. The average citizen can go about his or her daily routine and leave the "cost" to that small minority of Americans who themselves or whose loved ones are bearing the risks and making the sacrifices on behalf of all Americans for success in Iraq. One of the senior military leaders whom I encountered in Iraq, Major General John Batiste, now retired, made the telling comment that, upon returning from service in Iraq, he was "shocked" to find that "the country was not mobilized for war" and caustically suggested that "the only time [Americans] think about the war is when they decide what color magnet ribbon to put on the back of their car."[13]

The issue of sacrifice in a circumstance such as exists with our efforts in Iraq raises the important factor of determining the proper level of involvement and contribution to be expected of the American people in such an undertaking. In the early stages of the Iraq conflict, rather than being challenged to accept some hardship, Americans were encouraged to maintain robust economic activity as their contribution to the Iraq War. Practically speaking, since at the time the U.S. economy was just emerging from a recession, this was probably the most valuable contribution that the U.S. general public could actually make to the war effort. Economic growth would generate jobs and increase tax revenues to help pay the costs of the war. Thus, from a purely analytical perspective, an admonition to, essentially, "go shopping" as a contribution to the Iraq War effort made perfect sense.

However, from the perspective of public solidarity with those on the front lines, the Iraq experience has revealed the downside of having the U.S. public largely disassociated from such a crucial and difficult undertaking. In any war-fighting enterprise, there needs to be a recognition of the role of a psychological dimension to such a national undertaking, a dimension which would serve to connect the public at large with the important effort at hand. Perhaps some type of national service, or a program to reduce oil imports, or a multifaceted endeavor to assist families of deployed military personnel or combatants who return with disabilities, i.e., some broadbased national initiative coupled with the effort in Iraq (and Afghanistan) would provide a valuable link with average Americans to these challenging and costly undertakings and give them a sense of a shared sacrifice with those who are bearing the brunt of the fight.

The "economics" of the Iraq War itself contains a lesson about a new challenge to the United States in waging war in the current era. Just as the new information environment and the unprecedented (during wartime) fact of our having an all-volunteer military have presented new challenges to fighting our current wars, the level of affluence that the United States enjoys as it fights the wars in Iraq and in Afghanistan means that paying the costs of these wars requires only a small fraction of the nation's wealth. Even with the expenditures associated with the current military operations in Iraq and Afghanistan, coupled with the regular Pentagon budget, the United States is currently devoting just over 4 percent of its gross domestic product to defense expenditures.[14] At that level, such military activity can be conducted without requiring real sacrifice on the part of the

U.S. public. While in most respects this represents a very positive element concerning our nation's defense posture, it has negative repercussions in the area of maintaining connection and commitment on the part of the broader U.S. public to such military efforts.

Another disconnect that colors current perspectives and attitudes toward Iraq is that between the relatively small number of Americans who have seen duty in Iraq since the fall of the Saddam regime and the broader U.S. public. As discouraging as everyday life in Iraq can be, and as devastating as is the landscape of the country that one sees in daily life there, during my year in Iraq there was certainly an intangible sense of positive change, of hope among Iraqis that they now have an opportunity for a truly revolutionary turn in their all-too-tragic recent history. Certainly Iraqis are unhappy about shortages in essential services, about unemployment, and about violence and lack of security. A telling case in point involves a telegram from June 2006 sent from my former office in embassy Baghdad to the State Department that detailed concerns of the Iraqi staff of the office with the circumstances of their everyday lives in Baghdad (the message became very public when it found its way into the *Washington Post*[15]). The key issues raised in the telegram included the following:

- "A Shiite [woman] who favors Western clothing was advised by an unknown woman in her upscale Shiite / Christian neighborhood to wear a veil and not to drive her own car."

- "An Arab newspaper editor told us he is preparing an extensive survey of ethnic cleansing, which he said is taking place in almost every Iraqi province, as political parties and their militias are seemingly engaged in tit-for-tat reprisals all over Iraq."

- "Employees all confirm that by the last week of May they were getting one hour of power for every six hours without. . . . All Employees supplement city power with service contracted with neighborhood generator hookups."

- "Of nine employees in March, only four had family members who knew they worked at the embassy. . . . We have begun shredding documents printed out that show local staff surnames."

- "One Shiite employee told us in late May that she can no longer watch TV news with her mother, who is Sunni, because her mother blamed all government failings on the fact that Shiites are in charge."

- "Staff members say they assess daily how to move safely in public. Often, if they must travel outside their own neighborhoods they adopt the clothing, language, and traits of the area. . . . Since Samarra, Baghdadis have honed these survival skills."

The concern, fear, and discouragement reflected in this message are real and well founded. Baghdad, and Iraq, are in the throes of a violent struggle between the bulk of the Iraqi people who support a free and tolerant society and those on the margins of Iraqi society—and many elsewhere in the region—whose agendas are threatened by such an outcome for the country. To this has now been added the tragic element of Sunni-Shi'a tit-for-tat sectarian violence.

However, through it all, the Iraqis I came to know generally seemed to sense an empowerment through which, over time, they will now actually be allowed to apply their considerable talent and energy to creating a country and society in which the future is a far better place than the past. They are certainly not blind to the suffering and sacrifice that will still be their lot for some time to come, nor do they underestimate the effort that will be needed to achieve this revolutionary change. Nonetheless, they do see the prospect of creating a country in which their children will live much better lives than could ever have been expected without the international intervention that removed Saddam and his henchmen from power. The perception of this hope and optimism in encountering average Iraqis day in and day out certainly contributes to the well-documented high morale and strong sense of purpose among U.S. forces in Iraq. It is also this intangible perception which, I believe, separates those who have experienced it through intense involvement inside postwar Iraq from those who have not.

For those in my shoes, the operative frame of reference is the courage and determination of the heroic Iraqi people—suffering tragically as they are—to use the opportunity that they have been given to create a better country and a better society. "You can't understand unless you were there," a line that the *Washington Post* used to headline an article containing the reflections of returned military service personnel from Iraq, embodies a great deal of truth.[16]

COMMITMENT

When analyzing our current effort in Iraq from the perspective of internal dynamics within U.S. society, one must look at the commitment factor, broadly speaking, for such a difficult and costly undertaking. For those who argue for continued U.S. effort in Iraq, the justification for such effort is, presently at least, largely analytical: whether it is President Bush's assertion that we are fighting the terrorists in Iraq so that we do not have to fight them at home, or an assessment such as that by Senator Joseph Lieberman, who cites an ongoing war between "extremists and terrorists," on the one hand, and "moderates and democrats," on the other, and concludes that

> Iraq is the most deadly battlefield on which that conflict is being fought. How we end the struggle there will affect not only the region but the worldwide war against the extremists who attacked us on September 11, 2001.[17]

As such, and even though the analysis that led to the war includes real and horrific events such as the attacks of 9/11, this essentially theoretical justification for continued effort in Iraq is susceptible to dispute and skepticism. As the costs of the undertaking rise, in terms of both blood and treasure, the voices of dissent, not unexpectedly, become ever louder.

Ever since the U.S. experience in the Vietnam War—the first televised war—the challenge of maintaining public support for military action over a sustained period of time in view of the gruesome reporting and images that televised war entails has become recognized as an essential element in its own right in any decision to employ military force. In his analysis of what happened in the Vietnam War, former secretary of State (and former chairman of the Joint Chiefs of Staff) Colin Powell cites the closing window of public opinion toward that war as a key factor in our inability to prevail.[18] Powell's conclusion concerning the importance of maintaining public support for military action is not in itself new; however, his insight that this element in the use-of-force equation has become dominant, coupled with the fact of a new information and political environment that makes sustaining such support more challenging than ever, points to the importance of the U.S. "commitment factor" in the struggle in Iraq and the centrality of that factor in the thinking of our enemies.

This theme has been used frequently by al-Qaeda leaders and was also a part of Saddam Hussein's thinking and planning in connection both with the Gulf War in 1991 and the Iraq War in 2003. Moreover, this is not a secret or subtle element of our enemies' strategy against us. As noted in the discussion of democracy in chapter 4, they have been so convinced of our lack of will that they have openly and repeatedly taunted the United States on this issue as part of their strategy in confronting us. This is certainly one reason why our enemies in Iraq and elsewhere in the Middle East have been so steadfast in their efforts to raise America's stakes. Of course, as Saddam Hussein learned in 1991 and 2003, and the Taliban and Al-Qaeda in 2001, it can be very unwise to question American determination to deal forcefully with its adversaries. Senior officials spoke to this point in testimony before the House Armed Services Committee on February 7, 2007, when Defense Secretary Robert Gates and Chairman of the Joint Chiefs of Staff General Peter Pace put this issue into the proper American perspective. As Gates noted: "history is littered with examples of people who underestimated robust debate in Washington, DC for weakness on the part of America." For his part, Pace delivered the unequivocal and very forceful statement: "There is no doubt in my mind that the dialogue here in Washington strengthens democracy, period."[19] Nonetheless, to the extent that our adversaries—and our local allies—question that we as a nation are prepared to see through to completion the effort in Iraq as an aspect of the fundamental change that we seek to spark in the Arab world as the only true antidote to the root cause of international Islamist terrorism—the dysfunctional political and economic circumstances in that part of the world—this perception increases the difficulty of our accomplishing the mission.

YET ANOTHER PERFECT STORM

In the preceding treatment of the broad range of factors at play in America's current efforts in Iraq I have tried to draw, in some detail, on the experiences and circumstances—in the Middle East, in Europe, and in America—that, during the course of the past decade, have influenced my perceptions concerning how and why we have ended up where we are in today's international order, using the most pressing and problematic issue during this period—Iraq—as a prism for this analysis. At the risk of overusing the now well-worn metaphor of a "perfect storm," the foregoing analysis leads to the conclusion that a perfect storm is just what we have experienced during this period:

- With 9/11, a "theoretical" (if catastrophic) threat was revealed, subtle enough to allow those who wish to deny or ignore it room to equivocate in responding but of such potentially devastating impact that it led others—including President Bush and his administration—to decide to set out on a new and controversial course of action, including a pre-emptive security posture and the use of intelligence, law enforcement, and other government assets in new, and to many, troubling ways.

- At the time this new threat came to light, the United States occupied an historically unprecedented position of military, economic, and cultural primacy in the world, a circumstance that—independent of actual international circumstances and threats—bred resentment in some and anxiety in others and that led aggrieved parties around the world to direct their anger and frustration at this omnipotent America.

- The particular domestic circumstances in which the United States found itself just when the new threat and increased international ambivalence toward a dominant U.S. arose undermined the ability of the country effectively to address these new circumstances. A situation of one-party-rule and an accompanying atmosphere of political partisanship and acrimony largely ensured that, in the face of the other two elements of the "storm," domestic political factors in the United States would undermine the prospects for a unified national response to the newly recognized threat.

- These factors, coupled with an increasingly competitive and polarized 24/7 domestic and international media environment, helped feed unhelpful perceptions abroad concerning the United States and contributed to the intensity of the international rancor that the United States' response to the threat triggered.

THE APPROACHING END GAME

The autumn of 2006 saw, in essence, a de facto "good cop, bad cop" scenario unfold with respect to U.S. policy toward Iraq. This scenario conveyed to Iraqi leaders that while the United States and its coalition partners continued to be committed to providing support for the Iraqi government's efforts to reconcile its communities and defeat the domestic and foreign terrorists (the "good cop" of the Bush administration), now that viable political institutions are in place and Iraqi security forces are increasingly available to handle the country's internal security requirements, Iraqi government officials and the leaders of Iraq's communities need to make the hard decisions and compromises necessary to establish security in the country under Iraqi government authority or risk losing U.S. support (the "bad cop" of the Congress). In November 2006, I asked *Washington Post* journalist Anthony Shadid, who is one of the most astute American Iraq watchers and who had just been in Iraq, if the lack of progress on reconciliation in Iraq was due to the difficulty of finding the compromises that would allow such reconciliation to take place among parties genuinely committed to such an outcome, or rather was it due to a lack of true commitment to reconciliation by Iraq's leaders and the communities that they represent. Anthony candidly admitted that he could not answer that question.

This same uncertainty was revealed at about the same time in a document that the *New York Times* published on November 29, 2006. The document is the text of a memorandum attributed to National Security Advisor Stephen Hadley, prepared following a fact-finding mission that he had undertaken to Iraq earlier in the month. Referring to Iraqi Prime Minister Nouri al-Maliki, the memo is cited as stating that "his intentions seem good when he talks with Americans, and sensitive reporting suggests he is trying to stand up to the Shi'a hierarchy and force positive change. But the reality on the streets of Baghdad suggests Maliki is either ignorant of what is going on, misrepresenting his intentions, or that his capabilities are not yet sufficient to turn his good intentions into action."[20]

In early 2007, President Bush effectively decided to test the various theories spelled out in the Hadley memo by ordering 17,500 additional troops to Baghdad to help secure the city and extinguish the sectarian violence that took hold there in the second half of 2006. He also ordered four thousand additional troops to Al-Anbar Province to quell insurgent activity there and disrupt the insurgents' efforts to use that territory as a staging ground to rain terror on Baghdad's Shi'a communities. The rationale is that, if these efforts at improving the security climate in Baghdad succeed, this will provide Iraq's government with the conditions to make good on its promises of seeking reconciliation among Iraq's ethnic and sectarian communities, on disarming the sectarian militias, and on providing fair and equitable treatment of all Iraqis under a government and constitution committed to such a new Iraq.

Summary and Conclusions

The specific circumstances that led to the use of military force to remove Saddam Hussein from power in Iraq are very unlikely ever to be repeated. They include

- a superpower that was seeking to respond to the events of 9/11, the most devastating attacks on its soil in its history, attacks that were carried out by extremists spawned by circumstances to which a ruthless dictator who had murdered hundreds of thousands of his own citizens, used weapons of mass destruction, and invaded two of his neighbors was a primary contributor;

- a broad international consensus that the dictator continued to possess weapons of mass destruction, and this in a post-9/11 environment in which leaders now had to accept the possibility of extremists being willing to conduct terrorist activities on an apocalyptic scale;

- an international community that, through a lengthy series of UN Security Council resolutions, had established a basis under international law for taking military action against that dictator; and,

- a conviction by the superpower that it needed to spark political reform in the region that had produced its attackers and that removing the dictator and fostering a democratic government in his place would do just this.

As controversial as the policy of launching military action against Saddam Hussein has been, in a world of proliferating WMD technology, the possibility of a "nexus of terrorism and WMD" is likely to present even more challenging circumstances to national leaders and international bodies than those that were present in the case of Iraq, because future threats of this nature might not be coupled with behavior that sanctions international intervention, as was the case with Saddam Hussein in Iraq.

Today, in early 2007, the outcome of the U.S.-led effort to address fundamental U.S. and western security vulnerabilities by sowing the seeds of the Enlightenment in the Arab world through Iraq remains uncertain. It was understood that the post-Saddam political process in Iraq would be challenging, but the expectation was that with effective international involvement—as occurred in the Balkans and in Afghanistan—and enlightened self-interest on the part of Iraq's various communities, this process could be managed and would ultimately be able to be shepherded to success. It was also known that the restoration and reconstruction of Iraq's economy and infrastructure would be challenging, but the expectation was that with international support in terms of debt forgiveness and aid, and with revenues derived from the wealth contained in Iraq's considerable oil reserves, this too could be mastered.

What was not foreseen, however, was the impact of the fact that the effort was being undertaken along the Sunni-Shi'a fault line in the Arab world. This allowed elements of Iraq's Sunni community, with the support of the Sunni Arab world more broadly (including that world's own terrorist group, al-Qaeda), to employ large-scale and indiscriminate violence against Iraq's Shi'a community and, in effect, the newly emergent Shi'a political hegemony in Iraq, as a means of preventing those—Iraqis and non-Iraqis alike—who would be seeking to address the political and economic challenges in post-Saddam Iraq described above. Then, with the level of insecurity and violence that derived from this Sunni-led insurgency in place, others—notably Shi'a extremists (with support from Iran), and the thousands of criminals let loose by Saddam on Iraq's streets—would be able to use the prevailing atmosphere of violence and instability toward their own ends.

These unexpected developments required a change of strategy, necessitating an urgent effort to establish sufficient Iraqi security capabilities to quell the violence while at the same time continuing to encourage and cajole the Iraqi leadership and Iraq's various communities to make difficult compromises and find ground for reconciliation in order to move the country's political and economic evolution forward. As the leaders of Iraq's communities hesitated in scaling back maximalist positions on behalf of their constituents in the Iraqi political dialogue, space opened up for terrorists and extremists to drive deeper and deeper wedges between these communities, resulting in widespread ethnic and sectarian strife which is proving difficult to eradicate.

In the face of this sustained high level of violence, the high costs to the United States in terms of blood and treasure have undermined the U.S. public's will to give the nascent Iraqi political establishment and security forces time to establish security and achieve the communal reconciliation needed, or—alternatively, once sufficient Iraqi security capabilities have been developed—to demonstrate that, despite having the tools necessary to do so, they lack the will, or the ability (or both) to achieve these ends. It is this end game that is about to play out.

My own views on communicating where we are now on Iraq, and our approach to the Arab world in general, is to focus on the fundamental security issues at play, and lay out our playbook for all to see. Our message should be

- to remind the Arab world that we have not forgotten that it was nineteen Arabs who hijacked four jetliners in the United States and crashed them on September 11, 2001, killing some three thousand people, and that we see the political and economic conditions of the Arab world as major root causes behind these terrorists acts;

- to reiterate that we support freedom and democracy everywhere in the world, including in the Arab world, and will support those in that region who peacefully pursue these values in their societies;

- to announce that we will not use force to effect reform in the Middle East or elsewhere, in order to reveal for what it is the speciousness of the argument among some of the entrenched elite in the region that the threat of U.S. military intervention requires the suspension of reform efforts in their countries; and

- to put the regimes in the region on notice that we expect them to recognize the aspirations of their peoples for freedom and to fashion a process to reform their political systems by methods and at a pace that are appropriate to their circumstances but—importantly—that convince and assure their populations that such reform is coming.

My sense on this last point—freedom's arrival in the Middle East—is that it is not a matter of if, but of when and how, and that this fact is already recognized and accepted by the region's leaders and elites. It is out of this conviction that, in my view, an explicit U.S. statement renouncing force as a means to implant freedom in the region holds the promise of tipping the balance in favor of those who seek a gradual, controlled transition of their societies from authoritarianism to democracy.

My own experiences during the twelve months I spent in Iraq provoked an array of responses, from inspiration, to frustration, to a conviction that in many respects the course of future social and political evolution is on display today in that country. There will be many lessons learned from the experience in Iraq since March 2003. Nonetheless, while the individual circumstances involved in future instances of fundamental political transformation as is being tried in Iraq will certainly differ, in my view what we see today in that country—a conflict between a majority who support a restructuring of their society to incorporate such principles as accountable governance, tolerance, and freedom, and a minority who oppose such principles either out of vested interests, for personal gain, or based on perverted ideology—is, in broad outline, likely to be at the heart of the key challenges of the first half of the twenty-first century.

Notes

CHAPTER 1: IRAQ AND 9/11

1. *The 9/11 Commission Report*, 1st ed. (New York: W.W. Norton & Company), p. 66.
2. In this connection, the former head of the UN's Oil-for-Food program, Benon Savan, was indicted by a New York Federal Court in January 2007.
3. As one example of the cross-border ties involving Iraqis and their kin in neighboring states, Johns Hopkins Middle East scholar Fouad Ajami cites the following concerning Sheikh Ghazi al-Yawwar, who served as president in the Iraqi Interim Government: "Sheikh Ghazi hailed from the Shammar tribe, one of the great tribal federations comprising no fewer than five million people in Iraq, Syria, Saudi Arabia, Kuwait, and the United Arab Emirates." (Fouad Ajami, *The Foreigner's Gift: The Americans, the Arabs, and the Iraqis in Iraq* (New York: Free Press, 2006), p. 17).
4. The 9/11 Commission Report, p. 59.
5. Thomas Kuhn, *The Structure of Scientific Revolutions*, 2nd ed. (Chicago: University of Chicago Press, 1974).
6. Charter of the United Nations, chapter 1, article 2, section 4, at http://www.un.org/aboutun/charter/.
7. Prime Minister Tony Blair, speech given at Georgetown University, Washington, DC, May 26, 2006, available at http://www.number10.gov.uk/output/Page9549.asp.
8. U.S. government, The White House, *National Security Strategy of the United States*, introductory letter by President George W. Bush (Washington, DC: September 2002).
9. Ibid., p. 6.
10. Bob Woodward, *Plan of Attack* (New York: Simon & Schuster, 2004), p. 70.
11. Ibid, p. 71.
12. Woodward, *Plan of Attack*, p. 71.
13. Ajami, *The Foreigner's Gift*, p. 5.
14. Colin Powell, interview by Tony Snow, *Fox News Sunday*, Washington, DC, March 16, 2003.
15. Woodward, *Plan of Attack*, pp. 312–14.

16. President George W. Bush, "Iraq: Denial and Deception," address to the nation from the Cross Hall (Washington, DC: The White House, March 17, 2003).

CHAPTER 2: THE END OF THE COLD WAR AND THE EMERGENCE OF A UNIPOLAR WORLD

1. President George W. Bush, "Discussing Freedom in Iraq and the Middle East" (speech, Washington, DC: Chamber of Commerce, twentieth anniversary of the National Endowment for Democracy, November 6, 2003).
2. Although it applies in a different sphere, the argument parallels that expressed in the oft-cited phrase from Supreme Court Justice Robert H. Jackson in a 1949 dissenting opinion that "the Constitution is not a suicide pact," i.e., a government should not be expected to adhere to its principles so rigidly as to cause its own demise.
3. President Jimmy Carter, State of the Union Address (Washington, DC: The White House, January 23, 1980).
4. Josef Joffe, "Who's Afraid of Mr. Big?" *National Interest* 64 (summer 2001): pp. 43–52.
5. Thomas L. Friedman, "The Post-Post-Cold War," *New York Times*, May 10, 2006, p. A25.
6. Richard J. Schmierer, comments at Tufts University, Fletcher School of Law and Diplomacy (Medford, MA: May 20, 2006). The remarks in their entirety can be found at http://fletcher.tufts.edu/news/2006/05/schmiererspeech.shtml.
7. Prime Minister Tony Blair speech, at www.number10.gov.uk/output/Page9549.asp.

CHAPTER 3: THE ARAB WORLD AND THE INFORMATION REVOLUTION

1. Reuel Marc Gerecht, "Selling Out Moderate Islam," *Weekly Standard*, February 20, 2006.
2. In Baghdad, we received inquires from colleagues in Europe, Turkey, and around the Arab world concerning reports that U.S. forces had used "nuclear weapons" in retaking Fallujah from the insurgents, all arising from second-hand use of erroneous (and agenda-driven) reporting from Fallujah.
3. Pew Global Attitudes Project, cited in Stephen M. Walt, *Taming American Power* (W.W. Norton & Company, Inc., 2005), pp. 85–86.
4. John Mearsheimer and Stephen Walt, "The Israel Lobby," *London Review of Books*, vol. 28, no. 6 (March 23, 2006).
5. Ibid.

6. For example, see Michael Isikoff and David Corn, "Hubris: The Inside Story of Spin, Scandal, and the Selling of the Iraq War" (New York: Crown Publishers, 2006), pp. 115–16.

CHAPTER 4: DEMOCRACY AND ITS DISCONTENTS

1. *The 9/11 Commission Report*, p. 349.
2. Ibid., p. 349.
3. Ibid., *The 9/11 Commission Report*, p. 350.
4. Robert J. Samuelson, "Why We Ignore the Risks," *Washington Post*, September 7, 2005, p. A25.
5. CNN, September 8, 2002.
6. Ron Suskind, *The One Percent Doctrine* (New York: Simon & Schuster, 2006), p. 62.
7. James Madison, "Federalist Paper No. 10," in Charles Kesler and Clinton Rossiter, *The Federalist Papers* (New York: Signet Classics, 2003), pp. 71–79.
8. President Bush made reference to "dead or alive" on September 17, 2001, while addressing employees at the Pentagon, and again on December 14, 2001; he used the phrase "bring 'em on" on July 2, 2003.
9. International Crisis Group, "In their own Words: Reading the Iraqi Insurgency," *Middle East Report*, no. 50 (February 15, 2006): p. 14.
10. President Bush, speech on the war on terror and *Operation Iraqi Freedom* (Cleveland, Ohio, March 20, 2006).
11. David Brooks, "Multiple Reality Syndrome," *New York Times*, December 4, 2005.
12. Thomas L. Friedman, "Iraq: Politics or Policy," *New York Times*, October 3, 2004.
13. Packer, *The Assassin's Gate*, p. 114.
14. Jonathan Rauch, "Divide This Government: When one party rules, both parties fail," *National Journal* (November 6, 2006).
15. James A. Baker III, *Work Hard, Study, . . . and Keep Out of Politics!* (New York: G.P. Putnam's Son's Penguin Group, Inc., 2006), p. 301.
16. L. Paul Bremer III, *My Year in Iraq* (New York: Simon & Schuster, 2006), p. 59.
17. Thomas E. Ricks, *Fiasco: The American Military Adventure in Iraq* (New York: Penguin Press, 2006), p. 163.
18. Ibid., p. 145: The reluctance of military commanders to destroy weapons stockpiles was almost certainly influenced by the occurrence in March 1991 when U.S. military personnel were exposed to nerve agents during weapons demolitions at Khamisiyah, Iraq.
19. David Brooks, "From Freedom to Authority," *New York Times*, May 14, 2006.

20. Eric Shinseki, speaking at a Senate Armed Services Committee hearing, 108th Cong., 1st sess., February 25, 2003.
21. Andrew Bacevich, "Trigger Man," *American Conservative* (June 6, 2005).
22. Secretary of Defense Robert Gates' confirmation hearing before the Senate Armed Services Committee, 109th Cong., 2nd sess., December 5, 2006.
23. Paul Pillar, "Intelligence, Policy, and the War in Iraq," *Foreign Affairs* (March/April 2006).
24. "Richard Clarke Terrorizes the White House," *Salon.com*, March 24, 2004.
25. For example, Ricks, *Fiasco*, p. 103.
26. James Fallows, *Blind into Baghdad: America's War in Iraq* (New York: Vintage Books, 2006), p. 52.
27. Michael R. Gordon and Gen. (ret.) Bernard E. Trainor, *Cobra II: The Inside Story of the Invasion and Occupation of Iraq* (Pantheon Books, New York, NY, 2006), p. 159.
28. Thomas L. Friedman, "Dubai and Dunces," *New York Times*, March 15, 2006.
29. Accountability Review Boards came into existence in connection with the Inman Commission legislation in the 1980s. The Inman Commission was convened in the aftermath of the April 1983 bombing of the U.S. embassy annex in Beirut, which killed sixty-three occupants of the building, including seventeen Americans. For those of us working at American embassies at the time (I was serving in Bonn, Germany), the Beirut embassy bombing was a watershed event: From that day forward, embassies that had until that time been relatively open to the public implemented stringent screening and access procedures for all visitors and vehicles.
30. See: http://www.poweroftravel.org/media.aspx.
31. Both the Fulbright Program and the International Visitor Leadership Program have been operated under State Department auspices since the formerly independent U.S. Information Agency, which had run them, was incorporated into the State Department in 1999.
32. Prof. Ramadan's remarks can be found on the conference Web site at www.awsummit.org.
33. Scott Smallwood, "U.S. State Department Revokes Visa of Muslim Scholar Who Was to Teach at Notre Dame," *Chronicle of Higher Education* (August 25, 2005).
34. Jonathan S. Landay, "Biden Seeks Review of State Department Screening," *McClatchy Washington Bureau*, at http://www.realcities.com/mld/krwashington/14262890.htm. In response to this concern the State Department Office of the Inspector General (OIG) reviewed the program. The OIG issued an inspection report in September 2006 stating that it "examined whether there was a 'litmus test' for speaker selection in the U.S. Speaker Specialist Program" and "determined that no such test exists." Rather, it found that

"there was undue attention to the speaker selection process, resulting in Bureau of International Information Programs (IIP) staff self-censorship in the vetting and selection of speakers" ("Report of Inspection: U.S. Speaker and Specialist Program Review," Report Number ISP-C-06-52, U.S. Department of State, September 2006, p. 3).

35. The report is available at http://www.state.gov/documents/organization/24882.pdf.

36. James A. Baker III and Lee H. Hamilton, *The Iraq Study Group Report: the Way Forward—a New Approach* (New York: Vintage Books, 2006), p. xiii. The full report is also available at http://www.usip.org/isg/iraq_study_group_report/report/1206/index.html.

CHAPTER 5: IRAQ AND THE U.S. MILITARY

1. The CIA World Factbook, citing the most recent defense expenditures available, lists U.S. defense spending in 2005 at $518.1 billion. This equals approximately the amount spent on defense by the next 41 countries listed. See: https://www.cia.gov/cia/publications/factbook/rankorder/2007rank.html (accessed on February 5, 2007).

2. Walter Laqueur, "The Terrorism to Come," *Policy Review* #126 (August-September 2004).

3. Michael Mandelbaum, *The Case for Goliath* (New York: Basic Books, 2005), p. 147.

4. Ricks, *Fiasco*, p. 346.

5. Robert Lieber, *The American Era: Power and Strategy for the 21st Century* (New York: Cambridge University Press, 2005), p. 73.

6. In *Cobra II*, Gordon and Trainor cite help from German intelligence agents in connection with information on Saddam's plans for defending Baghdad. They also outline other areas of German cooperation on the war (including those cited here) and then characterize Germany's role vis-à-vis the Iraq War as: "Germany was in an odd category. It was quietly contributing to the U.S. effort, but opposed to the war." (Gordon and Trainor, *Cobra II*, p. 123).

7. Richard Bernstein, "Germany and America: Soul-Searching Over the *Realpolitik* of the Iraq War," *New York Times*, March 12, 2006.

8. Department of the Army, *Counterinsurgency*, Field Manual No. 3-24 (Washington, DC: Department of the Army Headquarters, December 15, 2006), p. ix.

9. Packer, *The Assassin's Gate*, pp. 298–99.

10. Gordon and Trainor, *Cobra II*, p. 505.

11. Ricks, *Fiasco*, p. 190.

12. Kevin Woods, James Lacey, and Williamson Murray, "Saddam's Delusions: The View From the Inside," *Foreign Affairs*, vol. 85, no. 3 (May-June 2006).

13. As a personal anecdote concerning the issue of whether the civil disorder and looting following the fall of Baghdad were part of Saddam's planned strategy, in the summer of 2006 I had a chance to pose this question to an Iraqi acquaintance who was visiting Washington, DC, at the time, a Sunni whose family has lived in Baghdad for generations and is well connected with the country's historical political hierarchy. This individual's response was quick and emphatic: "Of course. Saddam himself had announced to the Iraqi people that if his regime was to be driven out of power he would ensure that he left Baghdad a smoldering ruin."

14. Fallows, *Blind into Baghdad*, p. 76.

15. Baghdad's Al-Mustansiriyah University traces its history to the year 1233 and is among the Arab world's oldest and most respected institutions of higher learning. It was this university that terrorists targeted with two bombs on January 16, 2007, killing some seventy people and wounding some one hundred seventy more.

16. Bob Woodward, *State of Denial: Bush at War, Part III* (New York: Simon & Schuster, 2006), p. 257.

17. Highlights of the Iraq Strategic Review (Washington, DC: The White House, National Security Council, January 2007), p. 6.

18. In my capacity as minister-counselor for Public Affairs at the U.S. embassy in Berlin, I served as vice chairman of the RIAS Berlin Commission from June 2000 through June 2004.

19. CBS, *Face the Nation*, November 19, 2006.

20. *Profile of Service Members Ever Deployed*, CTS Deployment File (as of November 30, 2006), pp. 1, 3. See https://www.dmdc.osd.mil/. CTS Deployment Files available on request.

21. For an analysis of the demographics of the U.S. military, see Tim Kane, "Who Bears the Burden? Demographic Characteristics of U.S. Military Recruits Before and After 9/11," *The Heritage Foundation* (November 7, 2005).

22. CTS Deployment File, *Profile of Service Members Ever Deployed*, p. 3.

23. "Some Facts about Members of New Congress," *Associated Press*, January 3, 2007; and Congressional Research Service, "Membership of the 109th Congress: A Profile" (Washington, DC: Congressional Research Service, December 20, 2004), p. 6.

24. Although today the participation of women in the military is also at an all-time high. The current division between men and women deployed in the military is 89 percent men and 11 percent women (CTS Deployment File, *Profile of Service Members*, p. 1).

25. Congressional Research Service, *Membership of the 109th Congress: A Profile*, p. 6.

26. David Brooks, "Savagery's Stranglehold," *New York Times*, June 8, 2006.

27. Ibid.

28. Joshua Partlow, "Path in Iraq Hard But Not Hopeless, U.S. General Says," *Washington Post*, February 11, 2007, p. A14.

CHAPTER 6: THE COALITION OF THE UNWILLING

1. *Le Monde* (Paris, France), September 12, 2001.
2. Robert von Rimscha, "USA rechnen bie Irak-Krieg mit Eskalation in ganz Nahost," *Der Taggespiegel* (Berlin, Germany), March 21, 2002, p. 1.
3. Speaking to Washington's foreign press corps at the State Department's Washington Foreign Press Center on January 22, 2003.
4. Testifying before the House Armed Services Committee (108th Cong., 1st sess.) on February 5, 2003, Rumsfeld said: "There are three or four countries that have said they won't do anything [in a war against Iraq]. I believe Libya, Cuba and Germany are the ones that have indicated they won't help in any respect."
5. From the episode "Round Springfield," first aired on the Fox Network, April 30, 1995.
6. In the lead-up to the Iraq War, the leaders of eight European countries—Spain, Portugal, Italy, Britain, Hungary, Poland, Denmark, and the Czech Republic—issued a joint statement calling for international unity against the Iraqi threat. They were subsequently dubbed the "European 8."
7. Shortly after the "European 8" issued their joint statement concerning Iraq, the foreign ministers of ten Central European nations—Albania, Bulgaria, Croatia, Macedonia, Romania, Slovakia, Slovenia, Estonia, Latvia, and Lithuania—issued a similar declaration calling for the "trans-Atlantic community, of which we are a part, [to] stand together to face the threat posed by the nexus of terrorism and dictators with weapons of mass destruction." This group became known as the "Vilnius 10."
8. John F. Burns and Kirk Semple, "The Struggle for Iraq: Iraq Insurgency Has Funds To Sustain Itself, U.S. Finds," *New York Times*, November 26, 2006.

CHAPTER 7: VIOLENCE IN IRAQ: THE INSURGENCY/SECTARIAN CONFLICT

1. Although the tales we heard in July of 2004 were undocumented, Col. USAF (ret.) Kim Olson, who served as executive officer to ORHA Director Gen. (ret.) Jay Garner, relates being shown a partially eaten human corpse when visiting the lion enclosure at the Baghdad Zoo, where Uday's lions had been relocated from their former home in the Green Zone, shortly after the fall of the Saddam

regime (Kim Olson, *Iraq and Back: Inside the War to Win the Peace* (Annapolis, MD: Naval Institute Press, 2006), p. 90).

2. International Republican Institute, "Survey of Iraqi Public Opinion" (Washington, DC: International Republican Institute, July 19, 2006).

CHAPTER 8: IRAQ AND THE MEDIA

1. Sean McCormack, State Department Daily Press Briefing (Washington, DC: U.S. State Department, April 21, 2006).

2. Jonathan Finer, "Press in Iraq Gains Rights But No Refuge," *Washington Post*, June 6, 2005.

3. "Dijla" is the Arabic word for "Tigris," one of the two rivers—the other being the Euphrates (Al-Fourat, in Arabic)—that sustain Iraq and that enabled Mesopotamia (Greek for "between the rivers") to become the cradle of civilization several millennia ago.

4. Donald Macintyre, "From football phone-ins to consumer complaints, Radio Dijla is flourishing within the constraints of a deeply unstable Iraq," *Independent* (UK), August 4, 2004.

CHAPTER 9: INSIDE IRAQ

1. Eric Davis, "Special Report: Strategies for Promoting Democracy in Iraq" (Washington, DC: United States Institute of Peace, October 2005), p. 1.

2. Suskind, *The One Percent Doctrine*, p. 327.

3. Richard Cohen, "Civil War? What Civil War," *Washington Post*, August 8, 2006, p. A21.

4. Woodward, *Plan of Attack*, p. 111.

5. Ricks, *Fiasco*, pp. 64–65.

6. Gordon and Trainor, *Cobra II*, p. 546.

7. Ibid., p. 546.

8. Karen DeYoung, *Soldier: The Life of Colin Powell* (New York: Alfred A. Knopf, Inc., 2006), p. 459.

9. Dafna Linzer, "Iraq and Analysis, Revisited," *Washington Post*, February 3, 2007.

10. David Ignatius, "Raw Politics in Iraq," *Washington Post*, February 17, 2006, p. A19.

11. Joshua Partlow and Bassam Sebti, "Iraqi Leader Outlines Plan for Reconciliation," *Washington Post*, June 25, 2006, p. A17.

12. In early 2007, CPA Administrator L. Paul Bremer III acknowledged that in some respects the overall approach to U.S. reconstruction efforts in Iraq might have been differently conceived: "[I]n requesting American money to help rebuild Iraq's economy, I put too much emphasis on large-scale projects when smaller ones would have

shown quicker results to the average Iraqi," he wrote. (L. Paul Bremer III, "The Iraqis Must Step Up To the Plate," *Wall Street Journal*, January 11, 2007, p. A15).

13. The report of the Iraq Study Group cites a variation on this phenomenon: "There are ample reports of Iraqi police officers participating in training in order to obtain a weapon, uniform, and ammunition for use in sectarian violence" (*The Iraq Study Group Report*, p. 10).

14. Solomon Moore, "In Corruption, New Government of Iraq Faces a Tough Old Foe," *Los Angeles Times*, May 23, 2006.

15. John F. Burns and Kirk Semple, "The Struggle for Iraq: Iraq Insurgency Has Funds To Sustain Itself, U.S. Finds," *New York Times*, November 26, 2006.

16. Sudarsan Raghavan, "Violence Changes Fortunes of Storied Baghdad Street," *Washington Post*, September 18, 2006, p. A1.

17. Peter Galbraith, *The End of Iraq: How American Incompetence Created a War without End* (New York: Simon and Schuster, 2006), p. 224.

18. Bret Stephens, "Can There Be a Liberal Iraq?," *Wall Street Journal*, February 6, 2007, p. A16.

19. Cited by BBC news, "Survey Finds Hope in Occupied Iraq," March 16, 2004.

20. Francis Fukuyama, "The End of History?" *National Interest* (Summer 1989).

21. Ronald Inglehart, Mansoor Moaddel, and Mark Tessler, "Xenophobia and In-Group Solidarity in Iraq: A Natural Experiment on the Impact of Insecurity," *Perspectives on Politics*, vol. 4, iss. 3 (Cambridge University Press, September 2006): p. 7.

22. Ibid., p. 9.

CHAPTER 10: IRAQ'S NEIGHBORHOOD

1. Lee Smith, "The World Turns: Bush, the Great Shiite Liberator," *New York Times*, May 1, 2005.

2. There are twenty-two countries in the League of Arab States, which includes Palestine.

3. The case of Syria is interesting in this regard, since the country's leaders are from the Alawite sect, which is an off-shoot of Shi'a Islam; however, the tenuous connection between Shiism and the Syrian Alawite government is such that most observers would not characterize Syria's government as "Shi'a" in its identity. In former times, however, there were Shi'a-led dynasties in the region, most notably the Fatimids in the Maghreb and in the Levant in Islam's early years.

4. In the same article, Friedman also conveys his overall take on post-Saddam Iraq as fundamentally defined by the Sunni-Shi'a schism: "The short history of the Iraq War is that the Sunnis in Iraq, and in the nearby Arab states,

refused to accept one man, one vote, because it meant bringing the Shiite majority to power in Iraq."

5. The name of the company was changed to Saudi-ARAMCO following its purchase by the Saudi government in the 1980s.

6. Packer, *The Assassin's Gate*, p. 66.

7. Ambassador Horan passed away on July 22, 2004, at the age of sixty-nine.

8. Woodward, *State of Denial*, pp. 270-71.

9. See a report by the Energy Information Administration, U.S. Department of Energy, June 2005, at www.eia.doe.gov, which states: Saudi Arabia's per capita oil export revenues remain far below high levels reached during the 1970s and early 1980s. In 2004, Saudi Arabia earned around $4,564 per person, versus $22,589 in 1980. This 80 percent decline in real per capita oil export revenues since 1980 is in large part due to the fact that Saudi Arabia's young population has nearly tripled since 1980, while oil export revenues in real terms have fallen by over 40 percent (despite recent increases)."

10. Zalmay Khalilzad, "Iraq: A Status Report," at the Center for Strategic & International Studies in Washington, DC, July 11, 2006.

CHAPTER 11: AMERICAN COMPETENCE AND COMMITMENT

1. Woodward, *State of Denial*, p. 387.

2. Ibid.

3. Rajiv Chandrasekaran, *Imperial Life in the Emerald City: Inside Iraq's Green Zone* (New York: Alfred A. Knopf, 2006), p. 16.

4. Special Inspector General for Iraq Reconstruction (SIGIR), "Iraq Reconstruction: Lessons in Human Capital Management," January 2006, p. 25, at http://www.sigir.mil/report/lessons/aspx.

5. Celeste Ward, *The Coalition Provisional Authority's Experience with Governance in Iraq: Lessons Identified* (Washington, DC: United States Institute for Peace, Special Report No. 139, May, 2005),

6. Packer, *The Assassin's Gate*, p. 184.

7. SIGIR, "Iraq Reconstruction," p. 20.

8. SIGIR, "Iraq Reconstruction," p. 46.

9. AFSA message to its membership, July 31, 2006.

10. Gamil Matar, "Rice on top of the world," *Al-Ahram Weekly Online* (Cairo, Egypt), Issue No. 785 (March 9–15, 2006).

11. These are two current U.S. government programs run by the State Department and aimed at supporting civil society development abroad.

12. Michael Rubin, "Is American Support for Middle Eastern Dissidents the Kiss of Death?" *Middle Eastern Outlook*, American Enterprise Institute Online, December 5, 2006.

13. Greg Jaffe, "The Two Star Rebel," *Wall Street Journal*, May 13, 2006, p. A1.

14. *CIA World Factbook*, at https://www.cia.gov/cia/publications/factbook/rankorder/2034rank.html (accessed on January 23, 2007).
15. "From the Embassy, a Grim Report," *Washington Post*, June 18, 2006, p. B1.
16. "Back from Iraq," *Washington Post*, May 14, 2006, p. A1.
17. Joseph Lieberman, "Why We Need More Troops in Iraq," *Washington Post*, December 29, 2006, p. A27.
18. Colin Powell, "U.S. Forces: Challenges Ahead," *Foreign Affairs* (Winter 1992/1993).
19. Dan Fromkin, "The Debate over Debate," washingtonpost.com, February 9, 2007.
20. Michael R. Gordon, "The Struggle for Iraq: Bush Adviser's Memo Cites Doubts about Iraqi Leader," *New York Times*, November 29, 2006.

Acknowledgements

My efforts to develop the material contained in this work owe a great deal to several colleagues in the State Department, at Georgetown University, and in various institutions in the Washington area. While they are too many for me to be able to name them all individually, I would like to thank some of those whose insights and comments particularly helped to improve this work. In some cases, their input reflected very different positions on the Iraq issue than those expressed here. These differing viewpoints were extremely valuable to me in revisiting my own assumptions and conclusions and in ensuring that the positions I was staking out were conveyed clearly and completely.

Among those who contributed their time and talent in commenting on earlier drafts of the monograph were two valued colleagues who worked with me in the Public Diplomacy Office at embassy Baghdad, fellow Foreign Service Officers Bob Callahan and Alberto Fernandez. Their meticulous reading of the work in draft form identified numerous areas for correction and improvement. The final product also owes a great deal to the contributions of two other Foreign Service colleagues, Ambassador William Rugh and Ambassador John Campbell. Ambassador Rugh is among the most experienced and expert U.S. diplomats to have served in the Arab world, and his advice challenged me to question assumptions and clarify several of the key issues treated in the work. Ambassador Campbell, while not specifically an Arab world expert, drew from his many years of foreign policy and diplomatic experience in offering suggestions that helped make the presentation more comprehensible to those not professionally immersed in issues of the Middle East.

The Georgetown University students in my graduate seminar on Iraq during the spring 2006 semester, and the undergraduates in my Iraq seminar in the fall 2006 semester, have been cooperative and supportive subjects for the testing of much of this material. Their comments and questions have often propelled me onto new and fruitful avenues as I sought to treat the daunting complexity of the Iraq issue. Despite the controversial nature of many of the topics and material covered, I found the students very open minded, reasoned, and nonpolemical; their response to the material represented a most valuable reality check.

The support and encouragement of my colleagues at the Institute for the Study of Diplomacy (ISD) of Georgetown University's Edmund A. Walsh School of Foreign Service have also been most appreciated as I have worked on this material over the several months of my time at the institute. Two ISD colleagues, ISD Director of Research James Seevers and ISD Associate Lieutenant Colonel William Mooney, provided very useful comments on an earlier draft of the monograph, leading to significant expansion and revision of several of the topics covered. Perhaps above all, I would like to acknowledge ISD Director Casimir A. Yost for encouraging me in developing and publishing this monograph.